A Modern Orthodox Life

Sermons and Columns
of
Rabbi Emanuel Rackman

Ktav Publishing House, Inc.

Library of Congress Cataloging-in-Publication Data

Rackman, Emanuel.
  [Selections. 2008]
  A modern orthodox life : sermons and columns of Rabbi Emanuel Rackman.
      p. cm.
  ISBN 978-1-60280-023-6
  1. Orthodox Judaism. 2. Jewish sermons, American. 3. Jewish way of life.
I. Title.
  BM197.6.R332 2008
  296.8'32--dc22
                              2008008761

Published by
KTAV Publishing House, Inc.
930 Newark Avenue
Jersey City, NJ 07306
Email: bernie@ktav.com
www.ktav.com
(201) 963-9524
Fax (201) 963-0102

Table of Contents

COLUMNS

ARTICLE

INDEX   297

Introduction

My father, born in Albany, New York in 1910, was the first Orthodox Jew to attend Columbia College. At the same time, he attended the Rabbi Isaac Elchanan Theological Seminary of Yeshiva University, from which he was ordained in 1934. (He also graduated from Columbia Law School and later was awarded his Ph.D. in Political Science from that same university.) He served various congregations on Long Island from 1930 through 1967, the longest tenure being at Congregation Shaaray Tefila in Far Rockaway from 1946 until 1967, when he assumed the pulpit of Manhattan's Fifth Avenue Synagogue. He also taught political science at Yeshiva University (where he ultimately became the Assistant to the President, Dr. Samuel Belkin) from 1962 to 1970 and he was a professor of Jewish Studies at the City University of New York from 1971 to 1977. During this time frame, he also served as the president of the New York Board of Rabbis (1955-1957) and the Rabbinical Council of America (1958-1960).

In 1977, my father was appointed President of Bar Ilan University and in 1986 he became its Chancellor; he is currently its Chancellor for Life. Thus, at the age of 67, he moved to Israel and took Bar Ilan, which was then Israel's smallest general university and more than quintupled the enrollment, to the point where today Bar Ilan has more students than any other Israeli university.

This book explores another side of this extraordinary career. It started out with a suggestion from a family friend, Blu Genauer Greenberg. Her father was one of my father's closest friends and they studied Talmud together daily for well over 30 years. She suggested that a book be published containing the best of my father's columns that had appeared in the *New York Jewish Week* in the 1970s, 1980s and 1990s. My daughter, Anya, helped gather many of the columns from the archives of the *New York Jewish Week* (and Gary Rosenblatt must be thanked for both granting access to those archives and reprint permission).

I am sorry that I do not remember who gave me the idea, but when I mentioned to this person that I was putting together a book of these columns, he asked whether I would be including in the book copies of my father's sermons. For the first 20 years, my father wrote out every sermon, but he rarely wrote out his sermons after the 1940s. Fortunately, the Rabbinical Council of America annually published a Sermon Manual and I was able, at their offices, to review all the sermon manuals. It turns out that my father had one or two sermons in every volume from 1947 through 1963 and I have selected a number of those sermons. (Thanks to the Rabbinical Council of America and Rabbi Basil Herring, its Executive Vice President, for granting reprint permission.) For those of us who had the privilege of hearing him preach, these sermons are probably the highlight of this volume, bringing back memories of hundreds of Sabbaths where in Far Rockaway the topic of discussion at the Shabbos lunch table was the rabbi's sermon.

Finally, I have included the last long piece published by my father in 1992, an essay on the Holocaust that appeared in *Theological and Halakhic Reflections on the Holocaust*, edited by Bernard H. Rosenberg and co-edited by Fred Heuman (K'tav, Rabbinical Council of America 1992).

The materials were selected with assistance from my brothers, Michael and Bennett, and are presented in chronological order (except for a few columns whose dates of publication are unknown). A topical index for the columns appears at the end of this book. The columns were not written as scholarly pieces and references have been inserted by my son, David, to the appropriate sources in many of the columns. And my niece, Jessica (Yocheved) Ingber, assisted with the design of the book cover. Also, special thanks to my wonderful assistant of many years, Carmen Denehy, for her work over a two year period in the preparation of this volume.

Last, but not least, I want to thank S. Daniel Abraham for subsidizing the publication of this volume. Going back to the days of the Fifth Avenue Synagogue, he has been a true friend of my father.

The title of this book is a play on my father's most popular book – it has been reprinted three times – *One Man's Judaism*, but taken together – these sermons, columns and essay, spanning five decades, reflect a Modern Orthodox life lived to the fullest. For all their considerable worth, they still are but a pale reflection of a man who led the way for so many. His students are legion and this volume will help remind them of that life and help to convey to others how Torah can be reflected in this world for the betterment of the world and for Jews in particular.

Joseph R. Rackman

SERMONS

Shabbat Shuvah
The Sabbath before Yom Kippur

In the Bible we find a very interesting contrast. The man who was most profuse in his good wishes for the people of Israel was Balaam – the Midianite prophet, whom we regard as one of our historic enemies. The man, on the other hand, who was most profuse in his threats and curses – was Moses, the greatest and most beloved figure of our past. Our sages commented on this contrast in the Midrash (Deut. Rabbah, I:4), one would have expected, they said, that a friend would bless us and an enemy would curse us. But the Bible indicates exactly the reverse. Balaam, who was intent on destroying our people, lavished praise and congratulations upon us. He regarded us as the undisputed favorites of God. Moses however, who set out to make us a great nation, did not hesitate to criticize us, to chastise us, to point out our deficiencies. Read the chapter of Deuteronomy in particular and you will come upon language one would never utter to a friend – if one cherished the friendship. The names Moses called the people of Israel would make an anti-Semite rejoice. The dismal future he predicted is a perfect blueprint for all Hamans and Hitlers to come. Yet, we regard Moses as the lover of his people, the man who best exemplified the love of Israel, an unswerving loyalty to his co-religionists.

To state this contrast, friends, is already to make the point of my message this morning. It is a point most of us have learned from bitter experience. Our best friends are not necessarily our most gracious flatterers. More often our severest critics are our truest friends. And what is true of individuals, is true of nations. Several years ago I pointed out that Balaam could not be respected as a prophet in the manner that the Jewish prophets are respected, for a real prophet helps his people to deepen their religious and moral experience, and does not lull them into a false sense of security as Balaam's wily tongue sought to do. And Moses was the forerunner – or rather the archetype – of Jewish prophecy. He loved his people so much that he even fought with God in their behalf. But instead of flattering them, he ever tried to make them aware of their short-comings, he even tried to make them better.

Yet, friends, as simple as this point may be, it would surprise you to learn what serious consequences it had for Judaism. Because Moses taught us that spiritual leaders must not be gracious flatterers of their people, we Jews have never had one important problem which Christianity has faced. We Jews never had social reform movements which had as their goal the destruction of Judaism, the termination of the political power of the rabbis, or the confiscation of synagogue property. Most European countries on the other hand, had such social reform movements with regard to their organized religions. Permit me to show you why.

When a clergy is like Balaam – flattering its constituents and assuring them that all they do is good – that whatever is has God's approval – you are bound to have a problem. When the clergy feels that the social and economic conditions which prevail, no matter how bad, enjoy God's assent, then anyone who seeks change must fight the clergy too. But Moses taught spiritual leaders not to nod "Amen" to everything that is, to everything their charges do. Rather spiritual leaders are to criticize and to improve the status quo. That is why Jewish spiritual leaders were always critical of the manner in which the rich treated the poor and the employers their employees. That is why Jewish spiritual leaders always advocated social and economic reform. They were always in the forefront of the battle to make social and economic conditions better, and righteous living more universal. And as such they did not have to worry about opposition from those who sought change.

Judaism, for example, did not tolerate slavery and say that if God made the slave a slave, it must be punishment for his sin. On the other hand, Judaism sought to abolish slavery. Judaism did not say that nothing should be done about poverty, hunger and disease because we had no right to frustrate what God willed. On the other hand, the elimination of hunger and disease became the greatest mitzvos we have. Our religion, instead of giving the stamp of approval to the status quo, always sought its betterment. And that is why it hurts us to hear our young people attack religion in general, including Judaism, because religion is on the side of existing power. If anything, Judaism, like Moses, was always critical of that which could be bettered. I repeat – Judaism and its spokesmen were not to nod "Amen" to all that was and bless God for it.

Such was our mood years ago. But what of the present?

In one way our rabbis today are not like Balaam, but rather like Moses. They could, for example, if they chose, flatter American Jews for all that was done for Israel. And the truth is that American Jews did do much. As I indicated once before, no other group in America can even approach our record for philanthropy. But rabbis do not flatter their people, for they know how much more can and should be done. We cannot be satisfied with a comparative standard. Rabbis will only congratulate Jews when they have given their very all, when they have given until it hurts, and then some more.

Rabbis could also, for example, undertake to congratulate Jews on the fact that on three business days of the year they cease completely from business activities, go to synagogue and even give generously to the support of worthy causes. But rabbis do not do this for they know that a three-day-a-year religion is inadequate and that the souls of Jews cannot be sustained by token observance alone.

Yes, rabbis could congratulate Jews, but instead, it is to their credit that they have chosen to be like Moses, and they scold and chastise. They want Jews to be still better and do more. This has been our historic role – to be like Moses, and not like Balaam.

I fear, however, that with respect to one thing at least, a change is setting in. I fear it, because once rabbis become like Balaam – flattering Jews and assuring their people that all they do is fine – we are headed for trouble.

We have come to an age when Jews, for example, prefer a rabbi who says that whatever they do is fine. As a matter of fact congregations now set out to retain rabbis who will give the stamp of approval to all the liberties they take individually regarding the Sabbath, regarding synagogue services, regarding even the laws of mourning which up to recently Jews were wont to observe rather strictly. Furthermore, Jews want to join or establish congregations whose policies are such that whatever the members decide to do is regarded as permissible.

I pray that no one will misunderstand me. Just because a Jew does not observe all the commandments does not mean that I cannot respect, admire and even love him. I know many such people in this very congregation and I respect, admire and love them. But I do not believe any of these self-respecting men could respect me if I said "Everything you do is fine. And even if you feel that there are some observances which you want to disregard, I will examine Jewish law to help establish a basis for proving that you are doing no wrong. And if I cannot find substantial proof I will change the law so that you need have no guilty conscience." Nor do I feel that any self-respecting man could respect a congregation whose policy it is to help him feel that all he does is right. Such a congregation should never have come into existence.

I believe that the Jew who is not 100 percent observant ought to respect his rabbi and congregation more, when instead of saying that whatever is inconvenient or not readily understood can be disregarded, the rabbi and the congregation help the man to see the value of doing the inconvenient, or help him to understand what is not readily intelligible.

If the rabbi becomes nothing more than an "Amen" nodder to all that his flock does, he will sacrifice his historic role. He will become simply an instrument to relieve Jews of all feelings of guilt.

Now I want changes in Jewish law. And I tell you that Jewish law was changed in the past, and will change in the future. But these changes were not made to relieve Jews of guilty consciences. We did not say, "Let us change the law whenever Jews don't observe it." We did not say, "Let us change the law so that instead of feeling like sinners, Jews will be saints in their own eyes." On the other hand, if Jews had a guilty conscience, we felt it was healthy. Their guilty conscience might help them to do better in the future. But if we continue to change the law only to appease the guilty consciences of Jews, we are making a farce of religion.

And that is what I want you to understand this morning on this great Sabbath of Penitence.

A guilty conscience is a healthy thing. It is healthy for our Jewishness. It is healthy for the survival of Judaism. If every Jew – and that includes everyone, rabbis and congregants – if every Jew has a guilty conscience, the day may come when there will be an improvement in our ways. But if we tell Jews they can do anything they like on the Sabbath, what hope is there that they will even make the Sabbath more meaningful to themselves, more inspirational, more conducive to family togetherness? If we tell Jews that they may eat anything they please, what hope is there that they will ever recognize what Jewish consciousness and consecration is induced by the observance of dietary laws? If we tell Jews that it is enough to pray once a week, what hope is there that they will ever experience the strength that comes from daily prayer or the dignity that is added to the table with the recitation of grace before and after meals? If we tell Jews that they may modify the laws of mourning as they please, what hope is there that they will ever appreciate the full value of the rules pertaining to Shiva and Shloshim with regard to the proper orientation of the living to the problem of life and death?

Yes, a guilty conscience Jewishly is a good thing. A man without a guilty conscience never becomes a better man. And a Jew whose rabbi has helped to deaden his Jewish conscience can never become a better Jew.

I remember during the last war how many orthodox rabbis had to counsel with soldiers who never desecrated the Sabbath or ate non-kosher food and found it impossible to continue their observance. The rabbis were wont to quote one famous sage who said, "If you have to do the prohibited, at least try not to enjoy it." If the soldier continued to have a guilty conscience, he might some day be restored to his earlier practices.

I also recall a non-Jewish general in Europe who expressed a similar thought. Like many others, his drinking habits were hardly honorable and his morals away from his family hardly praiseworthy. One day he expressed himself to his Chaplain, "I know I am doing wrong, Chaplain, but as long as you lead a decent life even here amid war conditions, you are my conscience. You are my constant reminder of what I should be. You are my reminder of the standards to which I hope some day to return. Don't you ever let yourself sink to my level."

And in my own chaplaincy experience I had a problem. I was stationed at Randolph Field and had no difficulty in observing Shabbos. As a matter of fact, I had regular Sabbath eve and Sabbath morning services. One day my superiors told me that they wanted me to forget the Sabbath morning services at Randolph and conduct them at Hondo Air Base 50 air miles away, for the men at Hondo could only attend services on Saturday mornings. A plane would transport me back and forth. I need not tell you how badly I felt, but before I could do anything about it, I happened to discuss the problem with my men at Randolph at a meeting of our chapel council. And a number of them did not hesitate to express themselves. "Chaplain," they said, "If you have to go to Hondo on Shabbos mornings we will take charge of the service at Randolph ourselves. But we hope you don't have to go. You are the one man who represents for us resistance to the desecration of the Sabbath. You manage in spite of military duties to represent for us what the Shabbos should be. Some day we too may be able to observe the Sabbath. But if we see you flying to and fro like the other officers, we will lose the one great reminder we had of what Shabbos is like." Their reaction floored me, and I was more determined than ever to find a way not to fly to Hondo. I moved heaven and earth and arranged for a service there on a weekday that I might personally observe Shabbos and at the same time not destroy what I represented to my men at Randolph. I was their conscience, even as they stimulated mine, and I could not let them down.

Yes, a guilty conscience is a good thing Jewishly. It helps to make us better – if not now – then later. Therefore, let us not ask rabbis to nod "Amen" to all we want to do. Instead, let us recognize our Rabbi as the reminder of what we ought to be and do. Instead of appeasing our consciences by seeking assurances that we are doing no wrong, let us see whether we can't improve upon our conduct and add to our observance. Let us see whether we can't do at least one thing better this year than we did the year before.

That is the appeal of the Sabbath of Penitence when we are to consider our potentialities of becoming better than we ever were – more observant, more charitable, more learned in things Jewish. That is my appeal to you – let us not deaden our guilty consciences. Let us not seek changes in the law only to appease feelings of guilt. Let us not seek different synagogues only because their policies help us to feel that we are saints, not sinners. Continue to be loyal to orthodoxy – and orthodox synagogues – and even if you feel guilty that you are not personally orthodox, the day may come when your guilty conscience will help to make a better Jew of you. Running away from your conscience to a place where you are told that you are a saint makes a farce of God and religion. And that no self-respecting person wants.

I pray that the day will come when all Jews will realize this, and while changes in Jewish law will come, they will come because of the demands of spiritual living – not because Jews want to be flattered into feelings of security that they are doing no wrong.

Judaism: A Social Religion

In recent years I have heard an ever increasing number of Jews refer to our current festival as the "Jewish Easter". Perhaps this new title for the holiday is born of the inability of our American co-religionists to remember the simple words Pesach or Passover. Or perhaps it is due to the remarkable perennial coincidence of the Christian observance with our own. This year, for example, our eight-day celebration coincides exactly with the interval between Palm Sunday and Easter, and that may prompt many of our people to seek to make themselves more readily understood to their non-Jewish friends by the use of Christian, rather than Jewish, terminology.

However, I cannot tell you how the phrase "Jewish Easter" would have offended the sensibilities of our ancestors. It would truly have grated against their ears to learn that the more ancient Jewish festival must be explained in terms of a later non-Jewish one – which seldom spelled anything but grief for them. I, too, find myself irritated by the phrase. But not so much for sentimental, as for intellectual, reasons. To me the association of Passover with Easter is an indication not only of Jewish inability to remember the names Pesach or Passover, but also of Jewish ignorance of the fact that the philosophies underlying the two holidays are antithetical as day and night. The significance of Easter is almost a contradiction of the significance of Passover. And for Jews to ignore the difference is to be oblivious of the unique genius of our faith and its eternal meaningfulness for humanity.

Permit me to explain. In the study of religions one frequently finds it advantageous to distinguish between what may be called private religion and social religion. Some religions are principally concerned with the individual man as an individual. They seek to furnish a way of attaining personal salvation. They seek to provide the means for assuring the immortality of the individual's soul. That is their principal goal. That is why I call these religions private religions. They may be the religions of millions of people but their primary concern is with the souls of individuals as individuals. There are, on the other hand, religions whose primary concern is with the group, with society as a whole, with humanity at large – not with isolated human beings – but rather with human beings organized into families, communities, nations. Private religions mainly ask, "What must a man do to make his peace with God that he may enjoy life everlasting?" Social religions mainly ask, "What shall man do in his relations with his fellow-man that God's Kingdom may exist on earth as it does in heaven?"

Now, Judaism is basically a social religion. It is more concerned with man's relationships to his fellow-man than with man's relationships to God. The principal aim of the Mitzvos we perform is to make us better members of the family, community or nation of which we are a part. Personal immortality is only of secondary importance. Christianity took over from Judaism some of this spirit but from the Greeks, the founders of Christianity took over the idea of personal salvation and made the yearning for immortality the central feature of their faith. In that way they made their religion more a private religion than a social religion. And while Passover is the holiday par excellence to symbolize Judaism's concern with the social importance of religion, Easter is Christianity's holiday to symbolize its preoccupation with the salvation of the individual. Easter is Greek in its significance – not Jewish. That it usually occurs so close to Passover is only because the alleged founder of the new faith was supposed to have been crucified a few days after Passover. But ideologically speaking, Easter has nothing to do with Passover. Nay, it is almost a contradiction of the Passover. For what person familiar with the Passover can overlook the fact that it is the greatest stimulus we have in the pattern of our religious life to evoke strong family and community ties, a moving regard for human suffering, and a passion for the liberation of the oppressed? Easter, on the other hand, is the holiday dedicated not to humanity at all – but rather to the quest of every individual man for either life everlasting or resurrection after death.

Think of the Passover. You can hardly visualize celebrating it alone. When God first commanded Jews to observe it, Jews were told to unite with the members of their families and their neighbors and together make the Paschal offering.

Every man must take a lamb for each extended family . . . and if the household is too small for a lamb, then he and a close neighbor shall take a lamb together.

Exodus 12:3-4

It was to be a feast for groups – rather than individuals. And from that there did spring the historic regard of Jews that no Jew – no matter how poor – shall be without a feast on this holy day.

Furthermore, because we were once slaves and God liberated us, we were never to forget the oppressed, we were to love the stranger, and do justice unto the exploited. The story of our bondage in Egypt, and our exodus therefrom, became the focal point of all Judaism. Freedom and justice became our slogans, and these are values for group existence, and not values for isolated individuals.

It would take hours to point out how extensive and penetrating is the significance of Passover for better group relations, for firmer family ties, for higher social, economic and political standards. All I ask you to remember is that this is the essence of Judaism, as it is the essence of Passover. Our religion starts with the family – not with the individual. Its very conception, its birth, is in a company of people – not with individuals in isolation. And this is the very opposite of Christianity's principal concern, and the very opposite of the meaning of the Easter. And that is why I cannot think of a Jewish Easter. We have no such thing as a holiday concerned with the hermit craving the peace of God and life everlasting for himself. And this, our sages also intended to express in their comment that Torah matters cannot be upheld individually. (Tal. B. Taanis 7a)

I call this to your attention this morning not because I want to recommend the avoidance of the phrase "Jewish Easter". As a matter of fact, I do not know whether many of our own members thus offend. It is rather to help you understand the practical significance of the distinction I have drawn between Passover and Easter.

First let me give you a simple illustration. There is a lawsuit pending at the moment which is attracting much attention. An American father is trying to get his children out of a Catholic orphanage to take them with him to Russia. The Church has refused, and is still refusing to return the children. From a Christian point of view, the argument of the Church is a good one. The Church asserts that only through Catholicism will the souls of these children be saved. How then can it normally give the children to a father who will take them to a godless country where their souls will be damned! That these children will be deprived of family ties, of the attention of their own father, matters not. That the father will suffer untold anguish because of his separation from his children is also of no consequence. That the Church is offending against every principle of social religion by destroying a family unit does not matter. It must worry about the children's souls.

This case may be exceptional. But in Jewish history it is not exceptional. It happened before – the famous Mortara case – when a Jewish child was practically abducted from his family, and baptized at the request of his maid. The child was never returned to his family though in fact nations protested. The child subsequently became a priest and a missionary to Jews. But even today after six million of our co-religionists perished at the hands of the Nazi beasts, it is estimated that at least ten thousand Jewish children in Europe are still in convents and monasteries and despite the claims of relatives the Church refuses to surrender them. After all, the Church is saving their souls by keeping them loyal to Catholicism and who cares that instead of having the affection of an uncle or aunt or cousin, or the memory of ancestors who are their real forbears, they have instead the mystical union of the Church! A Church concerned principally with salvation takes such an attitude. Judaism, however, could never take such an attitude.

Or take another practical illustration which happens often. The Church will marry two people unto each other even if only one is a Catholic. Protestant clergy will marry two people to each other if only one is a Protestant. And sometimes our Jewish children come to the Rabbis and say, "Why won't a Rabbi marry two people unto each other unless both are Jewish? A Rabbi would marry a Democrat to a Republican, or a Liberal to at Conservative. And why can't one's faith be like one's politics? Each member of the marriage can believe as he or she chooses, and why insist on Jews marrying only Jews?" The answer is again clear. If religion is a matter of personal salvation, then it matters not who one marries. One's religion is like one's politics – a private matter. But if religion is social, and closely tied in with a family, and a home, then how can you call the family a Jewish family unless both spouses are Jewish – unless the heads of the household stand for the same thing. We will not make religion a matter of personal salvation. Our religion only has meaning insofar as it has meaning for a social unit – a family, or a people. And mixed marriages destroy the social significance of Judaism. They mean that one or two individuals in the family may be Jewish but the family as a whole cannot be called Jewish. And if the family is not Jewish then Judaism can have no significance for it, and we will not give it a false Jewish character, by permitting a Rabbi to solemnize a mixed marriage. Let them become man and wife by act of law – or even by act of nature. But our marriage ceremony is to give their togetherness a Jewish character and that Jewish character a mixed marriage cannot possibly have.

But that is not all. I call to your attention the difference between the private character of Christianity and the social character of Judaism because there are times when it is important to caution our people. I believe no less than anyone I know in the importance of respecting every man's faith and permitting everyone the greatest possible freedom of worship. I believe no less than anyone I know that we all worship one God and that all humanity are brothers unto each other. I believe also that it is vital that we stress the ideals and the values that all religions have in common. But sometimes we stress our agreement with Christians so much that our children wonder why there must be differences at all. And for that reason I must just as often stress why I feel that all religions are not alike and particularly why I prefer Judaism – as a social religion – to other religions that, are rather private religions. I will defend every man's right to believe as he does – provided he does no harm to anyone. But at the same time I want to dispel the notion that one religion is as good as another. If they were all the same, why should we so struggle to maintain our own in the face of so much hatred and hostility? That is why I must constantly affirm that Judaism has a vital message which eludes other religions. And that is why I choose to be what I am, because I regard our message as one that humanity requires now more than ever. And that is why I thank God for Passover and its reminder to me of the social character of my faith. That is why I thank God for Passover – in this season when hundreds of millions of people have chosen to alter its emphasis and substitute a less significant one. That is why I thank God for the Seder and its reminder of the unique nature of Judaism – its concern for the social unit, the family, the community, the nation. And I pray that all the world may yet come to appreciate why a social religion is so much more to be preferred than a private one. Of this the Seder makes us mindful and to this end let us dedicate ourselves as Jews forever.

The Love of Jews

O urs is an age of specialists. As a wit once described it, it is a period when in every field of learning, the experts know more and more about less and less. However, long before we advanced to our present state of learning, we Jews also had specialists – but of a different kind. Many of our saints and sages decided that they would become specialists in a particular Mitzvah. (*See Talmud Shabbat* 118b) I need not tell you that they observed everything that the written and oral law required. But from the thousands of ethical, moral and ritualistic precepts that we have, they would select one with regard to which they sought to achieve perfection. One saint might choose tongue control, and he would become an expert in moral speech. He would never utter a word that might even remotely be regarded as slanderous. Another saint might choose benevolence and he would spend days and nights assisting the poor.

However, the history of Jewish morality indicates that not only individual Jews would try to become specialists with regard to a particular Mitzvah, but Jews as a whole would find that at different periods of their history, all of them would become perfect, or efficient to the maximum, with regard to a particular Mitzvah. For example, at one period of Jewish history, the entire world was depraved with idolatry. As a result, Jews felt impelled to become especially militant in their fulfillment of the Biblical commands to destroy idols and the last vestiges of pagan worship. At another period Jews found that the world at large was suffering from clerical domination and the universal ignorance that the clergy hoped to perpetuate. Jews therefore became all the more enamored of Talmud Torah – of study, and the propagation of learning among all classes of Jews. At still another period Jews found that the world was suffering from a resurgence of nationalism which became the greatest cause for bloodshed, conquest and exploitation. Jews therefore became experts in the type of nationalism the Prophets described – a nationalism which sought universal social justice as its goal. And if you should ask me what is the Mitzvah with regard to which Jews in the present period of history should become especially expert, I will give you the reply of the Gerer Rebbe – of blessed memory. This age, he said, is the age when the world has sunk to the lowest level in the history of anti-Semitism. In our day – more than in any other – Jews have been tortured and exterminated. In our day – more than in any other – the Anti-Semitism of the subtle variety, which is definitely the most venomous, dominates the hearts of almost all men in power. Therefore, if the world is sick with the hatred of Jews, then it becomes the moral responsibility of Jews everywhere to become especially expert in the Mitzvah of *ahavat Yisrael*, especially expert in the Mitzvah of loving Jews. Everyone of us must so discipline himself that our every thought, our every utterance, our every deed, must be one that will reflect our love of Jews. Such experts were the heroes of our Passover festival – Moses, Aaron, and the elders. Who were the elders whom God asked Moses to consult with regard to every move he made? How were they chosen? Why were they later honored to constitute the membership of the Sanhedrin? Says Midrash Rabba (*Bamidbar Rabba* 15:20) that they were the Jews whom the Egyptians made responsible for the quotas of bricks which our ancestors were to make each day. These foremen were punished for the failure of their co-religionists to meet the quotas but they reported no one and punished no one. They bore in silence the brunt of all the punishment themselves.

Aye, they loved their fellow-Jews and therefore earned their immortality. Aaron was the great peace-maker among his people. And Moses – Moses was the man who was chosen to liberate his people because he risked his life to prevent an Egyptian from killing a Jew. And this Mitzvah of loving Jews – even Jews with whom we disagree, even Jews who do stupid or sinful things – is one of which our Passover festival must make us mindful.

Moses was the man who exemplified the love of his people to a maximum degree. After their liberation, for example, he faced a situation which made him sick at heart. He had brought his people out of Egypt, into the desert, and had there furnished them with food and drink. But alas, the diet that he provided was terribly monotonous. It included no fish or meat and the Jews griped loudly. But as if that were not sufficient, they began to complain that life in Egypt was better than life in the desert. (*Numbers* 11:5-6) Mind you, they preferred the chains of slavery with its fish and watermelon chow, to freedom with only manna. God was angered and poor Moses did not know what to do. The Bible says, "In Moses' eyes it was bad" (*Ibid*. v. 10) and the commentators tell us that Moses felt more depressed about this situation than about any other problem that ever faced him because he could find no *Zichus*, merit for his people. He could find no justification for the way his people acted. And how would he defend them before God?

Can you visualize any Yemenite or Iraqi Jew trying to leave Israel now to return to Yemen or Iraq because Israel's food is poor? How then could Moses defend his people who had plenty to eat but only because the diet was monotonous preferred to return to slavery?

But Moses, in his love for Israel, found a way, and you must reread the text of his plea before God. "God," he said, "You picked the wrong leader for them. It is all Your fault. Had You picked someone who was closer to them – like a parent – or someone who was more patient – or someone who was more ingenuous in satisfying them – they would not now complain. And if, God, You did make me their leader, and I failed, kill me now and let me not behold my failure."

My interpretation of this plea, friends, is the one suggested by the weight of Midrashim and medieval commentators and it is a beautiful one. Since Moses found no way to explain his people's ridiculous complaint, he blamed it all on his own failure as a leader. That is how deeply he loved his people! The blame for any wrong they committed was his! And that is an illustration of what it means to become expert in one's love for Jews!

Alas, however, that we in our day – despite the plea of the Gerer Rebbe and the example of Moses – are not becoming as perfect in our love for Jews, as the non-Jew has become maximally effective in his hatred of us! Why do I say this?

I say this because you must be as disturbed as I am when you read in the newspapers how bitterly the Zionist Organization and the Government of Israel attack each other, or how at their Rabbinical Conventions, even Orthodox, Conservative and Reform Rabbis hurl uncomplimentary epithets at their adversaries. Now believe me friends, I am not naive enough to suggest to intelligent people that we can ever unite all Jews so that they will think and act alike. As a matter of fact, it would be most unhealthy for Judaism if there were not healthy differences of opinion. We Jews have always had sects and parties. We have always had groups who advocated new ideas, new proposals, and it was this healthy difference of opinion that vitalized Judaism and made it possible for a small group of people to make such enormous contributions to the progress of human culture. But what we must learn particularly in this day and age, when we are morally obligated to specialize in the Mitzvah of loving Jews, is that even as we differ with each other, we should do so with mutual respect and with love and understanding. When Moses could not find any justification for his people's fault, he blamed his own leadership. Perhaps we have no right to expect the Rabbis of today to be as great as Moses and take the position that if they have failed perhaps they are at fault. But the least that we can expect of every Jew, Rabbi and layman alike, is that our differences shall be expressed with mutual respect even for those with whom we differ.

Let us take the problem within the World Zionist movement as a whole. It is not so tragic that there are parties, because there do exist healthy differences of opinion between the different groups. The General Zionists may have reason to believe that Mapai has failed, at least with regard to its encouragement of private enterprise, and Mapai may have reason to believe that the reactionary General Zionists throughout the world and particularly in Israel cannot reconcile themselves to the fact that the State of Israel must be overwhelmingly socialistic in its enterprise. But the difference between the two is not so great that there ought be incriminations and recriminations in the press to embarrass us and create the impression that Jews fight their political battles on the same level of vulgarity which we are wont to see between Democrats and Republicans in the United States. The tenor of all the releases in the press is that the battle between the parties is only one for party advantage. It was made to appear as if Ben Gurion was involved in the controversy only because he wanted more jobs for Mapai members and as if the General Zionists wanted a chance to get their own party into power, and as a result each side tried to make the other side appear black and villainous. Wouldn't it add to the stature of the Zionist movement if we established a policy of speaking even of our adversaries with profound respect and admiration, without maligning their motives, and in that way help all Jews without party affiliations to understand that in the final analysis while there may be differences of opinion, the real motivation is a profound love of Israel and a desire to do what is best for the Jewish people.

An even better illustration of this controversy is the manner in which this fight is going on in Israel and in America between the parties on the extreme right and the extreme left. I am one of the Rabbis who does want Israel to be a land in which Torah will thrive, but I cannot reconcile myself to insulting and abusing the members of Mapam. As much as I might differ with them, I cannot march in parades and attend protest meetings to vilify them. And I cannot understand how any of my colleagues are writing tirades in the press and conducting protest meetings against the Government of Israel. But the left is also guilty of the same crime. In their hatred of the religionists, Mapam has gone to the extreme of denouncing Torah altogether and completely overlooking the fact that the great ideals which they themselves profess did not start with Karl Marx but rather with the Torah itself. When one reads their party newspapers one can see the extent to which they are blinded by their hatred of the Rabbis in Israel, that they cannot see anything in the Torah that might be the basis for their own idealism.

But it isn't only within the Zionist movement in America and in Israel that we detect this failure of Jews to recognize that our principle obligation today is to look upon our co-religionists with respect and admiration, and love them even when we disagree with them. It is also true of the religious sects in America.

The Torah Tour Committee of the Rabbinical Council of America urged all of its speakers, who traveled throughout the United States to present the position of Orthodoxy, never to attack Conservative or Reform Jews. These speakers were to state positively what they stand for and not to deliver tirades against those who disagree with them. Yet how distressed I was to read recently of the attacks made on the Orthodoxy of American Jews and all Orthodoxy in Israel by Conservative and Reform colleagues whose diatribes made the columns of the New York Times and the Herald Tribune. I cannot understand how a Reform Rabbi would make the statement that Reform Rabbis in Israel have no status when they heard here in New York from the mouth of the Minister of Religion that he had pleaded with several of the irreligious colonists in Israel to take a Conservative or Reform Rabbi and they refused. Particularly because the papers distort any statement we make about ourselves, we should be doubly cautious always to talk of our fellow Jews with respect and understanding. Nor can I understand how a Conservative Rabbi would say that Orthodox Judaism holds the law to be unchangeable when that very colleague sat with the greatest Orthodox Rabbi of America and heard from his mouth what is the philosophy of change and what should be the principle of change within traditional Jewish law according to Orthodoxy. But again, the effect of loose statements taken out of context and published in the press is just to create the impression that Orthodox Jews are just as benighted, as medieval as the Catholic Church and only the other groups represent progressive thinking. The net effect of this type of attack is to estrange our young people altogether and make them lose their love for Jews and Judaism as a whole. Why should they have any special love of their people when Jews fight with each other with the same venom and the same intolerance that characterize the most ugly political debates between Democrats and Republicans and between Catholics and Protestants. We cannot hope to win our youth back to a love of Israel unless we can impress them with the fact that by staying with us they are at least staying with a people who, if they accomplish nothing else, at least exemplify mutual respect and confidence.

Perhaps I am asking for a situation which is too ideal, but, friends, it troubles me no end. And I can at least talk to you Jews and say to you "if you agree with me that this is an age where we must combat the almost psychopathic hatred of Jews that prevails among the non-Jews, then we must cultivate in ourselves a profound love of Jews; then each of us must begin to learn how to discipline our tongues. When we talk of Jews and Jewish movements we must so talk that even when we differ it will not be in an ugly way. It will even be accompanied with an admission to the effect that the other side has a point too. The only Jews of whom we have a right perhaps to be intolerant, are Jews who hate their Jewishness, Jews who are anti-Semites themselves, and there perhaps we might even blame it in part on their background. But if we want to attract a younger generation to the fold, to love the people of Israel and all that the people of Israel have accomplished throughout the ages, then we can only do so by learning how to control that which we say about Jews and Judaism and I tell you this on the basis of long experience. I can tell you that more children learn to hate the Synagogue because of things said at home about the Synagogue rather than because of their disinterest in what takes place in the Synagogue. I can tell you that more children are estranged from going to Hebrew School because of what parents say about other Jews than because of the worst instructors we could possibly have. And therefore, I make this one plea and it is a plea I direct to yourself and myself. Let us learn to be cautious with regard to everything we say about our fellow Jews and particularly about movements within the Jewish fold and as we induce a love of Jews in the hearts of our young, they will love Jews and Judaism and return unto God with all their hearts, that our Redeemer might come soon, Amen!

1952
Slichot (midnight prayers on the Saturday
night at least one week before
Rosh Hashanah)

The Great Challenge of Our Day

You undoubtedly noticed how softly our Reader chanted the latter half of this past week's Scriptural portion. Twice a year he does that, when he reads the two *Tochachot*, Moses' great warnings to the people of Israel. On two occasions Moses told the Jews how they would be punished if they violated God's law. The punishments he described I will not dare to summarize. If you are not already familiar with them, you should read them, for no summary can possibly do justice to their overpowering eloquence.

Yet, one has cause to wonder. Why did Moses utter the warnings twice? And why did he do it differently each time? Do the two *Tochachot* in Leviticus and Deuteronomy refer, perhaps, to two different situations in Jewish history? Or do they perhaps refer to two different kinds of crises?

The great Nachmanides tells us that the first *Tochacha* is prophetic of the destruction of the First Jewish Commonwealth in the year 586 B.C.E., when the Babylonians conquered Judea, reduced Jerusalem to ashes, and exiled the Jews to Babylon. The second, he says, is prophetic of the destruction of the Second Jewish Commonwealth in the year 70, when the Romans burned the second temple and precipitated our dispersion to all the corners of the earth.

While Nachmanides' suggestion is very intriguing, the question remains whether one can support his opinion from the texts. And to this question, the greatest preacher of the last generation, Rabbi Amiel, formerly Chief Rabbi of Tel-Aviv, gives a truly brilliant reply. The texts, he points out, bear out Nachmanides' sug-

23

gestion. For, explains Rabbi Amiel, there are two kinds of national disintegration. There are two ways in which a nation tends toward collapse. One way is for a nation to lose the earmarks of nationhood. It can lose its land, its statehood, its independence. There is another way, however, which is even more tragic. The individual constituents of the nation lose their pride in their heritage, their faith in their ability to create things worthwhile. The nation then disintegrates, because its constituents have individually given up the fight.

The first *Tochacha*, says Rabbi Amiel, deals with that type of national collapse which comes from the loss of land and statehood. And that can be seen from the verses of the text in Leviticus. The warnings are all given in the plural, because they refer to the collective collapse of the nation. The warnings also refer to the destruction of the soil and the devastation of the cities. The emphasis is on the devastation that will come to the national shrine and all the national institutions.

In Deuteronomy, however, the warnings are directed principally to the disintegration of individual Jews. That is why the verses are all in the singular, "thou" not "you". And that is also why there is such a great emphasis on the collapse of individual faith. "Thou shalt have no faith in thine own existence."

And historically, that is what happened. After the destruction of the First Temple, Jews lost their land and statehood, but with the guidance of the Prophets, Jews, even in their exile, turned closer to their God than ever before. Babylon became a tremendous center for the revival of Judaism. The Synagogue became the great creation of our people and the institution of the Synagogue became a model for all of the western world and one of our greatest contributions to civilization.

After the destruction of the Second Temple, however, our greatest loss was the spiritual disintegration of most individual Jews. They lost faith in themselves and their heritage. A few remained loyal, but the overwhelming majority were dispersed, embraced Christianity or assimilated altogether. True, there were times in the past 2000 years when Judaism thrived, in the Golden Age of Spain and in the ghettoes of Eastern Europe. But generally speaking, in the year 70, there were at least five times as many Jews as there were in 1789 when the French Revolution began. This indicates a sad breakdown of the morale of individual Jews following the destruction of the Second Commonwealth. And that is why Nachmanides regarded the two sets of warnings in the Bible as prophetic of the two great destructions. The first, in the plural, referred to loss of land and state, but the second, in the singular, referred to the disintegration and "failure of nerve" of individual Jews.

Believe me, friends, there is much that we can learn for our own day from this comment of our sages. We have been privileged in our own day to behold one recovery, the recovery by Jews of their land and statehood. We have been privileged to behold the re-demption of the land – a miraculous and speedy rehabilitation of the soil of Israel, the reconstruction of its cities, the reforestation of its hills. But alas, we are very far from beholding *geulat ha'am*, the recovery of the people, the restoration of universal Jewish morale, the restoration of the faith of Jews in themselves, their heritage, their future.

Of course, millions of people get along all their lives without a faith to live by, but when we discover Jews in our day craving such a faith – particularly among our college youth who are groping, and among disillusioned intellectuals – what are the faiths to which they turn? Alas, it is seldom to Judaism that they rediscover an allegiance. It is usually to either Catholicism or Communism that they become all-out converts!

But while converts to Catholicism are few, the Jewish converts to Communism are many. In this instance, the conversions are reaching almost epidemic proportions. And make no mistake about it. When I say conversions, I mean exactly that. No reason-ing with these converts helps, for Communism is a real religion to them. What Moscow says is accepted on faith, no matter what the evidence. But these youths had been groping for a faith. They had no faith in their own heritage as Jews. They did not think that they could help the world by remaining Jews, as every mentally and emotionally healthy Jew should feel. And having lost faith in their Jewishness, they espoused a new religion.

American Jews are not the only Jews who must solve this prob-lem. Israeli Jews must face it also. I have no fears that Mapam will ever control the Israeli government. But the present govern-ment is finding it difficult to cope with the tactics of these pro-

Russian elements who are embarrassing the government at every step. These Israelis have also lost faith in their own Judaism. They have a new faith, the faith of the U.S.S.R.

And that is why I say, we are witnessing the recovery of land and statehood, but the Jew's recovery of his own faith, the recovery of the faith of the Jew in the potential of his own heritage for good, this the future must yet bring.

How it will come, I cannot say. But one thing I know. If we recognize this second recovery to be an important one, then we will do things we have never yet tried. And I speak to you in practical terms. Compare the cost of curing a man who is physically ill with the cost of curing a man who is suffering from a mental disorder. You know that to cure a mental disorder costs much more and takes more time. The same applies to the rehabilitation of a people. We know the cost of the physical rehabilitation of Israelis. Hundreds of millions have already been spent and there are estimates that it will take at least another billion and a half of investment capital to solve all of Israel's economic problems. But while billions are, or will be, spent on the recovery of land and statehood, we are spending meager millions on the spiritual recovery. What are we spending on Jewish scholarship a year, here and in Israel? A mere pittance. Without enormous resources how can we create the books, endow the schools, support the scholars, that are necessary for the recovery of our faith in our heritage? Compare what we spend with the millions the Catholic Church spends a year on its universities, its radio broadcasts, its literature, movies and plays, its missionaries, and its public lectures? That is why I say, first, if we are to solve the problem we must think in terms of appropriating hundreds of millions for higher Jewish learning as we have spent hundreds of millions to recover land and statehood. But second, a spiritual recovery consumes time and we are giving it practically no time at all. We cannot hope to accomplish the recovery of our faith in our heritage, so long as Judaism is a three day a year religion to the majority of Jews.

It is interesting, for example, that our ancestors who kept the faith, and practiced Judaism every day of their lives, who prayed thrice daily, uttering at least 100 blessings every day, and who observed Sabbaths, holidays and fasts, felt the need before the High

Holy Days to add to their Jewish living by rising before dawn for special services – the Slichot – before the New Year and Day of Atonement. And most American Jews, to whom the three days is the sum total of all Jewish observance, have felt no need for the Slichos. How can we possibly behold our spiritual recovery with such a minimum application of time!

I pray fervently, that we will earnestly consider the problem that is ours. I pray fervently that the day is not distant, when we will give serious thought to the recovery of our faith in our own heritage, even as we have been privileged to behold the recovery of land and statehood. I pray fervently, that you and I, in particular, will resolve this coming year to give more of our resources, of money and time to *geulat ha'am* – the redemption of our people's faith even as we have helped to redeem our people's land, Amen!

Altar and Courthouse

If one were to visit an old New England town, he would be apt to find two important buildings situated near each other in the public square. One would be a church, and the other, the town or county courthouse. It is not a pure coincidence that these two buildings were erected side by side. Rather was the practice based on a beautiful Jewish tradition which was known to the founding fathers of our beloved country. Indeed, the early settlers of New England relied heavily on Old Testament precedents for many of their institutions. And the proximity of the altar to the hall of justice was predicated on passages in the Book of Exodus. One passage describes the manner of building an altar. Immediately preceding, we have the Decalogue which we read today, and immediately succeeding, we have the civil and criminal codes of Judaism. Why is the passage dealing with the altar integrated with the most important legislation of the Pentateuch? "To teach us," say our Sages, "that the Sanhedrin – Jewry's highest court – was to sit and administer justice in a room adjoining the site of the altar." (*Jerusalem Talmud Makkot* 2:6) That accounts also for the nearness of New England's courthouses to her places of worship.

On many occasions, friends, our Sages pondered why our traditions required this proximity between altar and hall of justice. Our Sages found many parallels between the role of priests and the role of judges. They also suggested that in the performance of their duties priests and judges should maintain the same mood and the same dedication to high purpose. However, I find, in the association of divine worship with the administration of law, an even more significant message, and would only that Americans would heed that message today as their forbears respected the tradition in planning their town buildings!

For let us understand, friends, the nature of justice. The simplest form of justice with which all of us are familiar is what the philosophers call "corrective justice." If a man is killed, or his limbs are maimed, or his property is stolen, the offender must account to the law so that the law may correct or remedy the evil. The correction may take the form of punishment or compensation, but basically it is a wrong that must be righted. If the law did not do this, the peace of the land would be disturbed as persons who were wronged engaged in self-help to avenge themselves. The Law of Moses abounds in illustrations of this type of legislation.

There is, however, another form of justice which Aristotle called "distributive justice." Distributive justice is concerned with the fair distribution of worldly goods and services and the ready flow in society of that which is due unto every citizen. This is a higher form of justice for more developed societies. This type of justice – as conceived by the Greeks – is the justice of societies like our own, in which there always is an exchange of goods and services between people. The principal motif of this type of justice is that each man shall have what is due him and that what is due each man shall be fair and equitable. Long before Aristotle, our Torah projected more legislation in this connection than any other legal system in human history.

However, there is a third type of justice with which the Greeks and Romans were not familiar. It is the type of justice that made Jewish law the glorious body of law that it is. I choose to call this type of justice – empathic justice. It is the type of justice that seeks to make people identify themselves with each other – with each other's needs, with each other's hopes and aspirations, with each other's defeats and frustrations. It is the type of law that calls for empathy, and demands not only the righting of wrongs, and not only the distribution unto every man of the full measure of goods and services due him, but also the projection of every self into the condition of every other self. What other law, for example, would demand, as we read today, that slaves and not only masters, shall enjoy Sabbath rest? (*Deuteronomy* 5:13-14) What other law would demand that thou shalt not oppress the stranger "*because you know the soul of the stranger*," having been strangers yourselves in the land of Egypt! (*See Deuteronomy* 10:9) Because *you* know the distress of slaves and the loneliness of the stranger, justice requires that you project yourself into their souls and make their plight your own. What other law would demand that when you see your enemy's donkey collapsing under a heavy load, and you contemplate withholding your assistance, then remember that *"with him* you shall help!" (*Exodus* 23:5) Feel for the beast and feel for its master, and curb your own feelings for revenge. And what other law would require of a creditor who takes his debtor's sole garment as security to return it before nightfall lest the debtor have to lie without it! (*Exodus* 22:24-26)

So much of Jewish law is concerned with the projection of the human self into the needs and problems of every other human being that I feel that it was this conception that the propinquity of altar to courthouse sought to convey. For what was the altar? It was the place where Jews offered their sacrifices to God. And what were the sacrifices? Let us not be naive. God did not need animals to feast His heart, or incense to please His nostrils. Our Sages regarded the altar as the place where Jews could identify themselves with their God, share with Him the gifts that were theirs, dine from His table, and enjoy a sense of complete identification with their Maker. And as the altar was the symbol of their identification with their God, so the hall of justice was a symbol of their identification with their fellowman. That was the connecting link. And that is why altar and courtroom were side by side. They spelled identification – identification with God in the case of altar, and identification with one's fellow man in the case of justice.

And this empathic justice I should like to have you remember. I should like to have you remember it, not only because I want you on this festival of Shovuos to share the pride that is mine in the great legal tradition that is our own, but also because I want you to understand how deep are the roots that prompt us to resent, as we do, the tactics of McCarthy and his associates. When we read, for example, that Gallup's poll indicates that 49% of Protestants favor McCarthy, while the remaining 51% are divided between those who are opposed to him and those who are undecided; and when we read that 58% of Roman Catholics favor him, with the balance also divided between those opposed and those undecided, while at the same time only 15% of Jews look with favor upon him, with over 70% in opposition, then let us remember that this is not because any one of us yields to McCarthy in our loyalty to the American heritage or our hostility to all forms of totalitarianism, whether of the left or of the right, but rather because thousands of years of exposure to what I have called empathic justice have so conditioned us that we feel too deeply for the innocent people whose careers he ruined and whose reputations he besmirched. We cannot tolerate a man who brooks no interference when he is engaged in a villainous task, and crushes any individual who either asserts his constitutional rights or expresses the mildest dissent. We have had implanted in us a close association between the role of the altar as a means of self-identification with God and the role of the hall of justice as a means of self-identification with our fellow man. And instead of apologizing for the fact that we are overwhelmingly opposed to McCarthy, and instead of feeling embarrassed that "Time" magazine points to us as the sole religious group that feels so strongly about this cancer on the American scene, we should boast about it. We should proclaim that, just as two thousand years ago Jews conceived of justice in a manner that eluded even Plato and Aristotle, so today our conception of justice is still centuries ahead of the conception of most people, even our beloved fellow-Americans. Of this we should continue to remain proud, and we should continue to fight for the ultimate victory of our point of view.

But, friends, I call this to your attention on this festival also because I want you to consider how and why it was that our people developed and cultivated this highly refined conception of justice. It was not because our blood is different from the blood of other people. Nor are our genes superior to the genes of other people. There is nothing in our physical make-up that accounts for so great an accomplishment. It is rather that Jews recognized the study of the Law as the most important part of their education from the cradle to the grave. We have no objection to fairy tales, and no objection to Peter Pan and Pinocchio, to enrich the minds of our children and fire their imaginations. But we did not feel that that was enough. Rather did we want every Jew to become a master of the Law. And even if educators today cannot comprehend how eight and ten and twelve-year old Jewish children study the Law in the manner in which advanced seniors in a law school study law, that should not trouble us. It may be shocking to find Jewish youngsters involved in intensive and abstruse discussions with respect to civil law and criminal law and the ethical postulates of that law. But that was the normative Jewish education, not alone for lawyers and rabbis, but for every Jewish child. Children were nurtured and weaned and raised with constant exposure to the ideals of justice, and the rules of law which fulfill those ideals. The result was that all Jewish students were even more preoccupied with the nature of justice than they were with the nature of God. That is particularly important to remember on this festival when we rededicate ourselves to the Law. For if, for the next year, my flock will do nothing other than study the twentieth, twenty-first and twenty-second chapters of Exodus to which my sermon this morning refers, then they will become educated Jews and understand what it is that makes the Jewish conscience respond to empathic justice.

One great Russian jurist fifty years ago, Petrazhitski, proposed that a legal education was important for every citizen in order to cultivate that which was most necessary for the right kind of social and political living. We Jews were thousands of years ahead of him, and may God help us to revive that tradition so that there will not be in our ranks even fifteen percent favoring McCarthy and another fifteen per cent undecided. At the same time, may we win back to the fold of traditional Judaism those of our co-religionists who aped the Christians by rejecting the Law and denying its centrality in our ancestral heritage. Let our Reform brethren abandon their antinomianism and rejoin us in our dedication to the Law, that together we may hasten the establishment of God's kingdom on the face of the earth. For this we must pray even as we vow, on *Zeman Matan Toraseinu* [the time of the giving of the Torah], to study and fulfill that Law more frequently and more intensively than ever. Amen!

"The Yoke of the Law"

In the history of religion it often occurs that what superficially appears to be a minor difference of opinion becomes the basis for a schism of major importance. We Jews, for example, find it difficult to understand how Protestant denominations split so often on what appears to be minor differences in doctrine, while Christians find it difficult to understand how the problem of wearing a hat at Jewish religious services could precipitate a break between Orthodoxy and Reform. Yet so it was.

We read that the Jews went forth from Egypt. "In triumph" [literally, "with upraised arms"]. (*Exodus* 14:8) These words are translated by Unkelas, the great translator of antiquity, as meaning, with uncovered heads. Jews thus entered upon their freedom, by exposing their hair to the sun. In ancient times a slave covered his head while a free man did not. Therefore, to symbolize their freedom, Jews did the customary thing. They removed their headgear which was the badge of bondage. In subsequent years, however, they undertook once again to cover their heads as a sign of their submission to the will of God. They cherished freedom. Yet for their freedom to have direction, they accepted the yoke of the Law. And their acceptance of the Law they symbolized by covering their heads. As Rashi said, "Cover your head that you may thereby indicate your fear of Heaven." (Tal. B. Shabbos 156b)

However, with the advent of the Reform movement it was inevitable that the hat become an issue. Most Reform Jews were motivated by the fact that they wanted to do what Christians did. But scholars among them – and scholars there were – must have understood, that since the Reform Movement was rejecting the Law and the pattern of Jewish observance, it was only logical that they reject the practice of covering their heads, which symbolized acceptance of the Law. That explains how a seemingly trivial matter became so important. The hat became the symbol of the Law. Wearing it, meant acceptance of the Law. Not wearing it meant rejection of the Law.

I call this to your attention, not because we have any group in our Congregation agitating for the removal of hats. Not at all. On the other hand, so many Jews feel uncomfortable without the hat even in Reform synagogues, that most Reform synagogues now make the wearing of the hat optional. In only a few die-hard Reform congregations is the covered head forbidden. However, while the wearing of the hat is hardly an issue any more, the question of the acceptance of the Law is very much an issue. And it is high time that we came to grips with the problem.

Reform Judaism began with the view that what is important in Judaism is its ethical and spiritual message. The observances, it considered of little or no consequence. A distinction was made between Prophetic Judaism and Rabbinic Judaism. The former was cherished because it involved the ideals of peace and brotherhood and justice. But Reform Judaism was intolerant of the methods of the Rabbis to fulfill these ideals. Reform Judaism was intolerant of the legalists who developed the elaborate hermeneutics of the Halachah, the intellectual apparatus of Jewish Law. Alas, they forgot that they had discovered nothing new. They forgot that their view was precisely that of Paul, the first Christian, who also established a new religion. Paul wanted to make the ideals of our prophets acceptable to the pagans of the Greek and Roman world; and to accomplish this end, he too rejected the Law. And Reform Judaism did the same thing. But what was the result? Intelligent Jews could not long be duped, and soon they began to recognize, that if there was little or no difference between Christianity and Reform Judaism, intermarriage and assimilation could not be objectionable.

The same thing happened in America; and I remember how years ago, Reform Rabbis wrote and preached and lectured constantly, upon the differences between Reform Judaism and Unitarian Christianity, so similar were they that it became necessary to reiterate and reemphasize the differences. The arguments were not too convincing and intermarriage and assimilation continued to be so rampant that the leading Reform Rabbis in America today want to re-accept the Law. Not the complete Law perhaps, not the whole of the Shulchan Aruch, but some of it as revised by them. They want to create their own Law, a new Law, but they are at least giving up the idea of concentrating on Prophetic Judaism alone. They want Rabbinic Judaism too, some of it, at least, even if not all of it. And that is why there is the possibility that America, instead of having three groups – Orthodox, Conservative and Reform, may some day have only two. The left wing conservatives may merge with the reform group, while the right wing conservatives will join with the orthodox and constitute one united front of traditionalists. Yet what is becoming increasingly apparent is that all Jews, traditionalists and non-traditionalists, will once and for all recognize that Judaism without Law is not Judaism at all. It is Christianity. The unique character of Judaism will ever be that it calls for Law.

Now, friends, you may rightfully ask, "Why does Judaism so insist upon Law as a part of the religious way of life? Why do we so emphasize the Law when spirituality should be a matter of the spirit?" And to this I answer most emphatically, "You cannot make men spiritual by simply preaching to them about high ideals and eternal values. How much brotherhood does the world now have after two thousand years of preaching about the brotherhood of man?"

Let us look at the American scene. When will Whites and Negroes even have the right to attend the same Christian church down south? When will they sit as brothers, even in pews, to listen to the Sermon on the Mount? Never, because preachers will have preached a million sermons on equality, but rather when a Congress will have passed Civil Rights legislation, making any overt act of discrimination punishable by law.

When will Jews enjoy equality in admission to college or in employment opportunities? Not after a hundred thousand Easters will have been celebrated with sermons on goodwill, but rather after one effective Fair Employment Practices Act or one effective Fair Educational Practices Act will have been passed.

When will scoundrels stop their scurrilous attacks on innocent people, even in the highest legislature of the nation? Not after they have attended a thousand communion masses, but after one law will have been passed making legislators responsible for their malicious attacks on innocent victims. One law would silence where everything else has failed.

We could talk forever in generalities about Jewish ideals, or more specifically about Jewish consciousness and avail naught, unless we follow the Law to achieve our goals. We could talk to children forever about freedom, but nothing makes them as conscious of slavery and freedom, as laws with respect to Matzoh and Moror, and the observance of other Passover rituals prescribed by Jewish law. With regard to the equitable treatment and ultimate emancipation of slaves our sages did not rely on exhortations alone. Rather did they develop Hilchos Avodim, laws pertaining to slaves – and these laws were so effective, that a Rabbi once expressed himself to the effect that the Law so protects slaves, that it is better to be a Jewish slave than a Jewish master. And that is why I love law, and particularly Jewish law. That is why I love the yoke of the Law. It is hardly a yoke at all. It is rather the one truly effective way we have of translating ideals into realities. And that is why I am impatient with talk about freedom and brotherhood. I want action, legal action, legislation to achieve the desired goals. That is the spirit of Judaism and its method. That is the spirit of the Halachah. May God help us to appreciate this unique approach of our faith, to cherish it and to preserve it. For, alas, the world still needs it. May God help us to study and apply Halachah until the Messiah doth come and with him the age of everlasting justice and freedom.

Days of Awe

Our fast of Yom Kippur has begun and for some twenty-five hours we will mortify our bodies and deny them food and drink. Some Jews will even abjure sleep and remain awake all night reading the psalms and studying Torah. Yet, friends, one misconception I must correct. Too many of us are under the impression that the fast is punishment for sins we have committed. This conception is not authentically Jewish. One of my own great ancestors, Rabbi Ezekiel Landau of Prague, author of the classic "Nodah B'yihudah," protested vehemently against Jews who deem it important to torture themselves on the Day of Atonement and even add to the forms of suffering already required by the Law. Rabbi Landau argued that we fast only to induce that feeling of physical weakness and helplessness that will in turn induce submission of the soul to God and feelings of remorse for sin. The tormenting of the body for our sins is not penitence. Only masochists punish themselves. Judaism, on the other hand, seeks only that we cultivate the mood in which we may readily recognize our personal inadequacy, confess our sins and resolve never to commit them again.

Thus, friends, let us understand a basic truth. The purpose of the fast is to create a mood – a mood of helplessness and dependence upon God. And I know of no message that needs to be stressed more in our generation.

For let us ask ourselves – why isn't our generation as religious as generations that have preceded us? What has changed in human nature that makes us seek God so much less than our ancestors did? We are not all great intellectuals. And even among the great intellectuals of the past there were also many pious, devout people. The greatest of scientists and philosophers not only sought

God but prayed to Him. Yet we, who are neither as learned nor as profound, can get along for years without religion. And even when we do attend the synagogue occasionally, it is usually to perform a duty. We do not want to be conspicuous by our absence, or we do not want it said of us that we are evading our obligation to the Jewish community.

What has happened to us, friends, is not that we have become so much more philosophical than our ancestors were, but rather that our mood has changed. Emotionally we are different – and not intellectually superior. For basic in religious experience, basic in faith, is man's feeling of helplessness, man's feeling of personal inadequacy. Our ancestors had this mood. The problems of life and death, the challenge of raising children, even the need for making a living made them feel humble, and in their humility they craved guidance from God. But we, their children, are never humble.

What can't we do? We are masters of our fate and captains of our destiny. We control the air above and the earth beneath. We not only fly; we even make clouds and hope someday to dispel them as well. Perhaps we will soon engage in interplanetary transport and dominate the universe. The resources of the earth we magnify – even atomic power is at our command. We are proud of our achievements. Who did it all? We! We, with the might of our arms and the genius of our brains! Who needs God any more? Instead, man sits on God's throne. Man is king. And what appeal can religion have for us? On Yom Kippur we recite in our prayers a contrast between *Melech Elyon*, the Supreme King, and man, the *melech ebyon*, the lowly, pauperized king, but we do not mean what we say. We are, in fact, not sure that there is any God but ourselves. That we ourselves are gods we do not doubt.

That is why religion has no appeal to us. We are of an altogether different temperament than our forbears. They were humble; we are arrogant. They felt the need of God; we can get along without Him. We know how to do for ourselves all the things which once prompted man to search for God. Only when we are about to die do we, perhaps, realize that for once there is something we ourselves cannot control and we turn to God. But until we are about to die, we know it all and can do it all. And deaf are our ears to the prophet's demand that we walk humbly before our Maker.

Therefore, I say to you, friends, that the significance of this day lies not in the fact that we are to punish ourselves. Nay, this holy day is to induce a mood – a mood of humility and a mood of helplessness. As we become weak and frail in body, we are to learn that man is not king of the universe but rather a stupid, blundering fool who has learned to play God, and because he played God so long and so well, he now stands on the brink of his own destruction. Humble men don't go to war. Humble men don't seek world domination. Humble men also inspire humble children who do not crave the excitement of juvenile delinquency and even murder. Humble men are happy to share with others – for they know not when they themselves will be in need. But we are not humble. We rule the universe – we have no need of God.

If you agree thus far, my dear and beloved congregation, and you are prepared to tolerate still more my preoccupation on these High Holy days with the nature of religious experience, then let us ponder – What is it that died within us that has made us so arrogant? I cannot deny that ours is the right – even the duty – to conquer the universe. I cannot deny that ours is the right – even the duty – to end drought and disease. Yes – most decidedly yes. But, when in ancient times men made great discoveries, they felt something we do not feel. We simply have no sense of awe. We don't know what it is to stand before a grand spectacle – a beautiful sunset or a breathtaking Grand Canyon, and with awe, hail the Creator and His Creation. We don't know what it is to hold a baby in our arms and in awe meditate upon the miracle of a tiny egg grown into a live, pulsating, loving human being. We don't know what it is to fly in the atmosphere and in awe regard the vastness of space and our puny size by comparison. We don't know what it is to split an atom and in awe confess that we are like passing shadows before the Supreme Being who designed and made the atom.

We know more about nature than our ancestors did. But they stood in awe of what little they knew. We who know so much more ought to be even more impressed with God than they. But instead we become impressed with ourselves. We become impressed with what we accomplished – as if we created the energy in the atom – as if we created the process of gestation – as if we created the planets we shall soon traverse!

And without humility, there can be no awe, and without awe there can be no reverence. What respect do we or our children have for anything past, present or future? What respect for parents? What respect for sacred traditions or sacred objects? We all presume that we know more than our ancestors did. Why then should we revere them? We read the Bible and the prayer-book. For our parents it all made sense. But they were primitive! We have out-grown them. We do not want to accept their nonsense. And our children imitate us. We have no respect for our forbears and our children in turn have no respect for us. Who pauses to think that perhaps great wisdom and invaluable experience is being conveyed to us through an ancestral heritage which we might fathom if we had the humility and the reverence to study and master it!

And this, my friends, is the significance of the Days of Awe. Humility and reverence are their goals. Let us ask ourselves frankly, honestly – can we capture the mood? And if we do capture the mood, how will we retain it? What can we do to hold it for our daily living – and as an example for our children?

I haven't the whole answer, my friends. But two institutions remain in Jewish life whose principal goals are to induce reverence – the Jewish home and the Jewish synagogue. And alas, how these two institutions are losing their character in these days of arrogance and materialistic values. Every Jewish home was once a shrine. You entered it via a *Mezuzah* which signified that it was dedicated to the love of God. Its table was an altar. Salt was on it as a reminder of the salt that always reposed on the altar at Jerusalem. You approached the table with hands ritualistically washed as the priests wash their hands before they bless the Congregation of Israel. You ate and you drank only after having thanked God for your blessings, and when you had finished eating, you thanked Him again. You prayed before you retired for sleep and you prayed when you awoke. And even as parents now remind their children to brush their teeth, Jewish mothers once reminded their children that all that they were and are and ever will be was due to a great Creator whom we were to revere all our lives. Fathers studied Torah with their loved ones, inquired about what was happening at the Cheder, and sometimes would themselves communicate a beautiful thought or memory from their fathers or grandfathers. Children did not hail their fathers as the "old man" or their mothers as the "old lady." The table was not a place from which you hurriedly ran, especially on a Friday night, for a date or a movie. Home was not just an address and a place to park your car. Yes, our homes are more beautiful than ever, but they are houses, not homes, quarters not shrines.

And alas, the synagogue too is not what it once was. Synagogues have become big institutions without reverence. Generally they have become big and gaudy – with God playing less of a role than the rich patron, and prayer heard less often than idle gossip and even malicious slander. Thank God, our congregation has resisted the trend. We have striven hard to make our services inspiring. We have tried to make our services induce reverence. We have tried to teach Jews to respect and reverence a shrine of the Lord. We have tried to make the prayers moving and the sermons delivered from the pulpit a stimulus for reverence of the tradition of our people. But even the influence of our synagogue has not penetrated all the homes of our members.

On this goal let us meditate as we fast and let us recapture our sense of awe for ourselves and our children, for our homes and our synagogues, for America and all humanity, Amen!

Responsibility for Our Own Sins

Jews, alas, are not unfamiliar with the term "scapegoat". We have played the role too often and too well not to be aware of its tragic implications. In the middle ages, whether it was during a black plague, or after a Christian defeat at the hand of Moslems, we Jews were held to blame and we paid with countless lives for conditions over which we had absolutely no control. In modern times, it was a Hitler who held us responsible for Germany's defeat in World War I. It was a Sultan who holds us responsible for Morocco's difficulties with France. It is a Nasser who holds us responsible for Egypt's internal difficulties. The Jew is the classic scapegoat of medieval and modern history. But even that does not disturb me as much as the fact that Christians regard us as the people who created the idea of the scapegoat. They say of our Day of Atonement service that it is the source of the idea and it, therefore, behooves us to understand what the ritual of this sacred day purports to convey.

Yes, that ritual does involve a scapegoat – the sending of a goat into the wilderness, there to perish for our sins. As a matter of fact the term "scapegoat" is derived from this ritual and just as Jews in ancient times permitted a goat to bear the guilt of their sins, so in modern times the Christian world used the Jew as their own scapegoat. But this gave rise in Christianity to a doctrine which played a notorious role in Christian theology – the doctrine of vicarious atonement – the doctrine which recognizes that someone else's suffering can evoke forgiveness for my sins.

What I want to submit to you this evening is that the ritual which gave rise to the scapegoat idea is completely misunderstood. On the other hand, the ritual which Jews performed on the Day of Atonement in the Temple was specifically designed to teach the very opposite – it was intended to teach us the doctrine of free will and individual responsibility – the doctrine that every man has it within his own power to decide whether he will be saint or sinner, whether he will be angel or devil. Paraphrasing the words of the poet, we are the captains of our own fate, the masters of our own destiny.

How did the ritual dramatize this basic thought? The immortal Rabbi Samson Raphael Hirsch provides the answer. Two goats, identical in appearance and size, were bought and brought together. Lots were cast. One was chosen for the Holy of Holies. The other was chosen for Azazel. One was chosen for the loftiest and most sacred purpose imaginable. The other was degraded beyond the lowest degradation. One attained unto the holiness of the holiest compartment of the temple. The other was sent to the wilderness rejected, laden with the sins of all. The one stood for the peak of spiritual ecstacy, the other for the totality of a community's evil.

These two extremes are also available to man. Man too can aspire and reach the Holy of Holies. Or he can so sink that he merits the hate and ostracism of his fellow-man. Animals are not so. They have an almost negligible margin of choice. They are what they are and cannot change anything about themselves. The poisonous snake cannot help being what it is nor can the loyal dog fail to respond to its affectionate master. But for the human being there is a choice so wide that it ranges from the saintliness of a Moses to the treachery of a Hitler. Ours is the power to soar to the highest or sink to the lowest.

This point is beautifully illustrated in the story told of Rabbi Chaim, the Zanzer Rabbi. He once addressed his disciples and said, "When I will have to face my Maker on Judgment Day, I am not afraid that he will ask me why I was not a Lawgiver like Moses. I will simply tell him that I did not have the genius of Moses. I am also not afraid that he will ask me why I was not a philosopher like Maimonides. Again I will tell him that I was not as gifted as Maimonides was. But what will I say to the Lord when he says to me, "Reb Chaim, why weren't you simply Reb Chaim, why weren't you what you yourself could have been? To that question I will not be able to reply on Judgment Day."

And that is the challenge of the ritual of the Day of Atonement. What will any one of us say to our Maker when He asks us on

Judgment Day why we weren't what we ourselves could have been! Aye, we cannot all be geniuses. We cannot all cure cancer or polio. We cannot all master Torah and write philosophy. We cannot all compose music or create art. But every one of us can be a saint or a devil. That Judaism teaches. And of that the Day of Atonement reminds us.

But I explain all of this tonight, friends, not only because I want you to know that the Day of Atonement emphasizes individual responsibility, but also because this message needs special emphasis in our day. And it needs special emphasis because there is no end to the present use of scapegoats. Not only on the international scene, but in every personal and social situation, we look for a scapegoat to assume the blame for what we fail to be.

We fail as children or as students – our parents are at fault.

We fail as parents – our children are at fault.

We haven't the finest character – then it must be our older or our younger brother or sister that corrupted us.

We do not espouse the finest values – our friends are at fault, our society, our milieu.

No matter what the sin or failure for which we are called to account, we invariably have our scapegoat. True it is that much can be blamed on our families, our surroundings, our society. But there must come a halt to this pretending that the human being is incapable of responsibility for what he himself is or becomes. We must call a halt to the notion that nothing is within our control. Judaism teaches the reverse – everything is in God's hands except the character that you and I shall have. We are the captains of our fate and the masters of our destiny. And let us not seek scapegoats forever and ever.

And now, friends, you will understand one other important point with regard to the story of Abraham's sacrifice of Isaac with which I began my holiday preaching.

In Judaism, we are taught that Abraham was prepared to sacrifice his son Isaac to prove his love to God. Mind you, it is man who gives of himself to prove his love of God. In Christianity, however, the basic idea is that God sacrifices His alleged son to atone for man's sins. God's alleged son is the scapegoat for the sins of Christians! No wonder that for centuries thereafter the blood of

Jews could also be used as scapegoats to atone for the sins of non-Jews! But the difference is characteristic. We Jews affirm that we individually must decide for ourselves, and atone for our guilt. Christianity started with an alleged son of God atoning for them and continued seeking further scapegoats ever after.

Helping God to Use Us

Some time ago, it was my privilege to discuss religion with a number of young people. They were all devout and observant. I asked them whether they had ever considered what approach they would take to convince others to share their views and live as they live. What ideas would they have to communicate to those who differed with them in order to establish a basis for belief in God and Torah? One suggested that it would be necessary first to convince an irreligious person that there is a God. If one could but carry conviction with regard to the existence of God, then everything else that religious living required would follow from the one premise. Another suggested that it would be most important to convey to a non-believer a belief in the existence of a soul, the belief that there exists independently of the body a spiritual essence which could survive the body after death. Particularly in an age which is so preoccupied with psychosomatic medicine and the interdependence of body and spirit, it was necessary to indicate that while there may be this interdependence, there nonetheless is an entity which survives the physical substance of man. This person felt that if conviction with regard to the existence of the soul could be communicated to the irreligious, they, too, would accept the truths and the practices of religion more readily. The third youth indicated that it was difficult to communicate conviction with regard to the existence of God or soul, but the one point which he would stress most is that God communicates with man, that God reveals Himself unto man. This premise is especially important to Judaism, for without the belief in Revelation, the Torah would lose much of its binding power.

The answers which the children gave me were very impressive. However, I shocked them when I told them that I would start with none of these approaches. I told them that I would begin with an altogether different premise. I would want to convince the non-believing Jew first and foremost that the Jewish people as a people have served a unique purpose on the face of the earth; that they have served this purpose even unwittingly; that they have served this purpose most often without even participating in the process; and that by merely being Jews, they have played a unique and significant role in human history. If I could but convince people of this unique role of the Jewish people, I could then proceed to ask them who gave the Jewish people that role. Once I had convinced them that the role was given unto them by some Force beyond themselves, I would be in a position to bring conviction with regard to the existence of God and the existence of a spiritual substance in a person which might constitute the basis for the independent existence of a soul. I could also explain the unique role of the Jewish people by reference to a unique work, our Torah, given unto the world by God.

Friends, it is precisely this thought that I should like to convey to you this morning in my message for the new year. I should like to have you share with me the conviction that the Jewish people, whether they will it or not, have always played a unique role in human history and that they are still playing it 'Twere as if from time immemorial, we, by merely being Jewish, were to serve as the gadfly of the conscience of the world. 'Twere as if we were an irritant, a challenger, a heckler, to what in every age has been the accepted God for worship or the accepted philosophy for living. Abraham, our first patriarch, served that very purpose in his day. Everything he said and did represented a challenge to the prevailing ideals of his time. But also after Abraham, the same situation prevailed. Let us take Rome, as an example. There was a time that Rome dominated virtually the entire civilized world and the Romans represented a point of view that was progressive. They boasted that they did not interfere with the religious convictions of any of the peoples that they conquered and ruled. They were experts in international law and administration. They were empire builders. In the achievement of imperial purposes, they wanted the people under their control to enjoy a modicum of autonomy, provided they paid homage to the central authority at Rome. This was a form of international organization which was so successful that for eight centuries peace was preserved in the Mediterranean world. That peace became known as the Pax Romana. Yet, friends, as we study Roman history, we discover that while the system was acceptable and workable for all peoples, there was one notorious exception. The Jews could not be made to fit into the system. This central authority ultimately called for its adoration and worship. What started as a democracy, ultimately became monarchy and empire. And because Jews could not accept the respectable thesis of the day, Jews were persecuted, and the central authority of Rome felt impelled to suppress the Jewish religion. We had many martyrs in that age, many of whom we memorialize in our High Holy Day prayers.

Then the Roman empire collapsed and there came in its stead the age in which Christianity dominated the scene. This was the faith of the Mediterranean world, the faith that presumed to bring unto all humanity a God of love who wanted human brotherhood. This was the faith that regarded the Old Testament as inadequate, because it did not sufficiently stress the importance of love. This was the faith that preached the gospel of loving one's neighbor as one's self. Again, however, with one exception — love for everyone but Jews. By merely being Jews we were again a gadfly and an irritant. The love could not extend unto the one people. On the other hand, there had to be discovered some kind of rationalization for the hate that persisted in the hearts of Christians for the Jewish people. This rationalization ultimately took form in the Christian idea that Jews should suffer, because this is evidence of their sin in rejecting the son of God as the L-rd. Somehow the Jews again became a gadfly to the respectable thesis of the Christian world that it represented the God of love and the ideal of brotherhood.

With respect to Mohammedanism, we have the same situation. Even when we come down to the age of the Reformation — the revolt against Rome and its church in the days of Martin Luther, we discover that Martin Luther complained about the way in which the Catholic had treated the Jew. He thought that it would have been so much better had the Jews been treated with kindness. With kindness, the Jews might have become converted to Christianity. However, when Martin Luther, presumably a man of toleration, became annoyed that even his gospel had failed and that his toleration had yielded no results with Jews, he became as bitter an anti-Semite as ever the world had known. From the very beginning of Protestantism, too, we have been an irritant and a gadfly, from Martin Luther down unto the present, when many Protestants meet in international conventions and wonder whether the existence of the State of Israel is not a threat to their ultimate hope that Jews will be converted to Christianity. From Martin Luther to the present, we have been a challenge. 'Twere as if we were a perennial heckler of the rest of the world, a perennial heckler asking them whether they really mean what they say, whether they really are sincere with regard to the convictions they profess having.

That applied, however, not only to Christian groups. We can turn to philosophies that are presumably not at all committed to a religious ideology. There came the age of democracy with its glamorization of equality and fraternity. There was to be absolute equality irrespective of color, or creed. Yes, in a measure that has been achieved, and we Jews are certainly passionately devoted to the cause of democracy. We are passionately devoted to it because of our own tradition, because the ideals of democracy are derived from the heritage and the ethic that are ours. But somehow even into the democratic scheme of things, the sincerity of the democratic peoples is challenged by this perennial heckler, the Jewish people, the gadfly of the conscience of the world. Absolute equality there shall be for everyone, but for Jews. With regard to Jews, there is always a problem. There always had been a problem and the problem continues. The United States, for example, our own beloved country, has decided that it must do everything in its power to prevent communism from taking over other nations, and so we are providing arms to all the nations of the earth that promise to resist Communism — to all nations in Africa, Asia, and Europe, wherever they may be — to all countries but one. The State of Israel. Somehow the State of Israel is in a different position, and our State Department finds itself in a position where it can hardly explain the situation. But so it is! One step further. When was it ever heard that the American uniform worn by all American soldiers should not be entitled to respect by everyone? The

American uniform was always a badge of pride and honor. Everyone who wore it knows that it was so described and so glorified. Yet the American uniform can be a badge of honor for everyone, but a Jewish soldier who, when wearing it, may, nonetheless, be denied an opportunity to serve his country in countries like Saudi Arabia, where the United States is willing for oil to sacrifice the dignity and the honor of its uniform, when it is worn by Jews. So even in democratic countries, we Jews have been a heckler.

I do not say that we have been the only heckler, but throughout history we have been the most consistent and the most perennial of all the hecklers to the conscience of the world. This summer it was, alas, my sad privilege to have visited in a country with a totalitarian philosophy, but still a philosophy committed to the equality of all peoples, a philosophy committed not only to political and civic equality, but to economic equality as well — equality for everyone, no matter what his national or ethnic background. But again, not for Jews. Jews are in a different position. Somehow the Jews even there became the hecklers, the gadfly to the conscience of the Communist leaders. Perhaps it was because Stalin did want to become what the emperors of Rome once aspired to become—gods of the universe, that he had to depress the condition of Jews. Jews from the time of Abraham were the professional hecklers of all those who pretended to diety. Perhaps that was his reason. But again, by simply being Jews, we had become a gadfly to the conscience of the Soviet Union. It was not because Jews weren't willing to embrace communism. Indeed, it was not because Jews weren't willing to do everything that was expected of them, even if it meant forgetting God and their religion. However, simply by being Jews, we constituted a challenge to the powers that be.

Fortunately, we Jews are not the only one to have recognized our unique role. About a century ago, a very distinguished senator of South Carolina, a non-Jew, recognized this same role that we Jews were playing in human history. I quote from a speech which he delivered. "There is a river in the ocean. In the severest droughts it never fails, and in the mightiest floods it never overflows. The Gulf of Mexico is its fountain, and its mouth is in the Arctic seas. It is the Gulf Stream. There is in the world no other such majestic flow of waters. Its current is more rapid than the Mississippi or the Amazon, and its volume more than a thousand times greater. Its waters, as far out from the Gulf as the Carolina coasts, are of an indigo blue; they are so distinctly marked that their line of junction with the common sea-water may be traced by the eye. Often one half of a vessel may be perceived floating in the Gulf Stream water, while the other half is in the common water of the sea, so sharp is the line and such the want of affinity between those waters, and such too, the reluctance, so to speak, on the part of those of the Gulf Stream to mingle with the common water of the sea.

"This curious phenomenon in the physical world has its counterpart in the moral. There is a lonely river in the midst of the ocean of mankind. The mightiest floods of human temptation have never caused it to overflow, and the fiercest fires of human cruelty, though seven times heated in the furnace of religious bigotry, have never caused it to dry up, although its waves for two thousand years have rolled crimson with the blood of its martyrs. Its fountain is in the gray dawn of the world's history, and its mouth is somewhere in the shadows of eternity. It, too, refuses to mingle with the surrounding waves, and the line which divides its restless billows from the common waters of humanity is also plainly visible to the eye. It is the Jewish race."

Thus it appears that God willed that we play this role, and anyone who studies the history of our people must be impressed with this fact. Now, friends, if we are playing this role, and we cannot help playing this role, then it must be that God has willed it. Indeed, God willed it long ago as His Torah revealed that we would serve this purpose. The truth of Torah is thus vindicated by history and not by faith alone, and the least that one should ponder on the new year is a return to Torah, the book that indicated precisely what would happen in years to come. While our ancestors accepted it on faith, we now have the evidence of universal history to substantiate its authenticity.

Yet, friends, it is more than our role in human history that I want to demonstrate to you this morning. I want to call to your attention something equally significant. If, whether we will it or not, we must play this role, isn't it much to be preferred that we play this role consciously rather than unconsciously? If God is going to use us as His tool, should we not prefer to become that tool with our fullest accord? Shouldn't we prefer that we become His partner in His use of us, instead of being nothing else but the unwitting instrument of His design? This to me is the significance of the great story which we invariably read on the new year festival — the story of Abraham's sacrifice of his son, Isaac.

Abraham was asked by God to sacrifice his beloved son, Isaac, in proof of his devotion. Abraham could have argued with God. After all, it was God who had promised that it would be through Isaac that Abraham would transmit God's will to posterity. Yet, Abraham did not argue. Abraham had already been chosen as the instrument for God's Will and he was prepared to make himself a part of that Will. He was prepared to place his own will in tune with the Will of God. For that reason, he climbed Mt. Moriah with profound resolve to perform God's bidding. That is the theme which we recount on every new year festival. We, too, ought to learn to place our wills in tune with God's. In the final analysis, He shall use us. He has used us, and He is using us. Won't our lives as Jews have so much more meaning if we help God do with us that which He wants done with us? Won't we even understand His ways better if we make ourselves a part of them? Even in suffering, whose suffering has more meaning — the suffering of those whom God uses against their wills, or the suffering of those who are sharing with God the goals that he sets forth?

Most people choose the current of their environment. Jews who are intelligent choose the current which is God's. God has made of us a gulf stream among the peoples of the earth. Let us be part of that gulf stream, leading lives that are exceptional in holiness, as well as exceptional in dedication.

Children of Three or Eight

In the literature of the Bible and in the literature of the Talmud, we are assured that whenever we want to return to God, the road is open. (*See Talmud B. Makkot* 10b) However, in a few instances, penitence is of no avail. Thus, for example, if a man should say, "I will sin and on every Day of Atonement I will confess my wrongdoing and obtain forgiveness," he is not forgiven. (*Rambam Hilchot Teshuvah* 4:1) Penitence involves genuine remorse and a firm resolve not to repeat the same transgression. Consequently, any conduct which reveals the absence of genuine remorse vitiates the possibility of atonement.

In still another instance, penitence is of no avail. We are told in Deuteronomy that the day will come when the Jewish people will suffer great hardship and they will understand that all the evil was visited upon them because they had forsaken God. Yet, though they will recognize that it is the hand of God that bears down heavily upon them, this recognition will not help them. On that day, God will hide His face from them and not come to their relief. (*Deuteronomy* 31:17-18) Now, why isn't their recognition of God as the one who is meting out their punishment adequate as penitence? Are they not thus acknowledging that their worship of false gods and their adoration of pagan practices have brought them to the brink of disaster? Isn't this awareness of the bankruptcy of idolatry enough to open the road to God's forgiveness? Why should God, nonetheless, hide His face from His people?

To this question, the great Chasam Sofer makes reply which has much meaning for us in our own day. The Chasam Sofer tells us that for Jews the recognition of God's might and power is not enough. The mere fact that a Jew is ready to acknowledge that God exists does not constitute penitence. For Jews, the true road to penitence is described in an earlier chapter of Deuteronomy in which it is said that after all their tragedies, the day will come when Jews will want to return unto God, and they will return. However, it shall be by *hearkening unto His voice*. (*Deuteronomy* 4:30) On such a day, it could be said that they will have practiced penitence. Simply to admit that God is, simply to concede that He exists, is not religion. For us, religion begins when one is ready not only to acknowledge God's existence, but also to fulfill His Will and practice in our daily lives. That is why it will never be enough for a Jew merely to allege that God is King, or that it was because of God's anger that disasters had befallen him. He will have to take one additional step. He will have to open his heart to God's word and fulfill God's Will.

Friends, it is this message that I want to communicate to you on this Sabbath of Penitence, for when we hear much discussion in our day about a religious revival, it is important that we understand what we mean by religion. True, the day has come when more and more people are willing to admit that there is a God. There are countless scientists who, because of their own research into nature, because of their own inquiries into the universe, have reached some kind of dead end which impels them to admit that there is a Creator. They must concede as a hypothesis that there is a force behind all forces, and a designer underlying all designs. All of the theological arguments which were discarded a century or two ago by philosophers are being restored to popular discourse. They are being given a new dress, so that day after day we read of new books containing the admissions of prominent and renowned scientists that their agnosticism or atheism of an earlier day is no longer intellectually respectable. However, that does not make the scientists religious. It may be gratifying to many pseudo-intellectuals to learn that scientists, too, are willing to concede that there is a God. It may even give some religious people an assurance that they crave that they are not being old fashioned when they believe in a God, since scientists, too, make the concession. Yet, this is not religion in any mature sense of the term.

Certainly we Jews who first brought to the world the conception of one Creator are grateful to the scientists for confirming that which we knew four thousand years ago. However, if we stop there, we are being disloyal to our heritage. We are only inviting that which was described in the Book of Deuteronomy as God's hiding of His face from us. To be religious, one must go further. If one does not go further, then our conception of God is so primitive that we indeed regard Him as some kind of prima donna who wants us to be aware that He exists and seeks no more of us. Yet, it is precisely that kind of religion that is prompting many to believe that there is a religious revival in the world. It is that kind of religion that is making many believe that we are on the threshold of a new era in religious living. But this is nonsense. I need but cite a few illustrations.

We know that throughout the country there are hundreds of thousands of people who are members of fraternal orders, Elks, Masons, Pythians, every one of which is dedicated to the cause of brotherhood. Every member must also admit that he believes in the existence of the Supreme Being, otherwise he could not take the oath of initiation. Yet, it is also well known that in all of these fraternal orders there is an appalling lack of brotherhood. Some of these fraternal orders have lodges which will not admit Jews or Negroes. Often, Jews and Negroes must organize lodges of their own. That every member believes in God means nothing more than that all give lip service to the Creator. However, to what extent has their belief altered their lives and prompted them to recognize their own hypocrisy within the halls of their own lodges?

Or, take, for example, the entire problem of desegregation in the South. How can a person who really respects religion feel when he reads the statistics that there are more so-called religious people opposing desegregation than irreligious people? How can one feel when one discovers that psychologists who studied the situation report that among church-goers there is a higher percentage of people who believe in the inequality of man than among those who are unchurched? Can one really regard this kind of church-going as church-going that is religious in character? Or is this the kind of church-going which involves only recognition of the fact that there is a God, plus a weekly perfunctory visit to a place to symbolize that one acknowledges His existence, without permitting that belief to challenge any of the prejudices or habits or attitudes which we have learned to cherish?

Or, take still another situation. We in this great metropolitan area were given the spectacle these past few months of hundreds of thousands of people going to Madison Square Garden for a religious revival. They sought the inspiration of a great preacher who would bring them God's salvation, and many were converted. Many were moved to admit that they know there is a God who forgives their sins. That was all. Yet, you know the tragic instance of one man who after having been saved committed murder within twenty four hours after conversion. Perhaps his being saved was a prelude to the crime, or perhaps it gave him the strength that he needed to consummate the crime that he had planned. This may be an abnormal instance, but at least it makes us realize the extent to which religion can be meaningless when it is equated with nothing more than the belief in God, the profession that He exists.

However, for us Jews the mere recognition of God's existence is not of great consequence. What is important is the performance of His Will. This insight has been captured in a few sentences written recently by one of the greatest psychologists of our day, Erich Fromm. Erich Fromm would have us understand that the conception of contemporary man with regard to religion is like that of a three year old child to his father. The child of three cries for the father when he needs him, but otherwise the child is quite self-sufficient when he can continue to play. Contemporary man's attitude to religion is exactly that. We cry for God when we need him, but otherwise we are quite self-sufficient, and as we do what we want to do, we ignore Him and His teachings. If we would rather be like men of truly religious cultures, we would try to be like children, who are at least of the age of eight and need their father as a helper but who also feel that the time has come for them to adopt the father's teachings and principles in their lives. That is religion on a mature level – the extent to which man, *because* he believes in God wants to change his life that it may be consonant with God's Will.

That is what the Chasam Sofer sought to teach us. Tshuvah – penitence –does not mean being a child of three, but at least growing up to being a child of eight. To practice penitence is at least to move up from one who simply recognizes God as a helper and otherwise is quite ready to ignore Him, to one who wants to change one's life because one believes in God.

That, friends, is the challenge that I must articulate on this Sabbath of penitence. How long will all of us continue to be children of three instead of growing up to be children of eight? How long will we think that we are religious simply because we admit that there is a God ? When will we recognize that we haven't begun to be religious until we make some change in our lives, until we abandon some habit, until we alter some attitude, until we do something that we haven't done before, or stop doing something which we had been doing theretofore? Not until then have we really proved that for us the belief in God is something more than mere recognition that He is, but actually a commitment that will change our lives in one way or another.

There is a very charming story about a man who drove up to the synagogue one morning, and as he drove up, he noticed that the people were beginning to leave. He was somewhat disturbed, for he realized that he had come too late. He addressed the first person that he met and asked the simple question "Is the service all done?" However, he was amazed at the reply that he received. The answer was not in the affirmative. The answer was, "No, no, not at all. The service is all *read*; we first start the *doing* now."

That friends, is an important point to remember. To come to the Synagogue and experience the sense of belonging to God is one thing, but that is not yet *doing* the service. That is not yet being religious. The real service – real religion – begins when we have left the synagogue, when we meet with our fellow-man, when we meet with the members of our families, when we establish our homes and conduct our business or our profession. It is there that we do the service that God wills us to do and that is the challenge that I leave with you on the Sabbath of Penitence.

To what extent will we only read services, and not practice them? To what extent will we continue to be children of three, rather than children of eight or ten in our outlook on religion?

Most of us are parents, and we feel peeved when our own children regard us as individuals from whom they need only take. We resent mature children who do not understand that parents would also like to have their wishes respected in the different areas in which parents and children have interests in common. How long will we continue to treat the Father of all mankind in that same shabby fashion? How long will we continue to call upon Him when we need something, and when the need is satisfied feel that there need be no further contact? We owe it to ourselves to consider what our relationship to God shall be. If it is no more than a relationship between a three year old child who wants things, then contemporary man will have to concede that his religious experience and motivation are infantile. If, however, God will help us to act at least as eight or ten year old children, who are aware of the fact that there should be a reciprocal relationship between parents and children and that it is important for children to reckon with the will of their parents, then contemporary man will begin to think of reckoning with the Will of God and do the things every day of his life which have no purpose other than to indicate that he is submitting himself to the Will of God.

With such thoughts, we could not help but become more observant. We could not help but add things into our home which are done only because we feel that we want God's Will to prevail and to enrich our lives, and as we do these things we will fathom God's Will more and more, and our lives will be enriched in more directions than we could possibly visualize. This should be our prayer and our goal on the Sabbath of Penitence.

Selflessness

T he story is one of our people's most beloved. It tells of the Tzaddiq of Nemirov who disappeared every year during the Slichot season. The members of his family were wont to leave the house long before dawn. He would remain behind, presumably for a bit of extra preparation. However, he would never arrive at the synagogue, and no one would dare embarrass him by asking what happened. Who would be so bold as to ask the Rebbi where he went or what he did! Who knows? Perhaps he even ascended to heaven each day to plead with God, that God's people might have a good year, "Aye, it must be that," said Chasidim. "Who, but the Rebbi could wring good decrees from God for Israel!" Yet there was a Litvak among them. A Litvak is never gullible. A Litvak cannot tolerate myths. And he decided that he would discover what the Rebbi did during the Selichoth season.

Late one afternoon, when the Rebbi's house was empty, he entered and hid under the Rebbi's bed. All night he lay there – waiting, hoping that he would succeed in exposing the Rebbi. A few hours after midnight the family rose and went to the synagogue and the Litvak was alone in the house with the Rebbi – the Rebbi on the bed, and the Litvak under it. Then the Rebbi began to stir. He rose from his bed, washed his hands, and opened a clothes closet. From behind suits and coats, the Rebbi fetched a peasant's outfit, a peasant's cap, and peasant's boots. With these he dressed himself, hid his earlocks in the cap and fastened a hatchet to his belt. Then with cord, the Rebbi walked to the end of the town and into the woods adjoining it. The Litvak followed close behind. Is the Rebbi gone mad, said he. And why this attire? Can it be that the Rebbi is a saint by day and a thief at night? And he continued to watch. The Rebbi chopped down many small trees, cut them into logs for firewood, then bound them with rope, and heaping them on his back, wended his way to town again. In a little alley on the outskirts of the town, there was a dilapidated hut in which there lived an old widow. The Rebbi knocked and the widow answered, "Who is it?" "It is I," said the Rebbi, "I Vassil the woodcutter." "What do you want, Vassil?" said the widow, "I have wood for sale," said the Rebbi, "and it is cold and you need fire." "Ah," said the widow, "but how shall I pay for it." "Foolish woman," said the Rebbi, "don't you trust your God?" "But even if I trust God, who will kindle the fire," said the widow. And with that, the Rebbi was in the house, while the Litvak peeped through the cracks in the door. The Rebbi unloaded the wood, and as he put the logs in the stove his lips moved as he recited the first paragraph of the Selichoth, and as he kindled the logs, he recited the second paragraph, and as he watched them burn, he recited the third. The Litvak was speechless. He returned to the synagogue.

"Litvak," they called to him, "did you find out where the Rebbi goes." The Litvak did not answer.

"Litvak, tell the truth, doesn't he go to heaven?"

The Litvak mused. "Does he go to heaven? Who knows? Perhaps even higher than heaven!"

It is of heaven that I want to talk to you on this New Year festival, for in the story that I have told you we have the most perfect definition of heaven that I could possibly convey. I know that for many people heaven may be a life of luxury or sensuous pleasure. Many of us may even dream of a heavenly rest or a heavenly trip and some of us are even such gourmets that we speak of heavenly foods and drink. But in our serious moments we know that nothing physical can really be heaven – we are bored too rapidly by even the most lavish of physical indulgences. Instead we crave that sublime or ethereal experience of which it can be said that is the ultimate in life itself. Indeed, when we have such a sublime or ethereal experience we want it to last forever. In such moments we could even die with ease for they are moments when we feel as if we had caught a glimpse of eternal life itself.

Yet how can we describe these heavenly experiences that we may have them more often? How can we really experience heaven on earth?

Philosophers have asked the question and many answers have been given. I could, for example, describe for you at length what the great philosopher Maimonides visualized as the bliss of immortality. Maimonides was a great thinker, a great rationalist, and he imagined that there would be eternal bliss in the contemplation of God. For still other rationalists, to experience heaven was to be able to hearken to the music of the spheres and the divinely mathematical perfection of their relationships unto each other. This is perhaps the kind of bliss which appeals to great musicians when they either create or reproduce immortal music. Yet, in all fairness to the common man, can it be expected that every human being shall have the capacity for such intellectual enjoyment? We have not been endowed by our Creator with the genius of a Maimonides and it is not possible for us to enjoy the visions of pure reason and architectonic mathematics that could appeal to Maimonides. And if God loved the common man since He made so many of them, He must have realized that we too must have a way of catching the Infinite in much simpler ways, and in moods that while equally elevating are moods available to every human being, no matter how erudite or ingenuous.

It seems to me that God must have intended a much simpler answer to the basic quest that is ours. And He did. And that is taught to us by the Tzaddiq of Nemirov.

When you and I perform a good deed that is absolutely selfless – a good deed of which only God and we have knowledge, we are in heaven – we are at one with God. We are even as deathless as He is.

No one, but God, knew what the Tzaddiq was doing. The poor widow thought he was Vassil, the peasant. The Litvak was an intruder and the Rebbi did not know he was spying. But the Litvak knew heaven when he saw it. When I give of myself – without regard to self – when I give of myself without the chance of a "thank you," without the chance of recognition – when I give of myself with only God aware of it – I am with Him. I partake of His Infinite Self.

It is in a moment of selflessness that one has a foretaste of heaven. Furthermore, it is the principal aspiration of religious living to make us as selfless as possible. And on Rosh Hashanah when we ponder the life and career of our great patriarch Abraham it is primarily to learn how to emulate him in his great capacity for selflessness. For Abraham was subjected to many trials and tribulations, as the Bible tells us. All in all, the Talmud records ten situations in which God tested Abraham's loyalty. (*Mishnah Avot* 5:3) Yet only the tenth – when he was asked to sacrifice his beloved son Isaac – is regarded as definitive. Why didn't the earlier trials satisfy God? Didn't God ask Abraham to leave his native land and go to strange parts? Was that easy to do? How many of us are ready even now – with Israel in Jewish hands – to leave our native lands and reside there? And didn't God try Abraham when He confided in Abraham that He was about to destroy Sodom and Gomorrah and Abraham had the courage to challenge God in the name of justice? Why was only the sacrifice of Isaac real proof of Abraham's loyalty to God? For one simple reason, Abraham was loyal – undoubtedly. But if Abraham was willing to go to Canaan, at least he hoped thereby to acquire a great land for his posterity. And if he argued to save the doomed cities, he wanted to save his nephew. Only once was he asked to perform the most selfless act imaginable – to give to God what he cherished more than his life – his own son – only then could God regard him as capable of selflessness. And that is why, in Rabbinic literature, Abraham is the only person of whom it is said that he served God "out of love." No other prophet or saint described in the Bible was that selfless.

But it is the function of religion to make us selfless – not that we can be selfless all the time but at least we must be helped to increase the frequency of occasions when we are selfless and thus have a foretaste of heaven.

This is not the hope and goal of religion alone. Psychiatrists, who up until recently were hostile to religion, have now emerged with a new approach and they tell us that the principal reason for all anxiety today is self-centeredness. Americans are spending between 100 and 150 million dollars a year on tranquilizers. Millions of us in youth, in middle age and in old age, are neurotic. And what is a neurotic: I read the definition of one of the world's greatest experts – "Any neurotic is living a life which in some respects is extreme in its self-centeredness. The region of his misery represents a complete preoccupation with himself."

There may be many reasons for our neurotic anxiety. "Some-times when we are hypersensitive, resentful or captious, we are indicating a fear that we will not appear to advantage in compet-itive situations when we want to show our worth. Sometimes we are indecisive because we are afraid of choosing the wrong thing and being discredited. Sometimes we are even over scrupulous or self-critical because we want to show how praiseworthy we really are." The sin of pride is one of the most important causes of our neuroses. And as we shift to selfless goals, our lives become sounder even if we cannot completely rid ourselves of our neu-roses.

Religion and psychiatry point in one direction. They aim to help individuals to become more selfless in order to enjoy better men-tal health and a foretaste of heaven.

The question is – can one really be selfless?

No. One cannot be altogether selfless. Even the parent who ben-efits his son does so because the son is part of himself, the sub-stance of his selfish hope and ambition. But God does not ask that we ignore our egos altogether. He asks only that we balance self-ishness with selflessness. He is a real man who knows how to pre-vent himself from becoming permanently enmeshed in his own lusts and desires and can transcend the self and say – No more.

This is the crying need of our day – in every area of life. This is the crying need – a greater capacity for selflessness and a curtail-ing of self centeredness.

Let us take the area of religion itself. Why can't religion do for you and for me what it did for our forebears? Why don't we derive from religion the spiritual security it once afforded our parents and grandparents? Simply because our religion is self-centered. We want religion to suit our tastes, our desires, our convenience. Religious practices and rituals are trimmed to suit the cravings of our own hearts. Instead of religion making demands upon us, we make demands upon religion. We want the rules of the *Shabbath*, *kashruth*, family purity, to conform to our self-interest.

Or take the area of education.

What are the goals of education in our day? Again self-centered ones. We stress self-advancement, self-development, self-expres-sion. Every goal involves the self. However, where does selfless-

ness fit into the picture? What do we do with our educational facilities to convey a greater preoccupation with the needs of others
rather than our own needs?

Or take the area of home. What are the values most empha-
sized in the home? Aren't they personal hygiene and personal appearance? Don't we stress the fact that we must help ourselves to
feel well and look good? But ponder again, aren't these precisely
the goals that make our children self-centered so that we subsequently have to complain that they are altogether incapable of selflessness and a readiness to sacrifice for others. It is always we who
are trying to shield them from too much Hebrew, too much prayer,
too much work, too much responsibility, and therefore, it is we
who lay the groundwork for the neurotic personality which is the
major problem of modern society.

Or take the area of our organizational activity. Here, too, the
emphasis is always on what we ourselves can gain by joining. We
ask, what are the privileges that membership affords? What are
the satisfactions and the gratifications that are the reward for the
payment of dues? Rarely do we invite one to become a member of
an organization exclusively because he can thereby do something
for others, rather than for himself. Even in our synagogues we
think in terms of the privileges of membership and rarely do we
say to people that they ought to join us precisely because we offer
them as individuals nothing other than indoctrination in self- sacrifice. True; if they joined us for no selfish reason they would acquire the greatest gift of all, the experience of heaven which comes
from selflessness, the glimpse of heaven which can be had when,
like the Tzaddiq of Nemerov, one does the good with only God
looking on.

This is the message of Abraham's sacrifice of Isaac. Abraham
reached the peak of his spiritual development on Mount Moriah in
a moment of selfless devotion to God. May more of us be helped to
have glimpses of Heaven in our own movement away from self-
centeredness to selfless devotion to God and His people.

The Sin of Habit

On this holy night of the year I want to discuss with you only one of the many sins with regard to which we must do penitence. That sin can be described generally as the sin of habit. True it is that human beings can hardly be expected to dispense with habit altogether. If we did not rely on habit we would find living well nigh impossible. Moreover, there are good habits which we ought to certainly cherish, and there are bad habits of which we ought try to rid ourselves. The sin that I want to discuss, however, is the sin that is ours because we so often do the habitual, because we indulge in routine performance, because we constantly accept sameness without seeking elements of novelty.

On the New Year I discussed with you one difference between human beings and animals. Animals have no enormous potential for good and evil as human beings do. Tonight I want to call your attention to the fact that another major difference between human beings and animals is that animals cannot help being creatures of habit and instinct. We human beings, however, can transcend the habitual, the monotonous. We can introduce diversity. We can reconsider a situation and adopt a new course, a new fashion, a new pattern, and even mould a new image. It is this creative capacity with which God endowed us that makes us superior to the beast. Yet in so many ways we reveal our basic animality, and without thoughtfulness, without inspiration, without individuality, we yield to the habitual.

I need not tell you that there is no woman in this congregation who would appreciate or respect an annual gift which her husband would give her on her birthday or anniversary if the gift came as a matter of routine, because the husband had left a standing order with his secretary to remember the occasion and place an order for some souvenir. No parent would appreciate this kind of remembrance from a child, nor would even a teacher cherish an expression of esteem from a pupil that was not spontaneous and not the result of some creative act on the part of the donor. Yet, to such an extent are we the creatures of habit that even intellectuals frequently find themselves adopting courses of action and embracing patterns of thought that are habitual. Even when circumstances change and the realities warrant a new look and a new approach, they find it difficult to extricate themselves from that which they had been doing for a long time. Take for example in our own day, a very great spirit in India and a distinguished religious leader, Ghandi, who had become aware of the effectiveness of the hunger strike in his strife with the British Empire. He was effective. Yet when he was asked about the plight of Jews in Germany he did not have the depth of heart or mind to consider a different kind of situation and make a new proposal. He thought that what the Jews should have done was simply to engage in a hunger strike against Hitler. He had one solution for the world's ills. Little thought did he give to the fact that while he was warring against the British Empire, he at least had a foe that had some respect for moral law, while Jews were engaged in a war with a foe who would have taken great delight in beholding their starvation. As a matter of fact, the Nazis themselves introduced starvation as a weapon for the extermination of the Jew and there was no mercy and there was no compassion. Similarly, Bertrand Russell, a distinguished philosopher, developed certain programs for pacifism during the first half of the century. His approach made sense in the 1930's – it made less sense in the 40's, and it makes no sense whatever in the 1960's when we are dealing with a foe who has no respect whatever for any of the values which we cherish as civilized human beings. Yet, Bertrand Russell with his sympathizers in the British Empire can only resort to techniques to which he was committed at an earlier date in his career as a philosopher and a political thinker, and somehow he cannot alter his position even in the face of a new reality.

In politics we encounter the same inability to change policies. The United States is engaged in a very desperate cold war with the Soviet Union. On every front we are losing. Yet our State Department finds it impossible to give its position a "new look." Almost all its personnel remain prisoners of habit. At Santa Barbara, in the Center for Democratic Institutions, new ideas are being advanced. We are urged to change our conceptions even of foreign aid. We are being cautioned that the word "democracy" cannot mean to Africans and Asiatics what it means to us. And yet with respect to these continents we are deporting ourselves as if we were dealing with Western Europe in the first half of this century. It is very difficult for even great men to change their point of view; they become addicted to a particular course and are ultimately plagued by sameness, by routine attitudes which have become very much a part of their lives.

Now in religion this plague has become one of our greatest curses. There are many who look upon Orthodoxy as requiring Jews to be the creatures of habit and routine. This is not true. On the other hand, while there are rituals in Orthodoxy that are mandatory, Orthodoxy tries to stimulate every Jew to inject an element of personal creativity into his performance. Routine and habit are deadly to the religious life and experience of all people, and especially to Jews. Orthodoxy would like to have every Jew inject into his Sabbath and his festivals an element of newness. Every Seder service should yield a new question and a new answer. Our prayers must not be perfunctory and every communion with God should always have some spontaneity about it. That is why we have a mandate in Talmud that one may not make his prayer a matter of habit. And that is why, as one of my colleagues, Dr. Melech Schechter, so well said, even our recitations of sins we do as a matter of habit and we do not mean what we say. That is why our Sages were wise enough to include in the list of sins one which deals specifically with the routine recitation of sins committed, the routine confession, the meaningless mouthing of words.

Our Sages tell us that this emphasis on newness is the very heart of Judaism. (See, for example, the emphasis in the daily prayer on blessing God for renewing each day.) It is for this reason that we fix all our religious festivals on the basis of the movements of the moon which is seen anew every month. It is because of the fact that in this instance we can, with our own eyes, behold an experience of newness in nature that we compute our calendar on the basis of that phenomenon. Moreover, our Sages say that this has been the unique capacity of the Jew. No matter how many times we felt defeated and frustrated, we were reborn and started anew. This capacity to introduce newness into one's life is therefore uniquely human and uniquely Jewish and we are not being human when we so live that all of our performance is the product of routine.

Now, on this holy night of the year, I am making a simple plea to everyone to become a human being who can transcend the habitual and rethink a situation, so that in everything we do there will be one aspect, one nuance, which represents the product of our own ingenuity. And in no area is there more routine performance than in the area, alas, of Jewish philanthropy. This should have been an area that requires constant rethinking of our own situation and other people's situations; our abilities and other people's needs; and yet in almost every instance when one approaches a Jew for a contribution his immediate question is, "What did I do last year?" Patterns are established at one time and no matter how needs and circumstances may have changed there is sameness in that which we do. I cannot tell you what tragic consequences this commitment to sameness can have.

This was brought home to me most dramatically when in Norway this past summer I became aware of a tragedy which is almost too dramatic for mere verbalization. In one of the concentration camps where Norwegian Christians and Norwegian Jews were being held there was a pile of some two hundred corpses. The surviving inmates of the camp noticed, however, that there was one hand moving in the pile of cadavers. They rushed over to the Nazi commander and said that someone was still alive. The Nazi commander said he could do nothing about it; he had already reported two hundred dead; all the papers had been made out; everything had been entered in accordance with the prescribed routine and he could not undertake to make a change. The hand continued to move, and finally one man said that he had an idea: there was another pile of cadavers in regard to which no report had as yet been prepared – why couldn't they take a cadaver from the unreported pile and exchange it for the human being who still lived? That was done – permission was granted, and that

human being still lives and is a very distinguished citizen of the
community of Oslo, Norway.

Friends, we may loathe and denounce the Nazis for their unrelenting discipline and the meticulous manner in which they follow through on every routine. Even in a matter of life and death
they do not care to deviate. But why should we loathe and denounce them when we are so similar? So often we, too, are made
aware of hands that are moving, hands that beg for rescue, hands
that beg for succor, hands that plead for salvation. Yet, our response is one of habit and routine. We are made aware of the fact
that a new situation has developed in one country or another, a
new need, or a new crisis, new refugees, new escapees. Hands are
moving, hands are clamoring, but each year we give the same
amount. We learn from the UJA, or from Federation, for example,
of new needs, new problems. Yet our response is the same. We invariably ask what did we do last year. Within our own congregation, too, needs change. The number of scholarship cases may
increase; the number of children using our club department may
increase; the complexion of a community changes. There may be
more and more underprivileged. There may be more and more
low-cost housing, and there may be a greater demand on our personnel and our facilities. But no matter how different the present
may be, so many of us are creatures of habit. We give the same
amount, year in and year out, without any consideration of
changes.

Friends, with regard to the sin of habit, I ask you to do penance.

However, it is not principally with regard to money that I make
my plea. I make it principally with regard to our religious life. The
one thing that prevents so many of us from coming closer to our
faith, closer to God, closer to the tradition, closer to our great ancestral heritage of learning, is habit. We are embarrassed to make
a change. Sometimes it isn't even laziness or indolence. It is simply embarrassing to us to have anybody think that we are going to
do something unusual – that we are going to do something different – that we are going to do something that our neighbors and
friends and associates do not do. And that prevents us from doing
the right thing even when we feel we want to do the right thing,
even when we want to start embracing so much from which we

have heretofore been estranged. And that is why I plead with you. Learn to transcend habit, learn to transcend routine. Remember that God endowed us with a spark for creativity, for originality, for novelty, and let us introduce some of it into our own lives. How enriched our lives will become! This is my plea to you on this holy night of the year. Let us make the New Year really *new*.

The Lesson of Not Seeing God

The next time one of our children wants to see God, let us not be alarmed. The child is not making a heretical request. The great law-giver Moses asked no less, and his words are recorded in the Bible unto eternity. He, too, craved to see God. However, God denied him that which he sought, and it is God's reply that I want to consider this morning.

God said that Moses would not be permitted to see His *face,* Only God's *back* could Moses behold. (*Exodus* 33:18-23) What is the meaning of God's "face" and God's "back"? Are we to assume that God is a physical entity whose front and back have a tangible quality so that the eye can view them if only God willed it? I need not tell you that our faith indulged in no such anthropomorphisms. What then is the meaning of these references to face and back?

One modern commentator suggests that God's back, which man may behold, represents the negative attributes of God, rather than His positive attributes. God permits us to understand what He is not, but we cannot fathom what He is. However, this interpretation is not acceptable for it is not altogether consistent with Judaism. We do believe that we know something about God's positive attributes as well as His negative attributes. We are to be merciful because He is merciful; we are to be just because He is just. (*Talmud B. Shabbat* 133b) Moreover, what philological link is there between the positive and negative attributes of God and the anatomical parts, face and back?

A much more astute commentator, the late Professor M. D. Cassutto of the Hebrew University, is wont to regard God's back as representing the effects of His Being. Thus Moses was told that he would never fathom God as *Cause.* Moses would only be privileged to know God through His deeds, through His performance.

71

Philosophers may see in this explanation an echo of the view of the famous English skeptic David Hume, who first tried to teach us that no human being is able to fathom with his senses the reality of any cause. The most, said David Hume, that we are ever able to observe are effects, consequences, but we never see that which is the cause of the something else that follows. Cause is only a metaphysical abstraction of our imagination. Perhaps, according to Professor Cassutto, that is what God said to Moses. Moses would never be able to understand the full meaning of God as First Cause. The most that he and other humans might fathom is that which ensues because God is, and because man has faith in God. Yet, as intriguing as this interpretation may be, it still does not explain how the word "face" becomes the equivalent of "effect." Linguistically our original problem remains.

However, friends, if we will go back to a much more ancient source, the writings of the immortal Maimonides, and not his philosophical work, "The Guide to the Perplexed," but rather his legal work, the "Mishneh Torah," we will discover that in the opening chapter of that work, in the section called "The Laws of the Fundamentals of Torah," Maimonides gives us as perfect an explanation as one could seek. Maimonides tells us that Moses wanted to know God with certainty, with that certainty with which one identifies a friend or an acquaintance. Needless to say, we identify people best by beholding their faces. Faces are different. It is by gazing upon the physiognomy of a friend that one knows his identity with certainty. It was this certainty about the existence of God that Moses craved, but God said unto Moses that that certainty he would never have. The most that Moses could have would be that vague recognition of God that can be compared to our vague recognition of a friend whom we identify because we have seen his back. We identify such a friend because we are familiar with his stature, his gait, his form. Yet, when we identify a friend by beholding his back we are never really sure; we are only quite sure, or almost sure, but never do we have that illumination with regard to his identity that spells certain identity.

And this, friends, will help us to understand why it was after, and not before, the Jews had committed the sin of the golden calf that Moses made his request of God. Perhaps you, too, have asked, why was it that Moses waited so long to ask God about His identity. Moses had communicated with God for many, many months prior to the account of the sin of the golden calf. Why didn't Moses make this request when God first appeared to him in the burning bush? Why didn't Moses make this request when he complained to God about the damage that God Himself had wrought by sending Moses unto Pharaoh? Why didn't Moses make this request on Mt. Sinai when God first indicated that He would give the Decalogue? There must have been some reason that provoked Moses into making the request precisely when he did, after the Jews had sinned. And, friends, in the light of the interpretation of Maimonides, we can answer this question. Moses realized that the Jews would continue to sin unless there were some way in which they could have certain knowledge of the existence of God. Only a few weeks earlier they had heard on Mt. Sinai that they were to make no idols and have no other God. Yet they flouted God's will and made a golden calf which they heralded as the god who took them out of Egypt. Moses knew the frailty of his people and he realized that unless there were a better way to make them solidly and unequivocably aware of God's reality, they would continue to commit the sin of idolatry. To protect his people against this sin, Moses pleaded with God to do something more, but apparently God knew better than Moses what was good for humans. God determined that man shall not live with certainty that He exists. Forever man would have to be a creature of faith. Man would never be indulged the gift of certainty by demonstrable knowledge. And that, friends, applies to all of human life. No matter how we try to avoid it in the area of the natural sciences or in the area of the behavioral sciences, in the area of law, or in the area of theology – no matter what the field of human endeavor – man is predetermined to live by faith rather than by that certainty that comes from absolute knowledge.

Now is not the time for me, friends, to engage in an excursus into all the realms of knowledge, but please take my word that any scientist who is not a pseudo-scientist, but understands his subject well, is very much aware of the fact that there is no such thing as absolute knowledge. There is no such thing as knowing something as a certainty. One of the greatest philosophers of our own day,

Morris Raphael Cohen, demonstrated that even in the area of mathematics which we always equate with pure reason, and always regard as a field which might yield certainty, there is no certainty. Even the symbols usually have meanings which are the product of environment. Thus there is virtually nothing that is not based on postulates, axioms and hypotheses, and with regard to none of these can we say of a certainty that it is absolutely true. The man on the street who knows neither science nor philosophy may think that science and philosophy are endowed with the attributes of certainty, but professional scientists and philosophers know better.

Colonel Glenn may orbit the earth in a capsule, and his is a brilliant achievement of man. However, he, and all those who prepared the way for him, relied on faith, on hypotheses and formulae, which they will revise as time goes on, but about which they will affirm nothing with the assurance that they are absolutely right.

Thus God denied us the capacity for absolute knowledge. Why did He do this? Why did He handicap us? Why must we live by faith alone? Friends, I think I know the answer. God knew man better than Moses did. If man were given the capacity for absolute truth, the capacity for certitude, man would be the most arrogant creature imaginable and there is no doubt that not only would idolatry persist, but man would dethrone God and substitute himself as the Creator. For the spiritual life of man, it was necessary that man be made to understand that he must forever remain the creature of uncertainty. Man must remember, as Schleiermacher once said, his creatureliness, his dependency upon God. Without this, man's arrogance would know no bounds. And while, friends, I will not speak of the arrogance of pseudo-scientists, I can speak of the arrogance of certain nations on the face of the earth. From my understanding of the political and social theory of the Soviet Union it is fair to state that there is no group of people that is as certain about the absolute truth of that which it affirms as is the Soviet Union; the Soviet Union is the most arrogant and self-centered of all the nations on the face of the earth. Arrogance is the hallmark of those who are absolutely certain, and God preferred to cripple us and handicap us with a limited capacity for knowing so that we would always have to be creatures of faith. Compelled to rely on faith, we become mindful of our limitations; and perhaps basic virtue, at least humility, may also become ours.

Rashi suggests a similar thought in connection with the creation of Eve. (*Genesis* 2:22-23) God created Eve, not only because it was bad for man to be lonely, but rather because God feared that if man, unlike other animals, did not require a mate, the male species would be arrogant. Thus, in order that man might learn that he has need of, and is dependent upon, someone else, and cannot play the role of God, God made man dependent upon woman. This, too, was to reduce man to size, and for this identical reason God denied us absolute, certain knowledge and made it necessary for us forever to rely upon faith in every area in which we seek to advance human progress, be it in the technological sphere, be it in the ethical sphere, be it in the aesthetic sphere.

And that, friends, is the meaning of God's refusal to be seen. Oh, how we would have wanted certain knowledge! Oh, how easy it would be if we could tell our children, with a certainty, that God is seeable! Alas, like us, they, too, must walk the road of uncertainty, believing, believing, and never knowing that they are absolutely right, except because they have faith.

Yet, friends, as I explain this to you, some of you might be wondering whether it was fair for God to cripple us as He did. Was it fair to make us creatures of faith, instead of creatures of certainty? And to this, too, friends, I want to make a bold reply – God may have crippled us in one way, but He knows better than we that the power of faith can be greater than the power of reason. We talk of faith that moves mountains, and this, friends, is literally true. I want to pose this question to you. Let me ask you whether you do not believe with me that while it might be that with mathematics and physics, which come as close to certainty as anything we know, we could build a bridge, yet could anything other than the power of faith have built the State of Israel? What man is there who proceeding only with the relatively certain knowledge of mathematics and physics would have undertaken to reconstitute a broken people, and re-establish them in their own land after two thousand years of exile? How would anything that we regard as rational have supported the madness of a Herzl and a Nordau, a

Weizmann, and a Mohiliver? It was only through the power of faith that on the ashes of Dachau, Buchenwald, and Bergen-Belsen, there could have been established that which it is now our privilege to behold.

And therefore, friends, God did not cripple us. Faith does give power and, in many respects, more power than does reason. God willed that we shall walk with uncertainty; but that did not mean that because we were predestined to be the creatures of faith, we were therefore to be impotent, without vision, without drive. Nay, faith can move mountains – it did, and it still does.

However, the existence of the State of Israel is only one instance of what faith has done in the case of the Jewish people, and this brings me to the magnificent portion we read this morning from the prophet Ezekiel – the Vision of the Valley of Dry Bones. (Chapter 37) Ask yourself, friends, is there another people on the face of the earth to whom reason and experience would have dictated that they ought to perish? Is there another people on the face of the earth to whom reason and experience would not have dictated that they ought be embittered pessimists with regard to the future of mankind? Who has suffered more than the Jewish people? Who has had more cause for loathing mankind? Who has had more cause for despairing with regard to man's ultimate redemption? Yet, we have been a people of faith. We did not live by reason and experience alone. We lived by the very faith that moves mountains, and we believed with all our hearts that man was good and could become perfect, that human life was sublimely beautiful – that the destiny of man is a perfect world in which even the dead will be resurrected. By this faith we lived, and by this faith we survived. We defied the mandates of reason and experience, and we lived in the light of a force which has given our heritage and our national character the magnificent values which characterize them.

That is why I say to you on this festival of our redemption that we ought recapture faith, discover its overwhelming power and make our lives sublime and beautiful until the time when ultimate redemption will come. Amen.

COLUMNS

Is Term "Goy" Pejorative?

Volumes have been written on the attitudes of Jews and Judaism toward non-Jews. Perhaps, like most people, Jews did not always live up to the lofty ideals which their tradition espouses. Altogether too often they had good cause to hate and resent Gentiles. However, a review of the philosophical and legal position of Judaism ought to put to rest, once and for all time, the notion that the word "goy" may be used pejoratively.

Jews frequently use the term with respect to non-observant co-religionists. Many also use it to denigrate those who do not share their faith or ethnicity. But the Halachic norm dictates otherwise. For all human beings are endowed with the "Tzelem Elohim" (*Genesis* 1:27) – the divine image. No person is without it and consequently the sanctity of every man, woman, and child is inviolate – according to Judaism.

Even pagans could bring offerings to God in the central shrine in Jerusalem. Their divine image was the warrant for this privilege and gifts that they made to the building itself in perpetuity were never to be altered.

So committed is the Jewish tradition to the equality of the non-Jew who leads a righteous life that it accords to him the coveted title of "Chasid" and assures him salvation just as it is vouchsafed to righteous Jews themselves.

Maimonides (*Helchot Teshuva* 3:5; *Hilchot Melachem* 8:11) distinguishes between a righteous non-Jew who pursues righteousness because it is the will of God and a righteous non-Jew whose pursuit of eternal values and moral deportment is derived from reason and natural law. The latter he calls a "Chacham" – a wise man; the title "Chasid" is reserved for those who are also God-fearing.

But whatever the title, the conclusion is that Jews did not feel impelled to convert non-Jews to Judaism. Commitment to Judaism was not the condition prerequisite for salvation for anyone but Jews. Non-Jews could achieve it by righteous living alone. And Judaism today is still fully committed to this view.

However, there were some institutions and laws from whose scope non-Jews were excluded. Marriage is one of the most important. Jewish law very much respected the family ties that non-Jews created among themselves. But to be a Jewish marriage, and for the family to be deemed a Jewish family, both spouses had to be Jewish.

This did not spell inequality for if one of the spouses was non-Jewish, even the Jewish spouse was not regarded as married. It was the marriage that was no marriage for either. The taboo against intermarriage was always one of the most effective ways to prevent total assimilation and the end of the Jewish people.

Jewish law permitted Jews to take interest from non-Jews while they could not thus profit from their own co-religionists. But this too is no reflection on the non-Jews. The Jew could also pay interest to non-Jews while he was prohibited from paying it to a fellow Jew. The Jews were expected by the Bible to constitute a fellowship that closely resembled a family in which the more affluent members help the less affluent. Among themselves they were to promote "free loans". (*Leviticus* 25:36-38)

Plato approved of this for Athenians whom he too would have wanted to constitute a close brotherhood. The profession of banking was to be in the hands of outsiders. Unfortunately, neither he succeeded in Athens nor Jews in Jerusalem or elsewhere. The Biblical prohibitions were subverted and capitalist enterprise holds sway. But one can hardly regard the rule as demeaning the non-Jew.

Much of Jewish law was designed to create strong kinship ties among Jews. Jews were ever to be responsible for each other as members of a family are responsible for each other. This also explains why it is that when a natural disaster takes place Jews feel relieved when no one of their own people is a victim. Certainly there is no basis for this sentiment in Jewish law.

Whenever God's creatures are destroyed we are to sense pain and anguish. Yet it is only natural that one feel relieved when a member of one's own family has emerged safe and unharmed. In the same way, Jews feel that they are all members of one big family and theirs is a sense of relief when no member of this very extensive family is hurt.

Indeed Jews have always cultivated a feeling of family kinship which is much broader than the conjugal unit. The Hebrew term "Mishpacha" has always spelled more than father, mother, and children. It meant all the generations in a clan. It included ascendants and descendants and collaterals.

The loss of this conception of family in our own day is unfortunate and accounts for much unhappiness. However, because among Jews the sentiment applied to families in the broadest sense of the term, the family ultimately came to mean all of the Jewish people. In the messianic era it will mean all mankind.

Jews do have strong kinship ties with their fellow-Jews. Their millennial history has certainly helped to forge these ties. Yet when permitted to live in peace with their non-Jewish neighbors Jews have made manifest the greatest magnanimity conceivable to better the lot of all mankind.

The Christian and Mohammedan worlds have great evidence of this. The poor and the sick of all faiths have been a Jewish concern all the time. And if, because of a major or a minor holocaust, one Jew or another hates the non-Jew, his hate should be understood. But the mandate of Jewish law is unequivocal – all share the divine image.

Appetite Satisfaction on a Higher Plane Is Definition of Kashruth

It was a great rabbi who first said he wished that Jews would be as concerned about that which comes out of their mouths as they are concerned about that which goes in. Indeed, I suspect that those who denigrate the Jewish dietary laws – including Jewish novelists and humorists – are more often guilty of slander and derision of human begins than those who observed them.

Our sages point out that precisely because the Torah wants to sanctify the human mouth, and its power of speech, that the dietary laws in Leviticus are followed almost immediately by the laws pertaining to leprosy – which the tradition regarded as divine retribution for the abuse of the power of speech. (Chapters 13 and 14)

Without trying to rationalize all of the many rules, one can readily discern how these rules contributed to the survival of our people and dignified and sanctified the existence of individual Jews. It is an indisputable fact that awareness of one's Jewishness – Jewish identity – was induced in Jewish children almost from the cradle by dietary laws. They learned from their earliest years what Jews may and may not eat – only because they are Jews. It was not Jewish history, or Jewish suffering, or Jewish ethics, or Jewish values that made them conscious of their separateness. This came later. In the beginning – it was the Jewish table.

Because of their separateness in the matter of food, Jews were compelled to seek each other out. When they traveled they had to look for Jewish hospitality. When they settled in communities they had to search for a shohet (a ritual slaughterer) and a kosher butcher. Sociologically speaking, the ties with their own people were forged and strengthened in connection with the most powerful of all instincts – the need for food.

Furthermore, they learned from childhood the meaning of self-discipline. For a disciplined people we have been. That was one of the secrets of our survival. But the self-discipline also evoked a special kind of pause – one always had to pause before gratifying the appetite and ask whether one may or may not eat what is placed before one. Was the food forbidden or permitted? One did not partake impulsively.

Leo Baeck once said that according to Judaism the real godlessness is thoughtlessness. A Jew simply does nothing without first thinking – does God approve or disapprove? It was not a "here and now" philosophy but a philosophy which insisted that one think of consequences – now and tomorrow and the day after.

Needless to say, the aversion for Jewish dietary laws today is due to a strong desire to abandon Jewish separateness and Jewish identity and especially any kind of curb on one's instincts – gastronomic or sexual.

However, there is still another important aspect to Jewish dietary laws – and other Jewish rituals – which one ought to appreciate.

Many years ago, I wrote, and I now quote: satisfaction of his natural desires shall be achieved on a higher plane – a reflection of the divine soul which man has. We do not eat as cavemen. The preparation and the serving of food must appeal to our eye as well as to our stomach. Aesthetic considerations play an enormous role – the floral settings, the dishes, the table ornamentation. In sexual intercourse, too, our erotic tastes and deportment are more refined – we hope – than those of beasts.

What the Law sought to achieve was to add considerations of holiness to the aesthetic. Satisfy the appetite, but do it in accordance with the divine will. The gratification of the instinct is thus transformed from an animal-like performance to one charged with dignity and sanctity. To the value of the beautiful we add the value of the holy. Eat and sleep and clothe yourself – even shave and build your home – as God willed that you do so.

Be aware of God even as you fulfill your basic needs and requirements. In that way you will transform acts that are presumably without spiritual value into acts that are religious in character – acts that link you with the Infinite. In that way, too, you will avoid the feelings of guilt and even disgust with yourself that frequently accompany the satisfaction of appetites.

The Talmud makes this point clear in a beautiful text discussing the purpose of the Torah – and the Torah is the Law. The Torah is compared to a drug; not an opiate of the masses, as Karl Marx thought, but quite the contrary, a life-giving drug.

"Twere as if a man had severely wounded his son and placed a poultice upon the wound, saying, 'My son, so long as this poultice is on your wound, you can eat and drink and bathe as you please, and you need not fear. If you remove it, however, the wound will become ulcerous.'"

"Thus spoke God unto Israel. 'My son, I have created Satan but I have also created Torah. Study and observe the Torah and you will not only be saved from Satan; you will become his master.'"[1]

Apparently, God had handicapped man by endowing man with instincts that could lead to evil. However, God gave us Torah. So long as one lives within the Law one can eat and drink and cohabit – one can satisfy one's basic impulses – but their satisfaction will not be the fulfillment of man's animality as a result of which he may even forfeit his self-esteem, but rather the dignification and sanctification of those self-same drives which would otherwise be regarded as the hallmarks of his depravity.

[1] *Kiddushin* 30b.

Talmud Flatly Forbids Criminal Record for Those Who Repented

One who has been convicted of a crime suffers endlessly even after he has paid his fine or served his prison sentence. Anglo-American common law protects him somewhat when he has to take the stand in his own defense for the commission of a subsequent crime. His earlier criminal record is regarded as irrelevant testimony unless he seeks to offer proof of his own good character. But the law offers little or no protection in countless situations in which numerous young people presently find themselves.

Must a student of law, for example, who has been convicted of a misdemeanor or felony make that information available to the character committee when he seeks admission to the Bar? Ought public officials be subpoenaed to compensate for his failure to do so? If the student is asked whether he was ever charged with crime must he make reply even if the charge was dismissed or he was subsequently pardoned?

Resistance to the military draft in the United States as well as militant social action with subsequent arrests have made "criminals" of many of our country's ablest and most conscionable young men and women. To what extent will they continue to be victimized by the state's agencies? That they must cope with social ostracism and employers' prejudices is one thing. However, shall the state's machinery also be the instrument of their oppression?

Jewish law has something to say about this issue. One might have expected this from a great religious tradition that glorifies penitence.

If one has committed a crime or sin and truly atoned for it, the Talmud forbids us ever to make reference to it again. (*B.T. Kidushin* 40b and *Baba Mezia* 58b) This rule is applicable to

85

everyone and the state's law-enforcing agencies are not exempt from its observance.

Certainly, the penitent himself must not be subjected to the requirement that he himself disclose the information. According to Jewish law a person enjoys not only a privilege against self-incrimination but his confession, even if voluntarily made, is a nullity. And even if a third party has such information, he may not impart it if he knows that the applicant has atoned for his sinful or criminal behavior.

However, is the rule any different if there was no penitence but only the fulfillment of one's punishment? In the case of militant social activists or draft resisters there usually is no penitence. The persons involved are proud of what they did and would not hesitate to act similarly again. Yet, by Jewish law they too should not subjected to the indignity of being compelled to reveal their past and others who have the information should also be barred from making it available. Why?

Because according to Jewish law he who has suffered the punishment for his sin or crime has sufficiently purged himself of his offense thereafter to be regarded as "your brother" (Mishna, Makot, III:15). The strongest proof that he is deemed completely rehabilitated is that he is competent to testify and take oaths in a Jewish court of law (Maimonides, Mishneh Torah, Hilchot Edut, XII:3). If he has been guilty of a crime of violence it may also be necessary to establish that he is a penitent (*ibid.* 4). However, it is rare that any of the students who are presently in difficulty with state agencies that dispense licenses to practice law, medicine or accounting, have committed a crime of violence.

The most difficult question that one must resolve is the propriety of concealing embarrassing information or even lying under oath that one committed no offense – or that one was never charged with crime. The same problem frequently confronts third parties who are called upon to give affidavits with regard to the good character of applicants for state licenses. What shall they do when they know for a certainty that if they reveal what they know they will place in jeopardy the future of the person they want to help?

Jewish law regards oaths made under duress as nullities. The duress need not be threats of physical harm alone. It includes any kind of unfair pressure that prompts the person making the oath secretly to resolve that he does not intend to be bound by it. Undoubtedly this is a very dangerous rule for a legal system to entertain. It will make a mockery of all oaths if mental reservations can vitiate them. However, Jewish law would rather risk this consequence and permit individuals to make what may be a truly ethical decision – not only to lie but also to swear falsely. Jews who have had abundant and intimate experience with all kinds of persecution would rather abuse the oath themselves than permit the use of the oath to extort property or information unconscionably. Every important ethical decision usually involves the balancing of many considerations. One frequently makes the wrong choice and may have to pay the penalty for it. Yet Jewish ethics are not Kantian ethics and occasionally to lie is more promotive of justice than to tell the truth. One may even face punishment for the lie or the perjury but one must often be a martyr in ways other than permitting one's self to be killed. The right decision may be costly and even dangerous but to live ethically is often to live dangerously.

Deprive Them:
Can Christmas permissiveness fail to weaken Jewishness of the coming generation?

A Jewish parent's lot is not a happy one at Christmas time. Even if one lives in a preponderantly Jewish community it is still impossible to keep one's child unaware of Christmas, Christmas trees, Santa Claus, Christmas carols and the themes and greetings of the season. These converge on everyone from the street, from the shopping centers, from radio and television, literally from every portion of the atmosphere.

If the family lives, as I did for the major part of my life, in preponderantly Christian communities, then the problem is aggravated by the presence of the child's friends in the street and his classmates in school. I sincerely believe that many Jewish parents simply found the challenge too difficult to cope with and that is why they indulged their children Christmas trees and dreams of Santa Claus.

I am not so sure that it was a genuine desire to escape their Jewishness or to commit treason against their ancestral heritage that prompted them to embrace Christmas and "be like all the nations." It was rather a sense of hopelessness in the face of an environment that engulfed them and against those pressures they felt like lost sheep.

For children too it has not been easy. One of my dearest friends tells the story about his four-year-old grandson in a Midwestern university town who attends a pre-kindergarten school run by University psychologists. He came home from school one day bubbling over with excitement about Santa Claus. His mother explained to him that he was Jewish and they did not believe in Santa Claus but while she thought the boy understood, he went out to play and came back a few minutes later only to say, "Mommy, maybe Santa Claus doesn't know we're Jewish."

What is one to do in such a situation?

I can only suggest several approaches but in the final analysis every parent must solve this problem in the light of his or her own way of life and within the scope of his or her own religious commitment.

The easy way out, already suggested, is to pretend that Christmas is an American holiday and that the child is simply acting as an American when he or she participates in what is the hallmark of his environment during the Christmas season. Yet the parent ought to be forewarned that while this course may be an easy one to take it is fraught with many evil consequences.

First, the parent is forfeiting the first real opportunity to make the child aware of the fact that he or she is different. The time to make the child aware of this is not when the child is prepared to assimilate and intermarry but rather when the child is young and in the process of having his or her character molded.

Second, the child will become aware of differences sooner or later and when that happens he will be angry at his parents for having concealed the facts of real life. Third, parents might thus induce in the child an ambivalence with regard to his or her own Jewishness and at the same time the child may lose his respect for his parents because they were spineless and without a sense of their own identification.

In addition this approach is an insult to Christians. For Christians, Christmas is a religious holiday and when Jews embrace it as if it were a national celebration without any theological implications we are demeaning the religious meaning of the holiday to devout Christians. That is why there are so many posters around reminding Christians that they should put the "Christ" back into Christmas.

This is a subtle "dig" to Jews who secularize the festival, commercialize it, reap profits of business, and denude the holiday of its profound religious significance. In that way we do damage not only to the child but to the image of the Jews in Christian eyes. Certainly such an easy way out, which has such dire consequences, is to be avoided.

Another approach which I used myself but do not regard as necessarily the best one is to make Chanukah so attractive in one's home and within the ranks of one's family that the glamour of Christmas is lost.

When my wife and I raised two young boys in a Long Island community which was preponderantly Christian we celebrated the eight nights not only with candles but with gifts every night and with parties and celebrations all through the week to such an extent that the Christian friends of our children wondered why they couldn't be Jewish. Perhaps this was a compliment to my wife's ingenuity and in that way we spared our children any sense of hurt that they were being disadvantaged because they were Jewish.

Certainly eight nights filled with presents and candle-lighting can compete favorably with one night even if several stockings are filled. We spared our children a sense of hurt and at the same time communicated to them a sense of Jewish identity which they never lost despite the fact that they spent at least a decade on university campuses and never lost their pride in being what they are. Yet I am not so sure that even that is the only or the best way.

Perhaps I should want to make Chanukah a very attractive festival but I am becoming more and more convinced that it is important that as early as possible a Jewish child should be made aware of the fact that to be Jewish also means to sacrifice, to be denied, to be challenged by privation.

I am becoming more and more convinced that we have failed as parents and grandparents because we did not allow our children often enough to be without that which they craved. Moreover I would want them to know that this denial is because they are Jewish. Of course it is important to have them feel their lives are enriched because they are Jewish but equally important is the knowledge that because they are Jewish they cannot have everything. They must sacrifice. They must even suffer.

Not too long ago I raised a very important question with my congregation. Indeed it was suggested by one of our members. Is it right to teach children about a God who wants Abraham to sacrifice his favorite son upon an altar to prove his devotion? What kind of a God is that? What kind of compassion does He have?

Recently this topic was discussed by a Christian woman who never wanted to hear the story of the binding of Isaac because she felt the story was so inhumane that it made her sick every time she heard it. She finally discovered after very careful self-analysis that she loathed the story because when she was a child she suffered from a very severe illness which required long surgery and she had the most vivid recollection of her father delivering her to the hospital to men in white who performed the surgery giving her only a local anesthesia. This horrible memory she always associated with Abraham placing his son upon the altar. She then understood why she never wanted to hear the story.

However, my problem was that this question has never been raised by Jews before. Why is it that in thousands of years of pondering the subject no one questioned the wisdom of narrating the story unto children?

It occurred to me that the reason this question did not bother Jews of antiquity was that they saw nothing wrong in having children understand from their earliest childhood that to live Jewishly means to sacrifice; to live Jewishly means to be prepared to do without.

I am becoming more and more convinced that it is important for Jewish children not to be sheltered. Perhaps that is why they are not prepared for Jewish living when they grow up. Perhaps that is why they are incapable of assuming leadership in the Jewish community even though they say they want it. They are simply unprepared for the sacrifices that leadership involves.

Even sacrificial giving is more often made manifest by Jewish adults than by Jewish youth. This is the consequence of our having been so careful for so long to see to it that our children had everything and were denied nothing.

Perhaps the Christmas season is the time to have children have their first experience with being denied something because they are Jewish. Because of the dietary laws my children have been denied for a long time many opportunities to eat what they might have wanted then, but a line was drawn. There were only some things they could eat and not others. Perhaps they coveted those who could eat everything. But that was the beginning of their Jewish education – knowing what it is to deny one's self because one is Jewish.

In any event only a fool would venture to say that he had all the answers. I do not want to be a fool. I have no final answers.

However, I submit all of these considerations for the guidance of parents who cannot help but be troubled at this season of the year because they love their children dearly. The ultimate question is: Do we not sometimes demonstrate our love more by denying than by giving?

Zealots Who Offend:
Can their ugly behavior be
devoid of blind hatred for other human beings?

Basic it is in Biblical and Talmudic literature that one must never serve God by trampling upon a human being or in complete oblivion of the feelings and sensibilities of one's fellow man. It is a sad reflection on the rabbinate that at this late date they have to be reminded of this elementary principle of our tradition.

With regard to Israel's controversy surrounding Chief Rabbi Goren, altogether too many have forgotten that in their zeal to protect God's word they are being nothing less than immoral in demeaning colleagues and laymen alike. The prophets of old would have told them that God has no regard for their loud protestations that they are doing what they are doing because they love Him and His Torah.

Recently I came upon a comparatively unknown text that demonstrates how careful our sages wanted us to be with regard to the feelings of other human beings. It is in connection with the Joseph story that this insight is brought.

The Bible tells us that after Jacob, the father, had died and was interred in the land of Canaan, the brothers approached Joseph and told Joseph that their father had instructed them to tell him that he should forgive them their sin against him.

This statement in the Bible could not help but create consternation. Nowhere in the Bible do we find that Jacob said this to his sons. What is more, if Jacob had knowledge of the sin that the brothers had committed against Joseph and wanted Joseph to be forgiving, he would have made this request of Joseph himself. It must have been obvious to Joseph that the brothers were lying for if the father felt that way he would have told Joseph about it at any one of their many meetings.

Indeed from Biblical literature it is not even apparent that Jacob knew what had really happened. Some commentators tried to find oblique and very inconclusive sources to prove that he knew. My own guess is that he did not know for I cannot imagine that when he addressed the sons on his deathbed he would have made so much of the crime of Simon and Levi against the people of Shechem and said nothing about the sin against Joseph.

It is far more likely that neither Joseph nor his brothers ever gave him the whole truth so that his old age would have been a miserable one as he pondered the tragedy of brotherly strife that had infested his household. Yet one may ask, if Joseph was so silent for years about the crime committed against him, what is it that made the brothers feel that after the father's death Joseph would be vindictive and seek to punish them? After all he had done so much to relocate them in Egypt and make them happy.

In the exercise of their creative imagination our rabbis read something into the story that is truly remarkable. What they visualized was that as Joseph and his brothers returned from the funeral of their father they passed the pit into which they had thrown Joseph. Joseph approached the pit because there is a Jewish law requiring one to pronounce a blessing whenever one passes the place where one experienced a miracle. (*Berachos* 54a, b) Joseph has been saved from that pit and felt a moral and religious obligation to approach it and thank God for the miracle that had occurred to him.

However, in the fulfillment of that religious obligation he forgot how his brothers might feel about it. They sensed that the detour he took at the pit may have been a sign that there were being renewed in him feelings of anger and the impulse for vengeance.

Therefore the rabbis said that it was wrong of Joseph to have done that which he did. To fulfill a religious obligation and thereby hurt the feelings of human beings around you is hardly to be either religious or moral and in this connection our sages cited the verse, "And ye shall be clean, 'pure,' with both God and the people of Israel." (*Numbers* 32:22)

What our sages are telling us is that we are forever bound to be aware of the impact our behavior will have upon those about us. If what we do will be hurtful to them, then even if what we are doing is something that God commanded, we should abstain. Perhaps we should obey God's will a little later, or a little less ostentatiously, but never when what we are doing can bring a sense of hurt or pain to those who behold us.

It is tragic that in our day we so often overlook this mandate of our sages. Christians, too, can use this message. What they are doing and saying in connection with their new campaign for religious revival is not being done or said with any special consideration for the feelings of non-Christians in the United States.

However, my principal argument is not so much with Christians as with my own co-religionists and especially my own colleagues. There are perhaps times when these zealots must speak up. However, before one justifies one's ugly behavior as a zealot, one must search one's heart and be sure that it has no motivation other than the love of God, that it is completely devoid of any hate for human beings, and that one is really prepared to lay down one's life for the cause as Pinchas and Elijah were in days of yore. Who is the zealot today who can pretend that all of this is true of him!

What they are doing instead is to give expression to anger and frustration in the name of God's law and their zeal to champion the integrity and inviolability of that law, and they do not care about those whom they crush in the process. For this our eyes must shed tears and our hearts must ache.

True, such zealots are a tiny minority and their loud speech and ugly demonstrations do not reflect the mood of the overwhelming majority of observant and committed Jews in either Israel or in the United States. Perhaps I do not even begrudge them their freedom of expression and their outraged feelings. I fear only that too many Jews and non-Jews will believe that they are representative and that they reflect what is the way of Torah.

Long ago our sages quoted from the Bible approvingly that the ways of Torah are the ways of pleasantness. (*Proverbs* 3:17) They even legislated on the basis of that maxim. (*Sukkah* 32a, b) Let us ever remember it.

Bodies Belong to Whom?
Judaism denies a person
the right to abuse or destroy a gift from God

The Twentieth Century has given rise to many moral problems which did not receive much attention in the writings of the ancients. One of these problems involves the so-called "Right to Choose Death." Should doctors prolong the meaningless existence of patients whose brains no longer function? Must doctors prolong life no matter how much suffering they inflict thereby on both the patients and the members of their families who must witness the torture?

Recently the American Hospital Association recommended a patient's "bill of rights" and one of the rights included is that "the patient has the right to refuse to take treatment to the extent permitted by law, and to be informed of the medical consequences of his action."

In the last few years an enormous literature has developed on this subject as well as many legislative proposals. Judaism, too, has its point of view which on the one hand prohibits the physician to administer medication that will kill but at the same time permits him to stop treatment which is only prolonging life pointlessly.

I know very well how difficult it is to draw the thin line between active and passive euthanasia. However, my concern at the moment is with the notion that the central moral problem revolves around what is called the patient's right.

About a year ago, a very distinguished psychologist wrote the following in the New York Times: "The law permits one the right to determine how his earthly possessions are used, and by means of a will to direct what shall be done with them after his death, but the law denies him the right to direct what happens to him

personally in the event he is stricken with a painful incurable illness or condition that renders him helpless and his only remaining wish is that his life be ended.

"If a person longs for the relief that only death can provide and
he makes a written witnessed statement of his wishes, why should
he not be permitted to choose to have the assistance of a physician in mercifully terminating his life?"

While it may be that in certain cases Judaism would approve of
passive euthanasia, we must remember that Judaism does not regard the human body as any person's property. One's body does
not even belong exclusively to one's self. Therefore the mere
thought that a moral problem may be resolved on the assumption
that my body belongs to me and I am the sole judge as to what
should happen to it is repugnant to Judaism.

This approach to the problem is one with which we have become familiar in recent decades when young people say that their
bodies are their own and therefore they can destroy it by drugs or
by sexual promiscuity as they choose, or that a fetus in a mother's
womb is her property and she can decide to do with it what she
wants precisely as she deals with her fingernails or her sheared
hair – this approach is an approach that Judaism frowns upon.

I may not make myself popular with young or old but for the
sake of popularity I cannot misrepresent the nature of our religious tradition and that for which it stands.

The gift of life that we enjoy is from God. Our bodies, without
which life is impossible, are from Him too. According to Judaism
I am only the custodian of my physical self. I may not mutilate
myself any more than I may mutilate that which belongs to some-
body else.

I owe God the obligation to take care of that which He has made
available to me for use and not for destruction. Furthermore, God
made my body available to me not only for my own enjoyment but
also for the enjoyment and blessedness of others. I am to use my
body and my soul to advance the welfare of mankind and to promote the eternal values which Torah represents. Therefore, my
use or abuse of my body must be related to God's will and the ben-
efits that He wanted to accrue therefrom not only to me but to all
mankind for the fulfillment of the values which should be espoused by all.

There are times when I am permitted to martyr myself and let that body be destroyed. For example, if I refuse to let myself become the instrument for another man's death and as a result suffer death myself, my self-sacrifice is not simply the exercise of my right to do with my body as I wanted, but rather the exercise of my duty to fulfill God's wish that through me no evil should befall another. (*Talmud B. Sanhedrin* 74a)

Similarly, if the mutilation of my body during life or after death will serve to benefit someone else immediately and not remotely, such mutilation is permitted. Then again, I am not exercising my right to give away my eye or my kidney but rather my duty to help another human being whom God wanted me to help.

By the same token I must sometimes reconcile myself to suffering not because Jews glorify or even approve of asceticism but because my clinging to life in spite of suffering is God's will. I cannot take my own life for that decision is His. Nor have I the right to ask anyone else to take my life and make that person live with feelings of guilt about that which they did.

I must not cause others to murder in my behalf. I may wish myself dead. Those who love me may pray fervently that I be spared the suffering. But from a long range point of view I may be serving mankind best by reconciling myself to the suffering without vesting in individual doctors or teams of doctors the power to decide who will live or who will die. Thus I must accept my fate in fulfillment of a duty to all mankind by not permitting my suffering to become the pretext for weakening the almost unexceptional taboo against the taking of human life under any or all circumstances.

Modern writers on the subject seem to think that Judaism is so sensitive about this problem because of our revulsion over the Nazi crimes which were performed by medical doctors who misappropriated the term euthanasia as a cloak for ruthless killing. However, this is not so. Our revulsion is much older than the nineteen thirties. Indeed our revulsion was so great in the past that courts found it very difficult even two thousand years ago to administer capital punishment despite the fact that the Torah made it their duty to do so. They felt that it was better to let society suffer the liberation and free locomotion of an alleged murderer rather than involve courts in acts of homicide.

Much more will yet be written about this subject. I have nothing especially new to say about the problem. However, my concern is with the false notion that what is involved is a personal right to regard one's body as one's own so that we can make decisions with regard to it as if it were our property.

Young people must learn this lesson in connection with the use of drugs, abortions, and sexual promiscuity. There is no right to do with one's self as one pleases. God's will and the interests of all mankind must be reckoned with as well.

Intellectual Idolatry:
Name of God taken in vain
when linked arrogantly to any empty ideology

In the Ten Commandments we are told that we should not bear the name of the Lord our God in vain. (*Exodus* 20:6) However, as simple as this commandment may appear to be, it bristles with difficulties.

Most Christians have been wont to regard it as a prohibition against the use of profane language and especially the use of God's name in connection with that profanity. Yet this interpretation is hardly a satisfying one. It is difficult to believe that such an innocuous sin as the use of foul language would be important enough to justify a place in the Decalogue. Moreover, the sin described in the third commandment of the Decalogue is one for which God says He will never forgive us. (*Ibid.*) Can it be that while other sins are forgiven the sin of "cussing" is without the possibility of atonement? For these reasons and others, Jews have understood the commandment quite differently.

One of the rather popular interpretations of the commandment is that it prohibits false testimony and the use of an oath in God's name to give credence to perjury. However, as heinous as is the offense of perjury it would appear that this is precisely what the ninth commandment deals with. That commandment ordered us never to bear false witness. Why, then, is there need for a separate commandment with regard to bearing the name of the Lord in vain? Why the repetition?

Some rabbis did suggest that the commandment against the use of the Lord's name in vain was meant to interdict any oath which was false and not exclusively oaths in courts of law. (*Ibn Ezra Exodus* 20:6) When it is day I must not swear that it is night. However, if I swear falsely with regard to some inconsequential fact, why should God have expressed himself so harshly that this false oath will be unpardonable and he who utters it will be denied forgiveness? How much damage will I have done to merit God's unremitting wrath!

There is still a fourth interpretation which strains the language a bit but at least it is charged with great significance. That interpretation suggests that no human being and no people should include in their name the name of God when in fact they do so in vain because they have no commitment to Him or His will. Thus the commandment is directed against hypocrisy.

The Jewish people, for example, are called Israel. The word Israel includes the name of God. And if Israel is not a God-fearing people they should not call themselves by His name. The same would apply to a Jewish state. It ought not to bear a name which includes the name of God if it is not committed to His existence or to the fulfillment of His will.

At least this interpretation helps one to understand why it is that the offense is so serious. It is the offense of sham and duplicity. It is the offense of living under false pretenses. Such an offense is serious enough to warrant God's sense of outrage. The Prophets of Israel always spoke out against hypocrisy and thus their invectives would be in the best tradition of the third commandment.

Yet there is a fifth interpretation which I call to your attention because of its timeliness. It is suggested by one of the greatest philosophers of Judaism in the twentieth century, Franz Rosenzweig. It is also incorporated in that translation of the Bible in which he and Martin Buber collaborated.

What they say is that the words are to be translated as follows: Do not apply the name of God to an ideal or a cause which is truly bankrupt and does not warrant being deemed an ultimate.

Thus the logical order of the commandments becomes most impressive. First, God introduces Himself as He who took the Jewish people out of the land of bondage. Then He prohibits the worship of idols, gods made of gold or silver or stone. Lastly, He prohibits His being identified with anything that does not justify dignification by the use of His name.

This prohibition then would mean that first, we must not use God's name in connection with causes or movements that are

"Nichts" but would like to be regarded as divinely inspired or divinely charged, and second that we have no right to regard as an ultimate that which is not an ultimate. Altogether too often ideologies have been expounded by all kinds of propagandists who are presumptuous enough to claim that they are in possession of the final, ultimate truth.

In our own day, communism, liberalism, and individualism have been such ideologies. Unfortunately, our generation has beheld the bankruptcy of all. Yet the proponents of those "isms" all regard themselves as having the ultimate, absolute truth. They deem their ideologies final ultimate ones. Sometimes they have been killed, tortured, and depressed, as crusaders fighting God's battles. Even when they denied the existence of God, they deified their own ideology and crowned themselves Prophets.

It is against this that the third commandment is directed. Perhaps this is what was meant by one great American editor who said that what united all Jews was the belief, not in God, but in the fact that other than God there is no God. This made the Jewish people resistant to all kinds of idolatry and all forms of hero worship.

As Jews, we could not fit into the scheme of things set by dictators of the left or the right. We were always too aware of our own infallibility and we dared to speak in the name of God only with the greatest awe and trepidation, and even then with grave doubts as to whether we had the whole truth.

It is never out of order to remind Jews and non-Jews alike that humility, uncertainty, and doubt are good for the human soul especially when they help us to doubt our own omniscience.

Rabbis too can use the reminder. We must never apply God's name to "Nichts."

Price of Exposure:
In all times, Jews have been
exposed to rival cultures and generation gaps

The most important theme of the Passover Festival is the Exodus from Egypt. However, there is another theme which receives almost as much attention, and that is our ultimate redemption in the Messianic era. Indeed, it is the opinion of many of our sages that the first half of the seder service is devoted to our commemoration of the liberation from bondage in the days of Pharaoh while the second half is devoted to our anticipation of a glorious future in a world that is completely just because of the advent of Elijah and the Messiah, son of David.

Even before we celebrate Passover – on the Sabbath preceding – we dedicate our thoughts to the perfect world and "that great and awesome day" of which the Prophet Malachi did speak. (*Malachi* 3:23-24) However, one may ask, What are the hallmarks of that great day? How will one recognize it? How will one know that it is nigh?

According to the Prophet Malachi we will know it is here when we see the hearts of parents and the hearts of children at one, reconciled unto each other, and beating, so to speak, with one beat. Does this not mean that the problem of the generation gap must be much older than the twentieth century and that as far back as the days of the Prophet Malachi he and his contemporaries recognized that a symptom of the unrest of the world and the evil which the Messiah is expected to eliminate is the alienation between one generation and another?

Malachi prophesied more than two thousand years ago. Yet he gave us one credential by which we might recognize the advent of the Messiah and that is the reconciliation of young and old and their pursuit together of that justice which the Messiah is to guarantee.

This thought held my attention even as I participated in the seder service. So much consideration is given to the different kinds of sons that parents have. The text in which we describe the wise son and the wicked son, the simpleton and the retardate, is also thousands of years old. It is based upon older verses in the Bible but the text itself is found in the earliest Tanaitic literature which is at least two thousand years old. There are versions of the text in the Babylonian and in the Palestinian Talmuds.

Thus, it is apparent that Jewish parents had to cope with different kinds of children thousands of years ago and some of these children were wise, cooperative, identified with their parents' hopes and aspirations, while other children were alienated, resentful and anxious to break away.

A very distinguished philosopher of law once spent many years studying Indians and he came to the conclusion that we overrate primitive society when we assume that in primitive societies there was no generation gap. He pointed out that in every society there always were the drifters and the drivers. There were those who drifted along with the stream. They were the conformists. They did what their parents expected them to do. However, there also were the drivers, the pushers, the dissidents, the non-conformists. This phenomenon is thus true not only of modern society but of all societies in the history of man. The generation gap that so troubles modern man, and especially modern Jews, is a phenomenon of ancient vintage and perhaps should not be as surprising as it is.

Yet if Jews spoke of it so long ago and recognized it so early in human history, it must be because Jewish society had a heavy dose of the malady. And it may be that Jews could have been expected to have more of it than others. It was in the nature of Jewish society that Jews almost always had to live in more than one civilization at the same time.

Ancient Jewish civilization was close to Egyptian civilization and the civilization of Mesopotamia. Jews had contacts with the Persians, the Greeks, and the Romans. Jews lived side by side with Christians and with Moslems. And whenever a people live close to other peoples and other civilizations and are in constant communication with each other, there will inevitably be centripetal and centrifugal forces that will prompt some to attach themselves tightly unto their own people while others are drawn away.

One might almost say that it is a price one pays when one is Jewish. One is always raising one's children in an environment which will expose them to strong forces that seek to pull them away from their people at the same time that their people create strong forces to keep them attached and belonging. And the results speak for themselves. At one and the same time we Jews have the strongest sense of belonging to each other, and simultaneously we sustain the greatest losses in alienation, assimilation, and intermarriage.

Perhaps because of our millenial history we became aware of this much earlier than other peoples and it was because of this that our sages spoke of it on Passover. Similarly it was because of this that the Prophet Malachi dreamed of a perfect world in which parents and children would be totally reconciled unto each other without the pain and anguish that is associated with the loss of loved ones to whom one has given the breath of life and whose thanklessness "is sharper than a serpent's tooth."

It ought to be helpful to parents who have suffered the alienation of their children to know that this is a price they are paying for being Jewish. However, there is also a very practical consideration with which the Jewish community must reckon. There are small groups of Jews who because they are aware of this phenomenon try their best to live in isolation and seal themselves off from the rest of the world. Indeed these are also the Jews who have large families and even if they were to sustain a loss or two, the percentage of alienated children among them would still be very small.

On the other hand, modern Jews who live in more than one civilization at the same time have small families and when they sustain a loss that loss represents a very large percentage of the total of their offspring, sometimes a third, half, or even more.

For that reason those who are responsible for the survival of the Jewish community must do two things. No matter what their personal philosophies are, they must do everything they possibly can to help preserve those Jewish families that want to be isolated. It may not be a philosophy which we ourselves can embrace. However, those Jews will in a way assure Jewish survival. Their birthrate is high and their percentage of losses is small.

At the same time, however, many of us feel that it is the hallmark of the greatness of the Jew that he has always lived in many civilizations at the same time and only in that way could be a light unto the nations, and we must do everything in our power to understand the risks that we are incurring, even as we try to reduce the number of our losses.

Of course a fine Jewish education is one of the best ways to insure that the losses will not be overwhelmingly great. But even a good Jewish education is no guarantee against alienation. Some of the most famous enemies of the Jewish people have come from good Jewish backgrounds and even graduates of yeshivas are to be found among those who are abandoning Judaism for other faiths and cults.

However, in addition to Jewish education we must give more attention to meaningful Jewish experiences and Jewish activism so that the Jewish youth whom we train to live in more than one civilization at the same time may realize that while contact with other groups can be enriching emotionally and intellectually, yet their own birthright and heritage can be most meaningful to them and help them to achieve the most gratifying kind of life available to any human being on the face of the earth.

Certainly the Passover festival must of necessity impress parents with the grave nature of their responsibility. The more I live the more convinced I become that there are no easy answers any more than there is an easy road to human salvation. However, the greater the challenge the greater is the personal gratification when one has coped with the challenge

One cannot promise Jewish parents in the modern age happiness and nachas. One can only say unto them that if they choose to be parents, let them prove themselves equal to the great responsibility they have assumed.

No Jewish Watergate:
Right to privacy was firmly established centuries
ahead of other nations

During the seven-week period that intervenes between the festivals of Passover and Weeks, Jews are wont to think of the Law – the great gift that God bestowed upon them when He gave them the Torah. Unfortunately, this year that seven-week period finds millions of Americans obsessed with a national tragedy known as Watergate.

It is not my intention to discuss the moral issues involved. That is being done by thousands of others far more conversant with the facts. Rather do I choose to remind Jews that the basic right involved – the right to privacy – while a comparatively new one in modern law, is a very old and cherished one in the legal literature of Judaism.

Indeed, it is surprising that it is hardly a century since Justice Brandeis in the United States wrote about the emergence of that right in American jurisprudence while Jews already had written about it thousands of years ago. And Jewish legal experts, the men of the Halacha, expanded that right from era to era. This is something to ponder as we thank God on the festival of Weeks for the gift of the Law. Judaism is always in the vanguard for the preservation of human freedom, dignity, individuality – and privacy. And let us take pride in our heritage.

According to our sages it was a non-Jewish prophet named Balaam who first observed that Jews in the wilderness pitched their tents in such a way that the entrances or openings did not face each other in order that each family, and especially each couple, might have privacy. He praised the Jewish people for this and proclaimed, "How goodly are thy tents, oh Jacob, thy tabernacles, oh Israel!" (*Numbers* 24:5)

It was, therefore, inevitable that when Jews in Talmudic times promulgated building regulations they insisted that no man build a home near his neighbor's home in such a way that the windows face each other. In those days, there were no blinds or shades and windows were simply holes in the walls. Consequently, a neighbor who wanted to build a home had to be sure that the holes in his wall did not face the holes in the wall of his neighbor lest they invade each other's privacy. The holes in the walls had to be at least six or eight feet above or below one's neighbor's. (*Choshen Mishpat* (Siman 154))

It appears from extensive discussions in the Talmud and in the codes that this right to privacy was ultimately extended not only to a home but to a court or patio shared by neighbors, who, when they decided to partition the court or patio, were also compelled to contribute to the cost of a partition to insure and safeguard the privacy of everyone in the area. In those days the courts or patios were used for cooking, baking, storage, arts and crafts, and sundry other occupations with regard to which an individual might cherish the right to privacy.

In time, the right was extended even to one's garden or orchard, in some instances even to a wheat field. It was felt that an individual is entitled to conduct his private affairs without the intrusion or viewing of neighbors.

Related to this development, but not exactly as a part of it, the Bible and the rabbis in the Talmud guaranteed that even a debtor who fails to pay his debts should not have the creditor invade his privacy in order to seize property in payment of that which is owed. The rabbis in the Talmud extended this right so that even the sheriff had to stay outside and wait for the debtor to go into his own home and fetch something which would be security for the debt and deliver it to the sheriff. A man's home was his castle and neither creditor nor sheriff had the right to invade that privacy and go into the home in order to make a search and seizure. (*Ibid.* 97:6)

Unfortunately, this rule was modified during the middle ages because there were too many debtors who apparently took advantage of it and the law had to protect creditors to a greater extent than had theretofore been necessary.

Yet, by the same token, in the middle ages there was an expansion of the right to privacy so that it included the privacy of communications. Anyone who opened letters which he should not have opened was excommunicated. It was not at all uncommon in the middle ages for letters to bear upon their envelopes a warning to the effect that any unauthorized person who would read the letter would be subject to excommunication under the ban of Rabbi Gershom. In time, the rabbis found ways to impose money judgments upon anyone who violated the privacy of a communication and in that way obtained information which was prejudicial to the writer of the letter and advantageous to the man who violated the right to privacy. Business secrets and secret processes thus began to enjoy a measure of inviolability.

What about the privacy of oral communications? Truly this is what was involved in Watergate. At the time that the Talmud was written there was no need to afford a man protection with regard to oral communications because it was assumed that anyone who wanted to enjoy privacy in that regard need only whisper his communication and no unauthorized person would have the information. In those days there were no means for the so-called "bugging."

However, now that whispering is no protection for the privacy of oral communications, it would seem that the right to privacy would be further expanded so as to include not only damage done by "peeping" into another person's domain but also damage from taping or recording information which would constitute an invasion of the right to privacy.

That the world was unaware of the extensive legal literature that Jews had with regard to the right of privacy can be attributed to the fact that translators of the Talmud and the codes did not call the right a right to privacy. They literally translated the phrase as it is found in Talmud as "damage from viewing." It would never occur to a modern lawyer to search an index of the Talmud or the codes for "damage from viewing."

The modern term is "right to privacy" and unfortunately, as I pointed out almost twenty years ago, the failure to translate both the Talmud and the codes by using modern equivalents of the legal concepts dealt with in the Talmud has continued to make the Talmud a sealed book as far as many people are concerned. However, if one wants information about the right to privacy in Jewish law, one need only look at the Talmudic Encyclopedia presently being published in Israel and one will find literally hundreds of folios on the subject.

This is one of many instances in which Jewish law was centuries in advance of other legal systems. It is also an instance which indicates the extent to which the morality of the Jewish community influenced its legal development. That families wanted privacy, that husbands and wives wanted privacy, contributed immeasurably to the development of the rights of neighbors vis-à-vis each other to enjoy that right in many situations.

On the Festival of Weeks we give thanks for the Law and there is not a day that goes by that those who study the Law and are obsessed with its grandeur do not reap a harvest of joy from the veritable mine of insights that it makes available.

America Vindicated:
Exposure of Watergate
seen as result of liberties this country maintains

Respect for law is one of the major concerns of every legal system. We would expect nothing less. One might almost say that what self-interest is to self-preservation, respect for law is to the legal order.

Judaism also is very much concerned that its adherents shall have respect for authority and understand how dangerous anarchy can be. That is why even the prophets urged Jews always to pray for the stability of the governments of the countries to which they might be exiled. In some ways, the prophets were revolutionaries but they were also committed to "law and order." In the second paragraph of the third chapter of "Ethics of the Fathers" we find that Rabbi Chanina, the Vice-High Priest, said, "Pray for the welfare of the government, since but for the fear thereof, men would swallow each other alive."

I want here call to your attention to an interesting insight of the great Rabbi Samson Raphael Hirsch who is regarded as the founder of neo-orthodoxy in the modern age. He pondered the connection between the first paragraph of that chapter of "Ethics of the Fathers" and the second paragraph. In the first paragraph we have the following:

"Akavya, the son of Mahalalel, said, Reflect upon three things, and thou wilt not come within the power of sin: know whence thou camest, whither thou art going; and before whom thou wilt in the future have to give account and reckoning. Whence thou camest – from a fetid drop; whither thou art going – to a place of dust, worms and maggots; and before whom thou wilt in future have to give account and reckoning – before the Supreme King of kings, the Holy One, blessed be He."

Is there any connection between the maxim of Akavya, the son of Mahalalel, and the maxim of Rabbi Chanina, the Vice-High Priest? He said that there was. If, he argued, all men were truly moral people and could achieve righteousness simply by reflecting upon the three things suggested by Akavya, the son of Mahalalel, then there would be no need for law or government. All men would be decent because they would be moved by the mere thought of whence they came and whither they were going and before Whom they would one day have to report on their sins of omission and commission.

Unfortunately, however, most men do not ponder these three things and are not moved by such thoughts to lead righteous lives and deport themselves in such a way that they never harm their neighbors. It is for that reason that there must be law and order, and a government to maintain both. For that reason, too, Jews must not only hope for, and, contribute to, the welfare of government but they must even pray to God that He will lend His hand to the achievement of that objective.

For the very same reason the Bible is so insistent, and tells us in so many places, that one must never curse the prince, the ruling authority or anyone who exercises executive power in society. It should be of interest that there are no such commandments with regard to the priests, or even the legislators. It applied only to those who exercised judicial and executive authority.

Apparently the Torah wanted to make sure that there would be no subversion of those who are responsible for the avoidance of anarchy, and the security of human life, limb, and property.

That did not mean that princes and judges could not err. Indeed princes had to bring special offerings even when they were only negligent. Everyone is accountable to God and man, no matter how high his status. However, special steps must be taken to insure the maintenance of respect for constituted authority and while there was always accountability, and there could also be extensive criticism – as prophets were wont to admonish even kings – nonetheless, there was a modicum of respect due those who were charged with the preservation of law and order.

These thoughts occur to me at a time when unfortunately all of us in America are disturbed by what is presently happening in our country and we must pray for the welfare of our blessed land. I would not suggest by any means that there be any diminution of the accountability of all those who once held, or presently hold, high office. There must be investigation and there must even be prosecution.

My concern is that too much attention is being given to the wrongs that were committed and we are thus causing too many people, young and old alike, to lose their respect for the institution of government and the processes of government, when indeed were it not for government and her processes there could be neither investigation, disclosure nor punishment.

I think it is unfortunate that those in control of the media are placing all of the accent on the wrongs because they are newsworthy and they are not glorifying, as they should, the very processes of government which made possible the discovery and the exposure of that which was wrong. Side by side with all that they have written and said with regard to the evils that have been disclosed, there ought to be at least as much emphases on the glories of the democratic system and the fact that as many men are free to speak as there are. If this were done, then the damage to the image of government as such would not be as great as it presently is.

Somehow we have lost in our day the capacity to be grateful for aspects of our governmental system which, despite its faults, is still one of the greatest on earth. That is why I personally reacted so negatively to the comments of Angela Davis when she was acquitted. She blasted the system without realizing that in the Russian governmental system which she admires she would have experienced an altogether different kind of trial and result.

By the same token, I would have felt much happier if at the end of the Ellsberg trial the defendants would have uttered a kind word about a system of justice that gave them their freedom instead of attacking the President. Perhaps in the case of these defendants and Angela Davis I can be forgiving because they all gave expression to their bitterness.

In the final analysis a trial is an ordeal even if the outcome is in one's favor. However, too many Americans who were not subjected to that ordeal and know only the blessings of American democracy are ingrates and thus destroy the image of government in the eyes of young people. Thus they undermine the prospects for the survival of our democracy which in the words of Abraham Lincoln is still "the last best hope of the earth."

A Convert's Status:
He has embraced the Torah
of his own free will and derives special merit

If I had to give this essay a title I would call it "Double Dealing With A Convert." Talmudic literature on the subject is very impressive and is based on a difficult verse in the book of Numbers. However, the important political and ethical insights to be derived from that literature must needs to inspire anyone familiar with it. (*Numbers* 5:8)

The verse in the book of Numbers speaks of an individual who has no heirs. According to Jewish law, it is impossible for a person who belonged to any one of the twelve tribes of Israel to die without heirs. If need be, one can trace heirs back to our patriarch Abraham. Of necessity, therefore, every Jew must be related to some other Jew in existence and thus has heirs.

Unlike our American law, the right of inheritance is not cut off at nieces and nephews. The right of inheritance belongs to any relative no matter how distant the relationship. Consequently, the only Jew who can possibly die without a relative is an individual who was converted to the Jewish faith and died before he had a chance to have children. What happens to the property of such an individual?

According to American law, the property of a person who dies without heirs belongs to the state. However, Jewish law did not want to aggrandize the power of the state and therefore regarded such property as ownerless. Anyone who saw it, could take it. It was truly a "free-for-all."

This rule in and of itself is important to bear in mind because it reveals how reluctant our tradition was to give sovereigns an inordinate interest in person's possessions. The judicial system of the state would certainly be much fairer in the distribution of an estate if the state itself could never profit by the distribution. This is a political and legal insight worthy of attention.

However, the Bible has much more to say about this. What would happen if an individual borrowed money from a convert and had falsely sworn that he did not owe the money; or was in possession of the property of a convert and had falsely taken an oath that he did not have it; or stole from the convert and again perjured himself by denying the theft?

In all of these instances the individual who offended against the convert has compounded his sin by taking a false oath. Yet when he wants to atone for his sin what does he do if the convert is no longer alive? The convert may have no heirs. To whom can atonement be made? To whom can the stolen property or the unpaid debt be paid?

The language which the Bible uses is quite clear. It must be given to God. (*Ibid.*) It is due God. God takes the place of the convert. Yet since God does not reach out His hand to take it, it is given instead to the priests, and one must also bring a sin offering to the Temple. Indeed our sages even pondered what would be the rule if the offender was himself a priest. Sometimes priests themselves were guilty of double dealing. Under such circumstances the priest would still have to return what he had unlawfully retained but he would return it to other priests while he himself could have no share in it.

What impressed me about this rule is that we have here one of hundreds of instances in the Talmud which indicate the extent to which Jews were expected to be considerate of, and compassionate toward, converts who embraced the Jewish faith. If need be, God Himself acts as their surrogate. Certainly they are not to be disadvantaged.

We are told many times in the Bible to love the convert. Indeed there is a charming text in the Midrash to the effect that in one verse in the Book of Deuteronomy God mentions the Levites and the converts almost in the same breath. Moses, to whom the verse was given, challenged God and asked God how He placed the sacred Levites and converts in the same category.

To this query of Moses, God is said to have made a charming reply. He said unto Moses that Moses ought to think of the shepherd who takes care of his flock from the time they are born until the time they are slaughtered or die. He gives them so much attention when they are young and raises them until they can fend for themselves. And then a deer comes along, full grown, and joins the flock. In the final analysis, the shepherd will love that deer for having spared the shepherd so much effort. So it is with human beings.

For us Jews God had to do so much until He made of us a people and gave us His Torah. However, when other people come along and embrace our Torah, of their own free will and accord, it is like the deer joining the flock of the shepherd and becoming a part of the chosen people without any special effort on the part of God.

Very often in the Talmud Jews are cautioned never to utter a word that would embarrass the convert and remind him of his pagan forbears. (*Bava Metzia* 58b) There is a special command not to oppress or disadvantage the convert. (*Exodus* 23:9) We must be especially cautious with regard to everything we say to, or do with, the convert, that the convert shall appreciate that even though he has misgivings as to whether he truly belongs to the Jewish people, he must be reassured and made to feel that he is very much a part of us. This is the Jewish ethic. We are always concerned about those who may feel that they have second-class status and we must act with special consideration for them.

The Talmud also tells us that one can always judge a man by three things: how he handles his purse, his liquor, and his temper. (*Eiruvin* 65b) I think the more important hallmark of a human being is how at acts toward those who are in a status lower than his. This ethical point Judaism always sought to stress. God is always on the side of the pursued even if the pursued is a villain and the pursuer is a righteous man. (Some of those extremists in the Orthodox camp who continue to vilify Chief Rabbi Goren and me and others ought to remember this.)

In any event this ethic is too often forgotten not only by Jews but especially by the nations of the earth. It amazes one that the nations of the earth cannot abandon their hostility toward Israel and treat her among the family of nations with the most elementary forms of justice. We had an instance only these last few weeks of what ought to really be regarded as bizarre.

An official organization of nations appoints a committee to investigate the air-plane crash over Sinai in which many innocent people lost their lives. The report of the investigators is so overwhelmingly in favor of Israel that one of the leading newspapers in Europe predicted that as a result of that report the nations that were formerly critical of Israel would apologize. However, despite the report of their own investigators and all the evidence that favored Israel, the nations voted unanimously to condemn Israel! It was as if a jury had come to the conclusion that the accused was innocent and the judge didn't care about the evidence and condemned and sentenced the accused! In any event, there is no regard among the nations for those with second class status!

Alas, Israel is still the pursued. God must be on her side if she is able to survive at all.

Sept. 6, 1973

Joy of Being Jewish:
It is enough to compensate for all
problems, trials and grim forebodings

Laymen very often say that they would not like to be rabbis because rabbis must please too many people and that is a role they do not cherish.

As for myself, that has not been my problem. I learned long ago that in every service profession one must find favor in the eyes of those whom one serves. Even businessmen must be mindful of the reactions of customers, suppliers, and associates. And rabbis, like Aaron of old, must also charm those whom they have chosen to lead. What is more, if they love people enough, they will not find this difficult to do.

The most difficult problem that I face as a rabbi is that I cannot answer the questions which Jews present to me. I do not refer to questions of Jewish law – most of these I can resolve. And I do not refer to moral issues. As for these I am usually able to provide a grey answer even if not an unequivocal negative or affirmative response. I refer to questions that are theological – why God does what He does, when He does, and how He does. People expect me to explain the inexplicable and I have no answers. In such situations I feel that I am letting them down. They look to me for light and my darkness is as impenetrable as theirs.

Why does God strike them? Why does an innocent child suffer a handicap or untimely death? Why is a righteous man subjected to the ordeals of Job while the wicked and corrupt thrive?

Jews ask these soul-shaking questions not only with regard to their individual lives but also with regard to their collective existence as a people. Why does everything bad happen to Jews? Why is all the world against us? Why must a cause like Zionism – which is perhaps the most just cause ever to make its appearance on the scene of human history – cope with a hostility that is psychotic in its fierceness?

Was not the year 5734 bad enough for all of us – with its Yom Kippur War, its slaughter, its loneliness? Did 5735 have to bring still more depressing tidings as Israel's one ally – the United States – also became alienated? How much more evil can 5736 bring? Another war? More gains for ruthless and truthless Arabs?

How does a rabbi cope with question such as those? He is expected to have the answers. If not he – who?

This summer I met a man who waged his private war with God. If there were a God, how could He tolerate what is happening to the Jewish people? And if He permits Jews to suffer as they do, then He deserves to be hated, not loved. It was easier for this man to live with the view that there is no God and that the Jewish people should disappear, stop bearing children, and once and for all time drop the curtain on their millennial history. All of this makes sense. It is not unreasonable. How does a rabbi make reply!

Professor Emil Fackenheim tells us that it is our moral obligation as Jews to live – to survive as a people – to make sure that Hitler will not have enjoyed a posthumous victory. His master plan to destroy us must be nullified – and by our very survival we accomplish that.

Yet, will one find it satisfying to live and suffer as a Jew only that one might prove Hitler wrong?

To all this painful soul-searching I have but one gut reaction. I love being Jewish, living a Jewish life and sharing the past, present, and future of my people, because it is the best way I know to be truly human, truly a creature in the divine image. And what I love I want my offspring to have. It is the most valuable heritage I can bequeath to them. I am grateful to my parents that they gave it to me, and I pray that my loved ones will feel that way about me, precisely because I did for them what my parents did for me.

What is more, my parents did not feel that they created this wonderful life and literature which mean so much to me. They received it from their forebears and their forebears from God. So I am grateful to God who made all of it possible. True, all of us have paid, and continue to pay, a high price for the treasure. But what great treasure does not require vigilance and sacrifice that it may continue to be ours! Is not the cherished democracy of the west being lost because the west has lost its will to defend it and would rather appease, accommodate, even surrender, than fight for ideals!

A new year is about to dawn. The outlook for Jews and for Israel is no better now than it was a year ago. We shall pray for better, but conditions may even get worse. Nonetheless on the High Holy Days I shall be obsessed by one thought – how wonderful it is to be a Jew, whose spiritual significance and grandeur are without peers in the life or experience of any other people, whose liturgy is incomparable in its poetic imagery and philosophical insights, and whose intensity exalts me above the mundane preoccupations of daily life and gives me a glimpse of heavenly bliss! What a thrill to be a Jew on the High Holy Days and with my family to ponder what did I do that I should not have done and what did I fail to do that I should have done. And in prayer, charity, and penitence, to make the coming year a more meaningful year than the one that has passed.

Of course the new year may bring problems, new crises, new defeats. Yet all human beings have problems, crises, defeats. Only vegetables are without problems. But for my problems I have the blessing of being Jewish, living a Jewish life, and beholding every problem from a Jewish perspective. True, because I am Jewish, I may also have more problems than others. Yet I need to be Jewish to fulfill the highest dimension of my humanity. And thus I choose to live; and want other Jews to live. I want them to bring more Jewish children into this world to be blessed with a Jewish existence. And ultimately I hope all the world will understand this and perhaps seek to enjoy what I already have.

Thus I face 5736 – but not without praying for peace for all mankind and especially our beleaguered Israel.

One-Sided Orthodoxy?
Passover message insists honesty
just as important as ritual observance

As I celebrate Passover this year with my family and my congregation, I shall try to focus attention on Passover's significance as a holiday to refine human character and promote the basic values of honesty and integrity.

Needless to say, Passover's central theme is freedom. God freed us from Egyptian bondage and therefore we must try to remain free and help liberate all who still do not enjoy that blessing. No one familiar with Biblical or Talmudic literature can be oblivious of that message. But this year I feel impelled to make that theme a secondary consideration. I will play it in low key. For unfortunately too many of us have abused the privilege of freedom. We forgot that freedom without a sense of responsibility is suicidal – destructive of ourselves, of human society, and of our natural environment.

In the name of free enterprise we have aggrandized ourselves whether by exploiting the disadvantaged, or demeaning truth, or wasting resources that should be conserved for our posterity. Nothing is more embarrassing to the Jewish people than the revelation day after day that the descendants of those who heard the Ten Commandments on Mount Sinai have forgotten their commitment to obey those laws forever and ever.

That non-Jews also misbehave is not an excuse. Jews are not free to ignore God's imperatives and we risk our very existence in the world when we undermine that moral code without which no society can long endure. True, only a tiny minority among us may be guilty but we are jointly and severally responsible for each other and we must stress as never before the centrality in Judaism of

God's will that in our dealings with our fellow-man we must be more meticulous than in our relationship with Him.

And Passover conveys this message. I cite but one instance. God hates those who use dishonest weights and measures in their business transactions (Deuteronomy 25:13-16). But when he ordered us to make sure that our scales are accurate, He reminded us that it was He who took us out of the land of Egypt (Leviticus 19:36).

And the Talmud explains the connection between the two. When God struck the Egyptian first-born and spared the Jewish first-born – immediately prior to the exodus from bondage – He knew how to distinguish between one tiny drop of semen and another – between the drop that made one Jewish and the drop that didn't. (*See Bava Metzia* 61b) In like manner He will know how to distinguish between one who gives sixteen ounces to the pound and one who gives but fifteen. That is not all. How will He punish us for such dishonesty? (*Ibid.*) In Deuteronomy we are reminded that for dishonesty the Amalekites – the Hamans – the Hitlers – will attack us. (*Deuteronomy* 25:17-18) How prophetic that was!

Throughout the millennia this point and countless others in the same vein were stressed in Jewish education. Yet I do not know how it happened that precisely in the schools that today provide maximum Jewish education this point is not receiving the attention it merits.

And that is why I recently urged the dedicated and committed devotees of a prominent leader to be less concerned at the moment with Jews who do not don phylacteries or do not have kosher mezuzahs on their doors and more concerned with those who though they do don the phylacteries and have the kosher mezuzahs are not setting good examples to their children, their associates, even their pupils, by their disregard of those portions of the Torah which mandate honesty and integrity in our dealings with all men – observant and non-observant, Jewish and non-Jewish. Indeed, they could start such a campaign in the very Yeshivot dedicated to the propagation of Torah.

Again I say – only a minority is guilty. But we cannot afford to tolerate even a tiny minority to embarrass all our people. And we must see to it that youngsters appreciate that cheating in any form is a more heinous offense than eating non-kosher food. And insulting a fellow human is more unforgivable than desecrating the Sabbath or eating on Yom Kippur. The Talmud so tells us. (*See Bava Metzia* 58b) And it is imperative that we learn this especially on Passover.

The leaven of which we must rid our homes is only a symbol of the leaven in our souls of which we must rid ourselves. (*See Berachos* 17a) That leaven is self-indulgence – the self-indulgence that goads us to advance ourselves at the expense of others – the self-indulgence that prompts us to acquire worldly goods by foul means – the self-indulgence that makes us insensitive to the standards of honesty and integrity that God Himself ordained.

Among the tiny minority that flouts the will of God there are, of course, non-orthodox Jews as well as orthodox Jews. But when orthodox Jews are the offenders the stench is more pronounced. Decent people feel more outraged when those who ostensibly presume to be obedient to God in one area, ignore His commands in another area. But these decent people should remember that villains of all persuasions have the need to camouflage their villainy.

They often seek a cloak of righteousness sometimes only to conceal their real purpose and sometimes to maintain a good self-image which is necessary for mental health. In a milieu in which religiosity is respected the villain will purport to be a religious man. In a communist society he will be a highly vocal worshipper of Marx or Lenin or Stalin. In the academic community he will shout the values respected in that circle – academic freedom or free, uninhibited research. Let us not forget that even Nero justified his burning of Rome to rid it of Christians. This is the pattern of evil men everywhere. They need masks. We must not condemn the masks but rather the men who use them. And when religious observance is the mask it is our duty not to demean religious observance as an ideal but rather to unmask or unfrock those who misuse it.

I write this message not because these men have done so much damage recently to the image of orthodox Jews. I write rather because of offenses which all we encounter so often in our daily dealings and which prompt us to question whether there is any correlation between religious observance and good character. That is what concerns me.

There was a time when a man who wore Tefilin was presumed to be an honest man. This was a rule of law. I want the return to that condition and no more.

Ethics of the Heart:
How pious men refused
to take advantage of common business practice

Basic Judaism is the notion that any person who aspires to be considered "religious" must also be "righteous." It would not be necessary to repeat this truth so often were it not for the fact that so many observant Jews forget it, and even worse, that so many non-observant Jews insist on using the adjective "religious" to describe people whose ethics are questionable. Such people are simply not "religious." They are "phonies" and "hypocrites" – but certainly not God-fearing, no matter how they may regard themselves.

However, it must be of interest that this problem is not of modern vintage. The prophets, thousands of years ago, encountered the same problem. And the Talmud too has a magnificent passage which reveals that its sages also had to deal with the same sad phenomenon. Human nature changes slowly, imperceptibly, if at all.

The Babylonian Talmud, in tractate Makkoth (23b and 24a) first cites the view of one Rabbi that God gave six hundred thirteen commandments to the Jewish people. Then it tells us that King David subsequently encapsulated all six hundred thirteen into eleven and these are listed in Psalm XV. Not one of the eleven deals with ritual. All are of an ethical character. Thus the essence of a rite that is in compliance with Torah is righteousness. There is no escape from this conclusion. However, Jews ought to be aware of some of the previous details cited in the Talmudic text.

In Psalm XV, for example, we are told that the man who would ascend the mountain of the Lord must "speak truth in his heart." How does one fulfill this criterion?

The answer: One emulates Rabbi Safra. Of him several stories are told. He maintained extensive trade between Babylonia and Palestine. On one occasion while be was reciting his prayers a prospective buyer announced an offer to buy some of his wares. The price was right and Rabbi Safra would have communicated his acceptance of the offer but for the fact that he would not interrupt his prayer.

The buyer thought that Rabbi Safra's silence constituted a rejection of the offer and therefore he increased the amount he was willing to pay. When Rabbi Safra concluded his prayer he told the buyer the truth that was in his heart. He was prepared to sell at the lower price and did so in fact. He would not exploit to his advantage the fact that he did not interrupt his prayer and while no one would have accused him of making an unlawful gain had he taken the higher price, God knew the truth.

The earlier offer was accepted by him in his heart. God was aware of it and one must always deport one's self so that one finds favor in the eyes of God and man.

On another occasion he was walking on a road outside the town and met Mar Zutra who thanked him profusely for coming to meet him. Mar Zutra never would have expected such a courtesy. But Rabbi Safra had to tell the truth. He said that he would have walked an even greater distance to welcome Mar Zutra but in that particular instance the meeting was altogether accidental and he did not want Mar Zutra to feel beholden to him for what was not in fact a courtesy but only a coincidence. (*Chullin* 94b)

These are simple illustrations of what it means to be conscious of God's awareness of what goes on in our heart. Before one deems one's self "religious" one must measure one's self by this standard: Are we honest even when none but God could possibly know of our dishonesty?

Or consider the phrase in Psalm XV, "he took no bribe against the innocent." (*Makkoth* 24a) The model here is Rabbi Ishmael, the son of Rabbi Jose. His tenant-farmer had been summoned to appear before him in a lawsuit. The tenant-farmer, to ingratiate himself with the man who would judge the case – his own landlord – brought the rent-fruit to the Rabbi on a Thursday instead of the usual Friday. The rent-fruit was due the Rabbi. The only added advantage tendered was delivery a day earlier.

Rabbi Ishmael refused to participate in the judicial proceedings lest the trivial courtesy extended to him influence him to favor his tenant-farmer. He designated other scholars to hear the case. And even as he listened to the proceedings he found himself unconsciously thinking of pleadings the tenant-farmer might have submitted in support of his case. "This itself proved how subtly corrupting the tiniest bribe could be," remarked the Rabbi.

One cannot resist asking how many people engaged in business today could even continue in business if they did not resort to tactics to corrupt the independent judgment of prospective purchasers or clients. Recently there was revealed to all the world how many millions are spent annually by American firms for bribes to men in power in other countries. Is it unethical for a judge to take a bribe but proper for industrialists and statesmen to give and take them, respectively?

The author of Psalm XV would not countenance a distinction. The "religious" man must, in his words, "work righteousness." Like whom? Like Abba Hilkiyahu. When he was employed to perform a day's labor he would not cheat his employer of his due even to the extent of interrupting his work to say "Shalom" to one he encountered. So honest was he with those who trusted him. Shall public officials be less so? (*Ibid.*)

Aye, it is much harder to be "righteous" than it is to be observant of rituals. Perhaps that is why so many seek the easier course. But to be "religious" means first and foremost to be "righteous", because God so wills it and then to be observant of rituals to keep one constantly aware of God.

Pragmatic Needs, not Halacha,
Hold Key to West Bank

Whether or not Israel should restore some of the West Bank to her enemies continues to be the most controversial point on Israel's agenda. Undoubtedly, the final decision will be made for political, economic, and military reasons. However, there has been considerable discussion of the issue from a religious, or rather Halachic, point of view. And the arguments on both sides should be of interest to Jews everywhere.

All of the land of Israel is sacred to Jews because it was promised to them by God Himself in a series of covenants with the patriarchs. Their return to that land was also vouchsafed by the prophets. However, in order to acquire or reacquire the land they would have to fight for it and in war there is the inevitable loss of life.

Consequently it would appear that though self preservation is one of the highest values in Judaism – and one may violate virtually all the commandments to save one's life – a major exception to the rule is the command to conquer the land of Israel. To conquer one must engage in war and thus the command to conquer means that one must ignore the threat to one's survival and fulfill the command even at the expense of life.

On this premise is based the insistence of many rabbis in Israel that Israel may not return any part of the sacred soil of Israel to her enemies in order to purchase peace therewith. For the sacred soil, one is expected to sacrifice one's life. One does not use it to negotiate for security. Martyrdom is the order of the day for either the acquisition or the retention of the land of Israel.

It is this position that prompted so many committed youth in Israel even to defy their government and its laws and insist on settling the West Bank. Needless to say they did so with the approval

129

of many outstanding Halachic authorities both in Israel and outside of Israel. And at least one major political party in Israel and
a small faction in another agree with them.

Yet there are many Halachic authorities who hold the view that
to save lives Israel may return even Judea and Samaria, which unlike Sinai, are unquestionably sacred soil. When Israel and Egypt
negotiated their disengagement agreement the issues were political, economic, military, but not Halachic. No sanctity whatever
attached to the land which Israel returned to Egypt. This is not
the case with the West Bank which is very much a part of the territory which is the subject of the covenant between God and His
people. And how do these authorities explain away the divinely
given obligation to fight and die for the acquisition or retention of
the promised land?

They argue that the obligation to martyr oneself for land is
binding on Jews only where there is a high probability of success
in that war. The Halacha does not ask for martyrdom which will
be to no avail. Therefore, if it is likely that Israel cannot prevail in
a war to retain the areas it once conquered, it is better to surrender a part in order to retain a part.

In Biblical times when Jews engaged in such wars they had the
assurance of prophets that God was on their side. Since that period
we dare not be so arrogant as to believe that God will perform the
miraculous and cause us to win against ever increasing odds – in
this case against the whole world. That is why they urge moderation, negotiation, and compromise.

Of course there are times when martyrdom is mandated even
when it will not produce any result other than the defiance of the
tyrant and a demonstration that there are values more sacred
than survival. Jews are expected to suffer martyrdom rather than
commit murder, incest or idolatry. Jews are also expected to suffer
martyrdom when governments try to extirpate the Jewish religion. Then a breach of even the most insignificant tradition is not
permitted. But the acquisition or retention of land is not in that
category. One wages war and risks life for land only when success
is highly probable or virtually assured. And this is a decision generals make, not rabbis.

Israelis will make the decision. We can help them make it but
in the final analysis they are the ones who are manning the de-

fenses. Yet one thought I should like to express. Somehow I would want any disengagement with Jordan to provide that as Arabs continue to live in Israel so Jews ought to be enabled to live in the West Bank even if the sovereign is an Arab and not a Jewish power.

All parts of the West Bank ought to be available for colonization by Jews who will nonetheless always be a minority there. But they will reclaim the sacred soil and cause it once again to bloom. Then the day may not be distant when at least in a federation the Jewish and the Arab states – with Muslims, Christians, and Jews in both – will show the world that international peace, which is the vision of our prophets, is not only conceivable but also capable of fulfillment.

Assurance of Future:
What else can explain continuity of identity?

Purim and Passover are Judaism's most popular holidays. And I am loathe to believe that this is so because of their taste appeal – because of the "hamantaschen" and "kneidlach." It is rather because these festivals deal with themes that are easily fathomed and appreciated by everyone.

Purim deals with anti-Semitism of which Jews can never be unaware. Hardly a time or a place has ever been without it. Passover deals with release from oppression and suffering. Of this too Jews have always had a full measure. Both holidays make one feel secure that the Hamans inevitably fall, and the oppressed do emerge to freedom. One need not be a philosopher to respond favorably to the hopes that are thus inspired. And that is why Purim and Passover are celebrated by so many Jews while festivals with subtler messages are neglected.

Yet even Purim and Passover warrant intensive study. They have much to tell us beyond their simplest significances.

For example, Purim, like Chanukah, pertains to problems of religious freedom. Was it proper for Mordecai to resist the order of a king which required only a trivial act of idolatry toward Haman? Should Esther not have resisted her selection for marriage to a non-Jew, even if he was the ruler of the empire?

Passover, of course, has many more themes and for this year I select one that is especially relevant.

How did the Jews in Egypt manage to retain their identity for centuries? The Black slaves bought from Africa to the United States did not remember their origins. No one would have expected that they would. But the Hebrew slaves did.

The Rabbis in the Midrash offer one explanation. They suggest that the Hebrews did not change their names, their dress, or their

132

language. (*Pesikta Zutrita Parshat Ki Tavo*) All three are important factors in ethnic identity. Chassidim today derive from this
point their own resolve to retain their distinctive attire and they
are the largest group of Jews wholly committed to the preservation
of the Yiddish language. But one has reason to question whether
as slaves the Hebrews wore anything other than rags. And as for
language, even if they spoke both Hebrew and Egyptian, how extensive could the vocabularies of illiterate, impoverished, masses
possibly be that their ancestral tongue should have so impressed
their psyches with the uniqueness of their heritage! Yet though
the rabbis of the Midrash may have been right, their answer is not
very helpful to acculturated Jews of today who dress as non-Jews,
and speak neither Yiddish nor Hebrew. Do the rabbis have any
other suggestion as to how the Hebrews remembered who and
what they were – a suggestion that might be meaningful to us
now?

Another Midrash does suggest that the Hebrew slaves remembered the covenant between God and Abraham and the promise
God had made that after centuries of bondage He would redeem
them. The Midrash says that they had scrolls which contained a
report of God's encounter with Abraham and every Sabbath eve in
Egypt they would comfort themselves with God's assurance that
one day they would march to freedom – and even take wealth with
them. (*Shmos Rabbah 5:18*) In other words, the memory of a
promise was powerful enough to sustain their ethnic identity and
help them to recognize – though not immediately – that Moses'
appearance was the fulfillment of that promise. If they did not feel
that way, it is difficult to understand what kind of idiocy would
have prompted them to follow Moses into the unknown – the dry
and deadly desert.

How powerful is a lover's promise to return and redeem! God,
of course, is the lover of His people and it is He who assured the
ultimate redemption of His beloved people not only from Egyptian
domination, but also from one exile after another. Many were the
nations who taunted the Jews throughout the millennia asking
whether the promise would ever be fulfilled. But the beloved had
faith in the lover and waited. It was a long wait but the beloved always knew that the lover would return. And He did. And faith in

the promise kept loyalty and identity ever present in the hearts of those who shared the faith.

When the Jews were exiled to Babylonia in 586 B.C.E. it might have been expected that that would have been the end of the Jewish people. Historians try to explain the mystery – why it did not happen. Professor Jacob Talmon of the Hebrew University suggests that the Jewish psyche received a traumatic twist when their belief in their own chosenness sustained the terrible shock of national disaster and exile. This shock may have made them impervious to the assimilating influences of their conquerors. But why resort to psychoanalytic explanations when there is a simpler one available? Jews had a promise – a promise set forth in a Bible which recorded not only their covenant with God but every detail of their past and future. That blueprint of their destiny influenced them and made their future what it in fact became. It was conscious commitment to a Book, and its Source, that made the difference – not subconscious sublimation of a trauma.

And that is the power of a promise by God. It conserved Jewish identity for thousands of years. And is not that promise still the best way to preserve Jewish identity when a combination of assimilatory influences and world-wide hostility to Jews threaten to bring an end to the eternal people?

It is the role of that promise in Jewish survival that I shall ponder this Passover. In. the face of all that now menaces the Jewish people in Israel, in the Soviet Union, even in the United States, I have need to reread the Book – the Book that contains the promise – and deepen my faith that the Promisor will redeem, and though He tarries, His beloved continue to wait.

"Denominations" Fail to Give an Accurate Idea of Jewish Life

There have been times in American history when one could identify a particular political party with a clearly defined ideology; A Federalist was committed to a strong, centralized, national government while an anti-Federalist preferred that more power reside in the State. Now, however, one finds in both major political parties numerous conservatives and liberals, backers of big government and little government, foes and friends of labor, and proponents of virtually every political ideal and program.

Alas, this lack of ideological clarity is almost as characteristic of the so called denominations in Judaism. The terms "Orthodox," "Conservative," and "Reform," are descriptive of very little. In each grouping there are many points of view on Jewish faith and practice and in recent years it has become increasingly difficult to embrace in any one organization the exponents of the very divergent philosophies.

Orthodoxy never had, and perhaps never will have, one umbrella group. Among Conservatives, the Reconstructionists never felt comfortable in their Rabbinical Assembly, and now that body is facing a schism on the question of the role of women in the synagogue.

The Reform group, which once split on the issue of Zionism, now contains within its ranks an organized group of dissidents who take a more conciliatory position on intermarriage. In all the groups the attitudes toward Halacha and conceptions of a personal God range from thesis to antithesis. So extensive is the diversity!

And how does one classify or describe the millions of Jews who are members of none of the three organized groupings? Are all of them secularists? I am not so sure. Many of them believe in God but in none of His American "prophets." Moreover, even Jewish secularists are not all of the same cloth. Should one not reckon with their different ideologies?

Just for the fun of it I sat down one day and tried to state how I would classify Jews – according to their beliefs and not according to their memberships, according to their ideology and not according to the institutional apparatus which dominates the American scene. I submit my classification for the benefit especially of those who are interested in making surveys on Jewish identity and commitment.

The following is how I would group our people:

A.   Jews who believe that as a people we have a special relationship with God Who revealed His will to us in the Written and Oral Law. These also believe that that will has been correctly transmitted to us by the sages of the mainstream of Jewish thought.

B.   There are also Jews who accept what Group A accepts but hold that in the process of transmittal there was vouchsafed a large area in which there always was, and can still be, creativity on the part of man and they want to exercise that creativity, cautiously but consciously.

C.   There are those who hold to the special relationship which Jews as a people have with God, and also believe that God revealed His will unto us, but they have strong reservations whether Jews always correctly recorded that will or properly understood it. Thus they try to revise the record or their comprehension of Revelation.

D.   Then there are those who believe that we are a unique people with a unique message for all mankind but that that uniqueness is the product of history rather than any special covenant with God.

E.   Without committing themselves to any notions of uniqueness there are Jews who simply cherish Jewish values and the forms in which these values were transmitted. In their eyes only the forms are unique, not the values themselves.

F.   Many of our people have no feeling for Judaism at all but do sense a gut identity with their brethren. They cannot explain it or justify it. It is simply there, and it is valid because it is natural.

G.   Lastly there are those who are with us simply because they are ashamed to quit us or abandon us to our fate.

Needless to say, I am not so naive as to believe that my seven groups are exhaustive of all the available nuances of belief and thought that are available. Nor would I be so stupid as to recommend the organization of seven groups, each with its explicit ideology. However, I engaged in the exercise only to suggest to my co-religionists that they first try to identify which statement most accurately reflects their point of view. Then when they approach another Jew it should not be with the altogether simplistic avowal, "I am Orthodox," or "I am Conservative," or I am ''Reform," but rather "I believe that...." Then the dialogue or discussion might make sense. It will make for a clearer understanding of what one's position is on any issue of Jewish faith or practice.

And Jews owe it to themselves to know where they stand. It ill behooves such an educated group – and Jews generally are well-educated – to be so confused as to where they stand Jewishly . "Know thyself" is still sound counsel for all of us.

Jews Racists?
Aid given equally to Jews and non-Jews

O n Law Day several weeks ago, one writer expressed the thought that our American legal system is protective of the rich but not adequately protective of the poor. On that very day in all the synagogues of the world the nineteenth chapter of Leviticus was read. It is, indeed, one of the Bible's greatest. And I could not help but reflect how unusual was the legislation it promulgated, especially for the benefit of the under-privileged.

The owners of fields during the harvest were ordered to leave the grain in one corner uncut so that the poor might come and take it. This became known as the law of "Pe-ah" — the law of the corner. In a slightly different form it was also applicable to orchards. And while the Bible did not specify how much was to be left for the poor, the rabbis established a standard of about two per cent.

Certainly this is a law for the benefit of the poor. And students of the Bible have admired it for thousands of years. However, there is much more to the verse than a first glance reveals.

Owners of fields are expected to make other gifts — to the priests, to the Levites, to the Temple. Yet there is a fundamental difference between these gifts and the gift to the poor which is involved in the law of "Pe-ah," the law described in the magnificent nineteenth chapter. All the other gifts were to be *given*. The owner could select those priests or Levites whom he wanted to favor. And he could have the satisfaction of being their generous benefactor.

If his ego required that gratification, it was available to him. Not so, however, with "Pe-ah." The grain in the corner was to be *left* there — uncut. It was available to whichever poor man came along, on a first-come, first-serve basis. And the owner was not the donor. It was taken by the poor as their own. The owner was not a benefactor. Indeed, he was prohibited from harvesting the grain in the corner for the benefit of any of his own cherished poor friends or relatives.

The rabbis sensed that this was the divine intention and they enacted safeguards to insure that this intention was fulfilled. They ruled that the "leaving" for the poor must be at the end of the field instead of permitting the owner in his own discretion to decide where in the field he wanted to make something available for the indigent. If the choice were left to the owner of the field he might wait for an opportune moment when no poor persons were around, and then within the hearing of only his poor relatives declare a specific area as "Pe-ah" and his own poor relatives would have an advantage over others similarly disadvantaged.

If, on the other hand, the owner was limited to one specific spot, all the poor would know when this part of the field was likely to be reached by the harvesters and they would be there in time to take their due. By thus restricting the owner another benign result was achieved. The time of the poor would not be wasted. They would not have to sit around and wait for the moment when the owner would designate "Pe-ah." They could themselves calculate approximately when the end of the field would be reached and be around in time for the take.

The owner too profited from the rule. Passers-by would not suspect him of having failed to leave "Pe-ah." If he left "Pe-ah" any place other than at the end of the field, they would find it difficult to see what he did in remote parts of the field and would have no way of knowing whether he fulfilled his obligation. However, if "Pe-ah" were always left at the end they would see it, as would the poor who were assembled near it. They would bless the owner, rather than curse him. Cheats too would not be able to claim that they left "Pe-ah" in other parts of the field. Since the law mandated uniformity, everybody leaves it at the end; the poor know when and where to expect it; and outsiders too will draw no false conclusions.

Such a fuss, one might say, about a little bit of grain! Needless to say, for the poor a slice of bread may be as important as a loaf to the rich man. But what counts here are the interests to be conserved — the dignity of the poor and the fair name of the owner.

The owner will not be suspect that he did wrong. And when he leaves the gift for the poor in its proper place for the poor to come and fetch it, the poor are spared the indignity of face to face confrontation with the benefactor.

Of course, there are even higher forms of charity about which the Bible, the Talmud, and the Codes, do speak. The highest form is to provide employment to the needy or a free loan that will save their enterprise and prevent their economic failure. (*Rambam Hilchot Matnot Ani'm* 10:7) Yet when there must be charity – the simple giveaway — then there must be concern for the self-image of the recipients. And this the Torah mandates. Don't give it to them. Leave it for them and let them come and get it themselves. You will not identify them and they will be spared facing you.

Another point in the verse that is worthy of attention is the fact that its beneficiaries include the "Ger" — the convert who is the equal of the Jew in every respect. And the rabbis extended the rule to all men — Jew and non-Jew alike! That is how "racist" our tradition is! Can our enemies match it?

Halacha Seen Viable Basis for Israel Despite Some Lacks

It was gratifying to learn that my recent piece on the importance of studying Jewish law was well received. It will be my privilege next semester to teach a course on Jewish law at the New York Law School and perhaps I ought to explain why – apart from very respectable academic reasons – I am excited about the opportunity.

I love Jewish law and I seek to share that love with as many others as I can. My deepest regret is that the State of Israel, as yet, is slow to respond.

Israel has revived much. The tongue of the Prophets has been resurrected there to become its official language. The study of the Bible was made universal. Even military experts profess their need of the Book of Books. Tourist guides refer to it in almost every comment. National contests involving demonstrations of its mastery attract thousands of spectators as baseball games do in the United States.

Rabbi Kook's prayer that the old shall be renewed is being fulfilled. But what of Jewish law? Will or can historic Jewish jurisprudence become the basis for the legal order of the autonomous Jewish republic of our day?

It may surprise many that this is not now the situation. However, except for family law and such cases as come before the rabbinical courts with the consent of all the parties, the legal system of Israel is a composite of Ottoman, British, and French doctrines and rules. The Israeli parliament, the Knesset, has not radically altered the pattern. Partisans of the Halacha (Jewish Law) have always urged the renaissance of the ancestral legal heritage. They feel that the revival of Jewish law would enhance the national revival even as the revival of Hebrew did. But as yet their success is minimal.

One of Israel's very prominent jurists, Supreme Court Justice Haim H. Cohn, cites at least three reasons why he is pessimistic about the future of Jewish law in the Jewish state.

First, he argues, most Israeli lawyers do not know Jewish law. However, one might hope that even as many of them mastered the tongue of the Prophets, so the education of the growing number of law students in Israel – and now even in the United States – will include what the older lawyers did not see fit to master.

Second, Justice Cohn says that "many of the provisions to be found in the Jewish codes are nowadays anachronistic and obsolete; and it does in no way derogate from the beauty and progressiveness and vision of those laws in the times, places and communities in and for which they were created, that they cannot serve the purposes and requirements of a modern welfare state."

However, all legal systems have provisions in their codes, which are "anachronistic and obsolete". The crucial question is whether the legal system contains within it the potential for growth and change. And it is precisely this that I look forward to demonstrating to my classes. Jewish law has this potential in great measure.

Justice Cohn's strongest argument against the reception of Jewish law by the Jewish state is that "the practical enforcement of the Jewish law of marriage and divorce by rabbinical courts has done very little, if anything, to encourage or justify such a goal."

About this point I could write a volume. It is simply not true that there has been no progress in the development of Jewish family law. The progress may not have been as rapid or as spectacular as Justice Cohn would have wanted it to be. But even in so sensitive an area as marriage and divorce, the Israeli rabbinate demonstrated the potential of Jewish law for growth and change.

What bothers me most, however, is that when people think of Jewish law what comes to mind is principally Jewish family law which is only a small fraction of the total corpus of the law. And because Justice Cohn is unhappy with what the rabbis are doing with Jewish family law, he would relegate to the antiquarian a vast and brilliant literature that can still enrich all mankind, and especially the Jewish people.

Jewish law pertains to every area of human existence. It is more comprehensive than any legal system with which moderns are familiar – American, British, Continental, Roman, or Russian. It involves private law and public law. It is charged with the ethical and the pragmatic. It can stimulate philosophical analysis and sociological speculation.

Name it and it is to be found in the legal literature of Judaism. Our sages said this many years ago and it is still true. Therefore, failure to make as much progress in one area as Justice Cohn would have wanted hardly justifies discarding the whole.

To students I shall try to communicate the love that obsesses me and perhaps, in due course, the demand for the renaissance of Jewish law will be irresistibly strong.

America's Jewish Debt Is Not to Jews of 1776, But to Judaism's Tenets

Unlike many of my colleagues I have chosen in this our beloved country's bicentennial, to focus attention not on what American Jews contributed to the revolution in 1776 but rather on what the heritage of Judaism contributed to the political thought of that period. It is my considered judgment that the American Revolution would have succeeded even if there had been no Jews in the colonies at that time. However, had there been no Old Testament and no Biblically based political ideals there would never have been a revolution nor any of the democratic institutions for which the United States later became the model for all the world.

Too often we overlook the fact that the very notion that one has the right to question the legitimacy of power is a Jewish perspective. Prior to Judaism no one ever thought, in the words of Professor Jacob Talmon, that "King, Parliament, even the sovereign people, even Pope and Council, must at all times exhibit their credentials in the face of divine or natural law." Everywhere it was assumed that the power of the ruler is as natural as the sun and the moon, the thunder and the lightning. Even Aristotle held that there were people who were born to rule while others were born to be ruled. Human slavery itself he deemed natural.

In the Soviet Union one does not dare question the credentials of the authorities in control. And even now her most famous rebels, when they do rebel, take their stance from the religious tradition. However, this religious tradition – which is essentially Judaic – yielded much more than the right to rebel. (I say essentially Judaic because Christianity was too often reconciled to giving to Caesar what was Caesar's as long as God had what was His. Judaism dared to question also Caesar's claims.)

And precisely because according to Judaism, no one was ever above the Law, there was in Jewish law the requirement that even kings and high priests must account for their deeds to human tribunals and not only to divine ones. Judaism also had the doctrine of judicial review. One could challenge the constitutionality of any legislative or executive mandate. Such a challenge was a challenge to the legitimacy of the power that was being exercised against a fellow human.

Furthermore, because Judaism always distinguished between spiritual power which resided in the priests, prophets, and rabbis, and temporal power which resided in kings, princes, "nesiim," and others, one can trace the doctrine of separation of church and state back to Judaism. No one other than Moses was entitled to hold the two powers at the same time and when the Maccabees later usurped both they were severely criticized for their breach of the Judaic pattern. Judaism preserved the right of the prophet to criticize the monarch while the monarch retained his claim to the prophet's respect and obedience.

It is from this position that one arrives at the notion that there is a difference between law and justice. Law is "what is"; justice is "what ought to be." What the ruling authority ordains is law; what he ought to ordain is suggested by the keepers of the conscience. Justice is the standard by which we measure the quality of law – the litmus paper to determine whether the rule of law conforms to the ideal. And this dichotomy is the heart of the theocentric law which Judaism gave to mankind and especially to the founders of the American republic. By its mandate, even the will of the majority is not the voice of God. That was the theory of the French Revolution, not the theory of the American Revolution. According to Judaism – and incidentally Hamilton, Madison and Jay – the majority must be made to do no wrong, and what is right and wrong is determined not by them but rather by a higher law, the "echo of the infinite" of which Oliver Wendell Holmes did write.

If Jews who immigrated to these blessed shores felt so at home here it was not because they came from democratic countries. On the other hand, they came from lands in which democracy was hardly known. But because of their Jewish background they could melt so readily into the American process which was familiar to them – it was Judaic in origin and character.

To be even more specific with regard to the Judaic roots of American political thought one could cite many more ideas.

In Judaism we stress the rule of law to such an extent that Prof. Zilberg points out that even God is bound by it. Having divested Himself of some authority by delegating it to the rabbis, He could not curtail the judicial power they were exercising.

Second, the violent resistance of the American colonists to the unlawful search of their homes and the seizure of their property stems from the Biblical injunction that even a creditor cannot invade the debtor's residence to collect a debt. He may stand outside and request security and that is all. Rabbinic law extended this prohibition to include even the court's sheriff. From this concern there ultimately emerged the right to privacy which Jewish law articulated at least two thousand years before western law embraced it.

And the right against self-incrimination, which is much more protective of alleged criminals in Jewish law than in any other legal system known to us, may have come from Judaism – not Lord Coke. Of this scholars have written and I need not labor the point. Suffice it to say that Maimonides rationalizes the rule by pointing out that it prevents mentally disturbed people from destroying themselves by confessing to crimes they did not commit. So great was the concern of Jewish law for the sanctity and dignity of human life that our sages were mindful even of those who did not cherish life!

Indeed, the greatness of America is her respect for the human personality which remains inviolate. This is also the hallmark of Judaism which teaches us that we were created in the divine image. The two traditions are kin – Judaism is the mother, and Americanism the daughter. Therefore, what American Jews did or could have done in 1776 does not intrigue me as much as the fact that Judaism came to this hemisphere before the Jews did and laid the foundation for a great civilization which will endure as long as Jews and Judaism have and will.

Letter to My Son[*]

Dear Son,

You may recall that when you began to study Torah more than a decade ago, your mother and I made a party in honor of the event. Jews were wont to do this in years gone by. Now you leave us to become a student at the university. And again we rejoice that you have attained a milestone, one which will help you deepen your learning, broaden your vision, acquire new skills, and cultivate new friendships. But this time we are also filled with misgivings – with anxiety. How will your new career affect your loyalty to our people and our heritage? Will your separation from family change your values-system? Will you exercise your new freedom to reject your past or will you exercise it to make that past more poignantly your own?

Indeed many of your peers wait precisely for this juncture in their lives to break with home and community – as if this were the longed for moment of emancipation. And that is why they sever the ties forthwith. They do not even wait for a challenge. They were never happy with their heritage and they exploit the first opportunity to shed it.

Perhaps that explains why I am impelled to write you now – before you leave us – and I do not wait for you to encounter the first threat to your affinity for the ways of our fathers. If I can, I want to avert your imitation of your peers. What is more, the response

[*] Editor's note: This column was written seven years after the youngest of Rabbi Rackman's children graduated from college. It was written at the request of a publisher and has been reprinted frequently.

of the Jewish student to his first challenge on campus frequently determines how he will cope with all that follow. And I want to prepare you for that response. If it will be one that will be an affirmation of your Jewishness, we and our people will be blessed. If, on the other hand, it finds you weak and vascillating then there will be a continuous erosion that will break our hearts – but even more it will ultimately plague you because you will have forfeited pride in yourself and your background.

There is a world famous academy for the training of military officers at which all students – prior to their first chapel session – are asked to line up for the particular denominational service they want to attend. Because the Jewish students are always a tiny minority in the group, there are invariably a few who hesitate to identify with their Jewish comrades. That hesitancy often costs them the respect not only of their fellow-Jews but also of their Christian classmates. Their first response is crucial. Either they stand up on the first call for what they are – or they never get another chance. As in the games of chess we were wont to play with each other – the opening often made the difference between victory and defeat. So it is with your first challenge in your new environment. Your opening declarations are most important.

Do not deny or conceal your Jewish identity and do not hesitate to be different. Yet, you may ask, why should one maintain a stance which makes one overly conspicuous? Is it not more normal to adjust and acculturate and don the coloration of one's environment? No, my son, it will be to your advantage even as a student to cherish the value of individuality, of personal uniqueness. You must not lose your identity in a pool of sameness with other human beings. Respect all mankind because of that which all men have in common – the inviolable endowment of personality – but be firm in the knowledge that you are what you are and must give expression in the classroom and in the dormitory, in social and intellectual circles, to your own feelings, views, interpretations, and your own mode of living. You have heard me say that the most creative spirits in human history, though very much influenced by their environments, were always somewhat alienated from them. And it was precisely this modicum of alienation that enabled them to be critical of their surroundings, and enrich human thought.

They innovated because they were alienated. Perhaps this also explains why Jews were, and still are, so creative. We were never truly at home anywhere. The feeling of at-homeness, conceived and nurtured in the cradle of uniformity, is not healthful for human progress. And by being yourself – Jewish in thought and deed – you will discover that your uniqueness will come to the fore in your response to every phase of learning in which you will engage.

I remember how I once shook a class and its instructor as he tried to point out that some parts of the Bible could not have been written in Moses' time because the ideas expressed in them were too advanced for that period of human history. Consequently he assumed that they were authored centuries later and interpolated into Sacred Scripture. This is a favorite technique of ancient historians. I simply challenged the assumption that in a given century we cannot find men whose ideas are as disparate as those of Adolf Hitler and Albert Schweitzer in our own era. If an atomic war should put an end to our civilization, and an archaeologist a millennium hence will dig up traces of what once was, would he also place Hitler in the Middle Ages and Schweitzer in the twenty-fifth century? A classic instance of what I mean when I urge you to be yourself is to be found in the way Louis Brandeis, a famous American jurist and Zionist, reacted to Plato's "Republic" when he was a student at Harvard University. While the professor heaped praise on the immortal Plato and his finest dialogue, Brandeis reacted as a Jew committed to the centrality of family in social progress and he demonstrated how ridiculous Plato's conception was. You will recall that it was Plato who projected as an ideal the elimination of family ties for the two upper classes of his three class society. But as Brandeis incisively saw, "Plato's fathers are to dearly love their children and sacrifice their lives for their sons and daughters – whom they have never seen, whom they can only suppose to exist. He imagines a class of men in his society who possess all the physical power, who enjoy the respect and admiration of the state, but who nevertheless have no desire to accumulate property, who have no tendency toward despotism, and this though all the nobler feelings which usually fill men's breasts have been killed at their birth or eradicated, although they have had no education in what is elevating and ennobling, on the contrary, whose greatest virtue is to be violent and brutal, whose pleasures debauchery, the emoluments of whose profession unlimited concubinage and mandatory infanticide."

Only an independent student, immune to the levelling pressure of the classroom atmosphere, can articulate a different point of view and expose the stupidity of that which so many before hesitated to challenge.

That is why I say that your readiness to be different will even make you a better student. But it will also make you a better man.

Political philosophers always dreaded the effects that democracy would have on individuality. And in our day, preoccupation with, and the worship of, science and technology are a greater threat than democracy ever was. Science has internationalized thought and enterprise, which is good, but at the same time the very internationalism and universality of its discourse and its symbols are a threat to the diversity of personal and uniquely human expressions of thought and feeling such as poets were wont to give us. Technology has been even more of a leveller. And by being human in a Jewish way of life we enrich the diversity which aggrandizes man's ultimate freedom to know and be himself. And need I tell you what this will mean to the survival of our people! Our survival as a people depends upon the readiness of at least a cadre of Jews everywhere who will have strong feelings of Jewish identity and will inspire others similarly to declare and be themselves.

While it is your initial response to your new environment that concerns me most deeply now, I am not so naive as to believe that once you have coped with your first challenge there will be nothing else to fear. You must also be made aware of the fact that you are entering the academic world which for centuries has demeaned Jews and Judaism. Today, fortunately, Jews gain admission both to the student bodies and the faculties. There was a time when even this was not easily achieved. But our heritage has not fared as well. For Toynbee that heritage was a fossil of Syriac civilization, and even if your professors do not verbalize their agreement with Toynbee, they share his point of view. They do not have to express their concurrence – they do it by their consistent neglect of the Hebraic component of western civilization. And I want to sensitize you to this intellectual dishonesty on their part. Even when they are Jews, they propagate the "big lie" that western culture is the legacy of Greece and Rome when in fact its greatest blessings are Hebraic in origin! That lie has been repeated so often that even Jews believe it, despite the fact that it denigrates them and their past. I could write volumes about this. I vividly recall how strongly I reacted, when I was a student, to the view stated in most textbooks that political theory began with the Greeks. I lived to see new textbooks edited which included selections from the Bible. However, that that same Bible was the source from which political theorists continued to derive their inspiration for the most revolutionary ideas of the Middle Ages and the modern period was rarely alluded to. In the development of both political and economic democracy it was the Jewish heritage that was far more significant than the Hellenistic heritage but even when that was recognized it was referred to as the gift of Christianity. Yet it was precisely the Old Testament, and not the New, to which the credit is due. The anti-Semitism of academia was of a "higher," subtler species, and you must prepare your antenna for it.

Let me cite a few simple illustrations. It was Judaism, and not Hellenism, that exalted man. Judaism gave man a divine dimension as it posited the creation of man in the divine image. Perhaps that is why Rennaissance scholars so cherished the Bible, and studied Hebrew that they might read it in its original tongue. It was also Judaism, and not Hellenism, that emancipated man from the grip of fatalism and enabled him to soar and conquer the earth, and the heavens as well. Our benevolent God gave Adam fire and bade him use it for his happiness. Unlike Prometheus we did not have to wrench it from the gods and suffer punishment for our daring. And it was Judaism and not even Rome, that placed justice and equity, goodness and morality, at the pinnacle of man's striving. There is virtually no area of the lives of western peoples that has not been affected by Judaism. True, the aesthetic dimension may have come from Greece. But the drive to the good and true is from us. Yet, the text-books you will use, and the lectures you will hear, will blithely ignore this. Who, in a world diseased with prejudice against the Jew, would care to acknowledge how much is owed to us! And this unrelenting ignoring of our contribution to civilization does incalculable harm to the egos of Jewish students. They imagine that all pastures are greener than theirs.

Even in an environment in which the knowledge of history is central to all disciplines, it is forgotten that both the preoccupation with history and the philosophy of history are Hebraic in origin. Michael Grant, the distinguished British historian, has demonstrated that the Hebrews, not the Greeks, wrote real history half a millennium before Herodotus. But the timing does not really matter. The fact is that Europeans were influenced more by the Bible than by Herodotus, and why the reluctance to give thanks where thanks are due!

I cannot anticipate the countless situations in which you will be confronted by the assault on your pride in your heritage. I only bid you to be aware of the fact that it will come. And Jewish professors as much as Christian ones will share the guilt. They craved acceptance in your new world and they had to pay the price that Heine paid in Germany, and Chwolson in Russia. I pray that you will have more integrity and be less gullible.

Unfortunately it is not only with regard to our past that there will be a continuous assault on your pride as a Jew, but even more so with regard to the Jewish situation in the present.

The fact is that the nations of the earth are giving increasing recognition to the right of all ethnic and racial groups in liberation and self-determination. The number of sovereign nations in the United Nations grows from year to year. Yet there is very little enthusiasm anywhere – even in the democratic countries and certainly not in the communist world – for the Jewish liberation movement and the right of Jews not only as individuals but collectively as a people to be captains of their fate and masters of their own destiny.

When other peoples seek what we seek they are accorded empathy and praise. But we are told to be content with a modicum of freedom wherever we live. We are to reconcile ourselves to the freedom we enjoy to be like others – but not necessarily to be ourselves. I hope I do not have to labor this point. But your classmates will need to be reminded of it. They will be in the vanguard of liberal, progressive movements. They will seek to enlist your help.

By all means identify with all causes that will redound to the advancement of universal peace and justice – but do not hesitate to seek it for your own people as well. One does not love humanity any less because one loves one's own too. Indeed those who can love only humanity at large – as Rousseau did – are usually incapable of loving any one at all – as he couldn't.

The Jew, with a strong sense of Jewish identity, who does not hesitate to lead his own distinctive Jewish life, and seeks to master much of human wisdom with a Jewish stance, can champion his people's cause as well as humanity's. He learns how to maintain a proper balance between particularity and universalism, which was the special gift of the Biblical prophets and their descendants. The university should not make you exclusively the universalist. Your vision will then be blocked by the forest and you will fail to seek the health of the individual trees.

With respect to one more issue, you will find your new environment quite devastating. Most universities in the west are committed to the philosophy of relativism in ethics. I will have more to say of this when I discuss your personal behavior. However, this philosophy – which is very much sustained in our day by the anthropologists – is also a threat to your Jewishness. Judaism is predicated on the existence of an absolute right and wrong, even if we cannot always fathom them.

I cite but one example from the writings of Professor Emil Fackenheim. A Jew cannot accept the notion that Hitler may have been right from his point of view, or from the point of view of his cultural milieu. A relativist in ethics might well argue that it may not have been so wrong that Hitler sought to liquidate six hundred thousand German Jews for the greater happiness of sixty million Germans. After all, what is so wrongful about sacrificing one mortal for the benefit of one hundred! Certainly the greater happiness of the greatest number was thereby served.

And Fackenheim is not the only modern philosopher to reject the modern point of view. In this connection there were Greeks too who believed that there was a right and wrong that transcended man. And Judaism is firmly rooted in that conviction. When your classmates or professors try to shake you in your commitment to that notion, use Fackenheim's argument. By the same token, I do not have to remind you that Judaism's ethics are not rigid. There must always be a balancing of interests or equities. Some values yield to others. Even some wrongs are occasionally right. The important thing is that you remember that the challenges you encounter are not new ones. Greater Jews than you and I have coped with them before. I plead only that you do not surrender your convictions, your pride, and your identity, without carefully examining the merit of the challenge. Be as much of a skeptic with regard to what you are being offered as you will be forced to be skeptical with regard to that which you bring to your university experience.

Yet how does one manage, in the face of so many challenges, to retain one's identity as a Jew and one's pride in the Jewish heritage? My son, the answer is one provided by the Bible – by the literal meaning of its mandates. You must choose to be different and permit Jewish observances to keep you aware of that difference. The Jewish way of life is our tactic to keep us continuously aware of our separateness – of our uniqueness – of our vocation as individual Jews and as a people. And if one truly wants to cope with the intellectual challenges of the university and not forfeit one's birthright as a Jew, then one must observe the commandments to make one continuously conscious of the role that one can and ought play in one's new environment.

You have often heard me give more philosophical rationalizations of the Jewish way of life. You have heard me explain the dietary laws as the Jewish way of sanctifying the very process of ingestion. You have heard me relate many of the specific rules pertaining to the preparation of meat to the problem of man's brutalization. As for the Sabbath you have heard me expound upon it as the greatest device yet conceived to preserve man's personal freedom, reconcile him with nature, emancipate him from the bondage of time and the machine, etc. etc. But I do not now stress these more sophisticated approaches to the Jewish tradition. It may be paradoxical but precisely when you are on the threshold of more advanced learning I become simplistic and stress the most elementary justification for the observances – their serving as a reminder to you as to who and what you are.

I do hope that you will not stop there. On the other hand, because you will be broadening your horizons it is very likely that you will discover deeper meanings for all that constitutes the Jewish way of life. My own preoccupation with social, political, and legal philosophy prompted me to appreciate our heritage more than I ever did before. Others have enriched their Jewish experience through the mastery of other academic disciplines – especially history, psychology, ethics – even aesthetics and biology. But you will discover the treasures the more readily if the search is one you are goaded to make all the time precisely because you are deporting yourself as a Jew.

It is only with a sense of uniqueness that an individual can live meaningfully and creatively as a person and that applies to a people as well. The greatest contributions to human progress have been made by men who opted to be different, who challenged the majority or dissented from the general consensus. The very existence of the Jewish people was, and continues to be, such a challenge and dissent. And because of it we enriched civilization in a measure totally disproportionate to the smallness of our number.

There are many sound philosophical and ethical rationalizations of particular commandments in the Bible but the overall impact of all of them is to make you aware of the fact that you belong to a group of human beings that is expected to be special and to do exceptional things for God and all mankind. And that also explains why daily prayer is so important. For one who prays regularly, God and His will are items of continuing, unrelenting concern. And it is that concern that I urge you to keep alive. I do not expect anyone to be immune to doubt with respect to God's existence or to ambivalence with respect to the efficacy of prayer. Yet even the moments of wrestling with one's doubts help to keep faith alive. Faith remains a live option to one who prays. And that is what is so important especially in one's youth. Experiences in later life deepen faith and make it meaningful. In youth one is more apt to dispense with it as unnecessary. However, even the habit of prayer will keep you involved at least in the process of religious thought and action and that is why I urge it so strongly upon you.

Moreover, as a Jew who prays you will be so helpful to other Jews in your new environment. I can assure you that will be needed at one time or another by classmates. And your availability and knowledgeability will help to form, on many occasions, a tiny Jewish community on campus. The sentiment of Jewish solidarity was always nurtured by prayer in a Minyan and you will be able to make a contribution to comrades and our people as a whole by your commitment to the routines of your life at home.

You know that I am not a Freudian but who will gainsay that the sexual drive is strong and perhaps in this connection you will find at the university the greatest personal challenge to the values and mores we have sought to transmit at home. What can I now add to that which your mother and I have said before?

Neither your mother nor I, nor anyone else for that matter, should invade your right of privacy. Thus what you will do is a matter of conscience between you and the girls you will meet. Except for truly heinous and criminal behavior you are accountable only to God and your own psyche for that which you will do. But not to your psyche alone. One overriding consideration must be what you will do to the psyche of the girls with whom you will establish relationships – social and sexual.

If you were a girl I would perhaps impart even stronger words of caution. But society being what it is, and especially men being what they are, women bear the greater burden in the consequences of sexual promiscuity. Yet men ought to act with a sense of responsibility. Nothing in our tradition is as important as respect for one's fellow-man. The use or exploitation of another human being exclusively for one's pleasure without regard to the evil done to that person is the cardinal sin of Judaism. It is abuse of another's divine image. And your peers are giving little thought to the significance of deferred gratification, avoiding harm to anyone now, and intensifying the pleasures of the future precisely because one can then live with one's conscience, and experience no self-destructive guilt.

Perhaps the standard ought to be: How would you want your own daughter to be treated by a male, when you will have a daughter? Of course one can retort that that is an old-fashioned idea. But what is old may be the encapsulation of universal experience. To have sex without love is degrading to both parties to the act. And if you love someone, the least you seek is not to do harm to the beloved.

In this connection Judaism is at one and the same time most permissive and most exacting. From the point of view of sanctions it is permissive – only incest and adultery are punishable. However, from the point of morality, it bids one, on one's honor, to respect the inviolability of one's beloved except when God even makes it a Mitzvah to unite body and soul in an act of love.

This is a high standard. I can only urge it upon you and pray that you will try your best to live up to it. But here, too, the observances of Judaism play a very subtle role. Living as a Jew will cause you to respect yourself. With a proper amount of self-respect one is loathe to demean one's self. Then one acts only in consonance with that self-respect and induces the same feeling in others. The vulgar and the base make one sick at heart and are avoided.

You will recall, dear son, that instruction given by Hillel to a prospective convert to Judaism. The sum total of the Torah is the Golden Rule – the rest is commentary.

The sum total of all that I have written is that I want you to perform the Mitzvah of Kiddush Hashem – sanctifying God's name in everything that you do. The essence of that Mitzvah is not martyrdom, although it sometimes calls for that. However, our sages define it differently. "So act," they enjoin us, "that all who behold you will say, 'Blessed is that man's God.'"

It is thus that I pray you will act. And you and we shall rejoice.
Love, Dad.

Concern for a Positive
Jewish Image Is No Heresy

Some people are impressed by the gains Orthodox Judaism has achieved in recent decades. But I believe that at least as many are depressed that the image of Orthodox Judaism in the world at large, and among Jews in particular, was never so bad. Not an issue arises but that it is made to appear that the Bible and the Talmud are the repository of all that is evil. These source books are considered intolerant, anti-democratic, narrow, benighted. They breed disunity, fanaticism, even violence.

Certainly, recent events in Israel appear to justify some of these conclusions. Yet people ought to be more circumspect. It would take volumes to make full reply and prove that the charges are unfair. Moreover, one must never forget that the traditional sources are like Scripture. They can be quoted and used by devils as well as saints. And the quotes reveal more about the person doing the quoting than they do about the tradition itself.

Nonetheless, Orthodox Jews ought to be concerned about their image and the image of the tradition. I know that there are many who could not care less. For them it is enough to know they are doing the Lord's work; how others see them or what they do does not evoke a thought. Yet is this proper? Is this the way the tradition would have us feel? Are public relations of no consequence at all?

Rabbi Joseph B. Soloveitchik once expressed the view that in halachic decisions one must reckon with public relations. The issue at that time was the propriety of instituting the draft of students of Yeshiva University to serve as U.S. military chaplains. That rabbis would not serve would be poor public relations in the eyes of non-Jews. That non-Orthodox rabbis would serve and Orthodox rabbis would not would be poor public relations in the eyes of Jews. Such considerations may not be the only ones or the most important ones, but one does not ignore them.

The same reasoning applied to the issue of Orthodox participation in such mixed bodies as the Synagogue Council of America. Would the image of Orthodoxy suffer if such participation came to an end?

In my life I have had to do many things which my non-Jewish colleagues found difficult to understand. I was concerned with the image of Orthodoxy in their eyes, and I always sought to put forth the explanation that they would most respect. And I found biblical warrant for so doing. Moses argued with God that He too must be concerned about what the nations of the earth would say about Him. When the Jews offended against God and God threatened to destroy them, Moses pleaded: "What will the nations say? They will claim that it was because You, God, could not deliver them to the Promised Land that You put an end to them in the wilderness. Consider what this will do to Your image!" (*Exodus* 32:12; *Deuteronomy* 9:28)

Consequently, if Moses was concerned about God's image in the eyes of the gentiles and his argument carried weight with God, who are we not to be concerned with our image in their eyes.

One rabbi sought to establish the same conclusion by referring to the fact that a Jew starts his prayers every morning with a verse that was uttered not by a Jew but by a non-Jewish prophet, Bilaam. Bilaam was the one who beheld the encampment of Jews and proclaimed: "How goodly are thy tents, Oh Jacob, thy tabernacles, Oh Israel." (*Numbers* 24:5) And the Jew enters the synagogue each day reciting that verse. Of all the beautiful verses in the Bible, why did our sages select one composed by a non-Jew, and hardly a friendly non-Jew? The answer one rabbi gives is that our sages wanted us to start the day with the thought that it is important that we ponder each day how we appear in the eyes of non-Jews, and not necessarily the kindliest ones.

Thus, to ignore the kind of impression that we are communicating to others is to flout the tradition, not to fulfill it. Yet there are many Jews who almost enjoy making spectacles of themselves and inviting ridicule by their behavior. They think that they are thus proving their greater devotion to God and His Torah.

They also overlook the fact that the basic notion in Judaism – *Kiddush Hashem* and *Chillul Hashem* – sanctifying God's name or desecrating it—are linked with the impact of our behavior on those who behold us. And often it is not only how we look that counts but what we say or do. One is not a hypocrite when one is careful not to say or do what may cause the non-Jew to have a negative view of Judaism. This is a message I have long tried to convey to many who glory in telling things as they superficially appear to be, without thinking of the effect their words are having on others. Sometimes they do this – as does Rabbi Meir Kahane in Israel – without even caring about the hurt they are causing their own people.

There were times in Jewish history when Jews even refrained from killing enemies lest the revenge be taken on coreligionists less able to defend themselves. So mindful were they of the importance of public relations!

From Jewish history we learn that when attacked, a Moslem minority in a Christian country could always threaten the assailants with reprisals against the Christian minorities in other lands, but Jews, even when they were in a position to deal a strong blow, found that they had to subordinate the destiny of their particular community to the welfare of the whole people.

They had a strong sense of solidarity with their coreligionists everywhere, and thus, for example, the Jews of Tulczyn in 1648 refrained from attacking treacherous fellow combatants among the noblemen. They chose to die instead when their leader exhorted them: "We are in exile among the nations. If you lay hands upon the nobles, then all the kings of Christianity will hear of it and take revenge on all our brethren in the dispersion, God forbid."

In our own century we have a tragic but eloquent example of what the Jews always dreaded. I refer to the bullet fired in 1936 by Herschel Grynzpan, whose story is beautifully told by Abram Sacher in "Sufference Is the Badge." At that time Poland was calling back all of her citizens and Grynzpan's parents were caught in a vise. After receiving a letter from his parents describing their distress, he decided to take revenge by destroying some great Nazi officials, made his way into an embassy in Paris, and killed a third-rate Nazi bureaucrat. That shot was the pretext for the dreadful pogrom of November 1938, which precipitated a reprisal against all the Jews in Germany.

All of this makes us mindful once again of a prayer we recite after meals when we ask God to help us "find favor in His eyes and in the eyes of man."

We must ever try to find favor in the eyes of both. Ignoring one or the other is bad religion. Considering both is good religion.

The Case for Israel's Prisoner Exchanges

I s Israel acting wisely when it releases hundreds of enemies – murderers, terrorists and saboteurs – in exchange for a few of her own soldiers, dead or alive? Furthermore, should Israel not restore the death penalty for those whose release may one day be sought by her enemies? Does she not encourage continuing extortion by keeping alive those for whom the extortion is effected?

I know that millions of Jews are wrestling with these questions – and perhaps millions of non-Jews as well. Alas, there are no black-and-white answers, only gray ones. But the legal literature of Judaism speaks to us on these issues, as it does with respect to almost everything else.

First, it should be made known that the mitzvah to redeem those of our brethren who have been taken captive is one of the greatest. The Talmud (*Bava Basra* 8b) so states, and Maimonides expands upon it and adds that "there is no mitzvah that is more important." A captive is in constant danger, and everything must be done to set him free. (*Ramban Hilchot Matnot Ani'm* 8;10) Yet at what price?

A thousand years before Maimonides, Jewish authorities ruled that the ransom paid must not exceed the price that would be paid for the captive were he to be sold as a slave. If this limitation were not imposed, those who take Jews as hostages would invariably bankrupt the Jewish community. They would fix ransoms that had no connection with the worth of the captive to anyone other than Jews, and Jews would give all they had to save a coreligionist.

The question was raised whether individual Jews, as distinguished from communities, could pay more than the economic value of the captive. The answer was that they could not. The only exceptions were husbands who were legally obligated by their marriage contracts to redeem their spouses if kidnapped.

Nonetheless, the limitations were not universally respected. The Talmud tells of one rabbi who ignored it to redeem a child whose ultimate promise as a leader in Israel impressed him enormously. (*Gittin* 58a) Yet one famous rabbi in the Middle Ages refused to let the Jewish community pay the ransom for his release and he died in captivity. (*Maharam of Rottenberg*) He knew that if he acted otherwise, Christian brigands would repeat the practice again and again – kidnap the rabbi and extort from Jews massive sums to obtain his release.

Yet even this precedent did not deter Jews from overpaying for individuals taken captive. It was not easy to justify this breach of Jewish law. In one instance the rabbi expounded the law but said that in that case the Jews should pay more than the hostage was worth. The reason was not that the hostage was so dear to the Jewish community; he was a villain. In the hands of his captors, however, he would convert to Islam and be a source of greater trouble to Jews than if he were restored to his people where he could be watched more readily.

In the 16th century, another rabbi did not seek a pretext for his breach of Jewish law and he permitted the payment of a ransom in excess of what the law allowed. Jews were simply too kind to permit a coreligionist to languish in the hands of captors. Thus, the Jewish heart prevailed over Jewish law. Can this also be said of the behavior of Israel's government in her negotiations with her Arab enemies?

And what about Jewish law and the resort to capital punishment for terrorists to prevent their release by extortions? It is well known that despite the general disapproval of capital punishment in Jewish law, its use in the case of terrorists is not only permitted but highly recommended in Jewish sources.

In the Middle Ages, Jews permitted the execution of fellow Jews who were informers on the theory that they presented a constant danger to their people; they were from a legal point of view *rodfim* – pursuers – and one may kill a pursuer in self-defense. Certainly terrorists are in that category. They are always a threat to humanity. Yet here too Israel is not applying the death penalty, though Jewish law would be very permissive with respect to it. Popular opinion does not support the government on this issue. But the government is not changing its position.

First, it argues that terrorists especially are not deterred from committing their nefarious deeds by the threat of capital punishment. Second, Israel is too much a respecter of the sanctity of human life to change its time-honored aversion to the death-penalty. Third, the enemy would retaliate and kill Jewish prisoners of war, in violation of international law. And fourth, Israel wants to be able to negotiate for exchanges, even though Israel pays exorbitantly for it. She still wants to have something to exchange, and for that purpose live enemies are better than dead ones.

I can readily appreciate the ambivalence of so many Jews with respect to the issues. Yet for me the most compelling consideration in justifying the two breaches of Jewish law I have described is Israel's obligation to her soldiers.

Israeli soldiers are assured that there is no price so high that Jews will not pay it to redeem them if they are taken prisoner. This is an important factor for the morale of the fighting man. If he is killed, even his remains will be brought home for burial. And if he is captured no stone will be unturned to achieve his freedom. This obligation the government must fulfill. And this obligation, from the point of view of Jewish law, is more to be respected than the legal limit on the price paid to redeem captives or the propriety of capital punishment for terrorists.

The decision is not an easy one. But important moral decisions rarely are.

A Step Toward Bridging
the Religious-Secular Gap

I do not like being called a *Dati, a religious Jew*. And I am not alone in disliking the term. Moreover, I shudder when a Jew feels that he must sheepishly confess to me that he is not religious. He may be more religious than I, though it may appear that I do more things that are identified with the tradition than he.

Indeed, no one should ever speak of himself as religious. To be religious is a goal to which one aspires and only one who is arrogant claims that he has already achieved it. Similarly, no Jew ought to affirm that he is not religious. Once he had identified with the Jewish people, he has already made himself a party to the Covenant. He may even deny that there is a God, but he already subscribes to one term of the Covenant – the responsibility of Jews for each other.

How I wish that I could eliminate the term from the vocabulary of our people! Christians are more astute. They speak of themselves as practicing or non-practicing. And virtually all Jews are practicing Jews – some more so, and some less – but once a person asserts that he is Jewish, he is already a practicing Jew in a very significant way. He has placed himself within the fold, and that is no insignificant deed.

One of the sad consequences of the use of the term religious is that it has taken on an obnoxious meaning almost everywhere. It is assumed that it refers only to commandments that pertain to man's relationship with God. Thus in Israel, for example, in a cooperative residential facility in which the owners have agreed to be "religious," a person who observes the Sabbath and dietary laws might not be expelled even if he is a proven thief or embezzler, while one who is honest and neighborly might be excluded because he parked his car there on the Sabbath.

Moreover, use of the term "religious" for the commandments pertaining to relationships between God and man enables some Jews to boast about being "more religious" than others. And this is usually not only arrogance on their part but a violation of the very tradition to which they profess loyalty.

For example, there has been a tendency in recent years to promote more meticulous observance of Jewish dietary laws. Frankly, I am no champion of this trend. It is usually described as the "glatt kosher" syndrome, and there are very cogent halachic and moral reasons for resisting it. To begin with, though, I want to stress that Jews are prone to equate "more religious" with this kind of concern and "less religious" with the lack of it. I would much rather relate the "more" or the "less" to the way a Jew conducts his business affairs, how meticulously honest he is in his concern for other people's money, how careful he is with his speech, how charitable he is, how neighborly, how civic-minded, etc. But we have come to equate showmanship with cleaving to God, ostentation rather than piety.

My late father discouraged use of two pairs of tefillin in prayer, though many Jews do just that. He relied on several giants of the talmudic tradition, who held that to be so observant gives the impression that one is superior to others. Modesty in one's religious observance is as much a cherished value as modesty in attire. Today we are witness to the rejection of both values, but not by the same people. The modest in attire are usually immodest in their claim to be religious, while the immodest in attire are usually very modest in denying that they are religious.

He was equally resistant to the glatt kosher movement. First, he felt that one ought not to encourage a practice which not all Jews can possibly observe. If all Jews observed it, the supply would never equal the demand. And for a Jew to engage in a practice which is unavailable to all Jews often serves only the ego and not one's spiritual excellence.

Second, to insist on glatt kosher is to denigrate what the sages have ruled is kosher. It is tantamount to a rejection of the oral law and its custodians, the rabbis and their published works. One of the greatest rabbis of the last century felt that it was a form of heresy to act in such a way that, in effect, tells the rabbis: "We question the validity of your rulings. We will do better."

To my father's reasons I add my own. When one day I shall face our Maker in judgment and He will accuse me of being lax with regard to the dietary laws, I shall at least apologize and explain that I was equally lax in my behavior toward my fellow man. I had no double standard. But what will those who want to be "more religious" say when they are confronted with their pursuit of the strictest measures toward God and the most compromising standards toward their fellow men?

There is one more reason why I dislike claiming that I am a Dati. By retaining that term and using it, I am contributing to the most serious division of our people in millennia, a division that threatens the future of Israel. The term is inviting civil strife.

I don't believe that anyone really planned it that way. It just happened. But the trend must be stopped. The *Datiim* and the *Chiloniim* can refuse to be described as such. Perhaps even political parties should cease to describe themselves as "religious." Movements may do so. So may schools. But political parties are organized for power and power inevitably corrupts. No "religious" political party ever succeeded in functioning with a view only to the realization of religious goals. And the state of Israel has provided no exception.

I have no solution to the problem of how religious movements in Israel will influence legislation without their own political parties as they do in the United States and Britain. But I do know that one immediate desideratum is to stop talking of ourselves as religious or irreligious. If all of us are simply practicing Jews, the so-called secularists will not have to organize to protect themselves against the religionists and the religionists will have taken a giant step forward to win the respect of those whom they would like to see cherish the Jewish tradition and its exceptional values and of life.

This would be step number one in the battle against a divided camp and enormous losses to assimilation.

Modern Orthodox Jews Keep Authentic Tradition Alive

W hen ghetto walls began to crumble almost two centuries ago and Jews had to confront the world that we call modern, there were many different responses ranging from assimilation and baptism on the one hand to total isolation and withdrawal on the other. Those who withdrew altogether from the challenge are still with us in growing numbers in Israel and elsewhere and they call themselves *Charedim*.

Their way of life, their dress, their social, educational and even economic institutions are almost totally unaffected by the rest of the world about them. Those, on the other hand, who opted for assimilation and baptism, are, of course, lost to us forever and the number that follow their example even today grows from year to year.

The majority of Jews, however, chose other alternatives, such as Reform Judaism, secular Zionism and Jewish socialism. Those who were loyal to the Halacha and at the same time wanted to participate especially in the intellectual currents of the day first embraced the so-called neo-orthodoxy of Samson Raphael Hirsch, whose influence is still very strong. He is, as a matter of fact, the inspiration of most orthodox Jews who do not want to return to the ghetto.

Unfortunately, today his approach is being modified in some quarters. Some of those who profess still to be his followers are trying to revise his clearly stated position. In the words of Rabbi Walter S. Wurzburger they are claiming that Hirsch "did not advocate his classical formulation of the synthesis between Torah and culture (*Torah im Derekh Eretz*) as an intrinsic religious ideal . . . but merely as an emergency measure in order to salvage those elements of the Jewish community that otherwise would have been completely overwhelmed by the onslaught of modernity."

I know descendants of Hirsch who are fighting this revision which dishonors the man. Yet the mere fact that such revision is suggested demonstrates how forceful have been the orthodox elements who want to rebuild the ghetto wall – at least with respect to world culture – and to live Jewishly without a symbiosis with modernity.

Those of us who, like Hirsch, feel that it is insulting to Torah to concede that it cannot cope with any challenge continue to follow Hirsch and other Jewish philosophers who manage the challenge – especially Rabbi Abraham Isaac Kook and Rabbi Joseph B. Soloveitchik. The thought of Franz Rosenzweig has very much enriched our perspective and here and there I too have tried to add a thought especially with regard to the legitimacy of the modern orthodox stance which I hold is authentically Maimonidean.

However, the symposium of modern orthodox thinkers published in Tradition reveals how apologetic many of them are. Dr. David Singer faults them very well for their lack of courage. In his contribution he defines "modern orthodoxy" with a quote from the same Professor Lawrence Kaplan (of McGill University) whom I quoted in my column last year. The modern orthodox Jew, says Kaplan, "attempts to justify his commitment to modernity in terms of his orthodoxy and, and at the same time, seeks to demonstrate the significance and meaningfulness of tradition and belief for modern man. On the one hand, his modernity informs his orthodoxy. Thus, he utilizes modern categories of thought to illuminate and deepen his understanding of the tradition and, in his study of sacred texts, makes use of the findings and methods of modern historical scholarship to the extent that they do not violate the religious integrity of these texts as he perceives it. But the movement of influence is not only one way. For his perception of the modern world and modern social and intellectual currents is shaped by his traditional perspective, so that his commitment to modernity is always critical and qualified."

Dr. Singer then submits that altogether too few of the so-called modern orthodox rabbis are doing what Kaplan and he try to do. Instead many of them beat their breasts that they are not as meticulous as the right-wing orthodox in certain areas of ritual and only Dr. Hillel Goldberg – in the symposium – had the courage to suggest that perhaps meticulous concern with regard to one's behavior vis-à-vis one's fellow man is as important as meticulous behavior with regard to ritual. And in the area of *Mentschlichkeit* certainly the *Charedim* do not take prizes.

What is even more disconcerting is that modern orthodox rabbis do not vigorously fight the image that their point of view is a "compromise" approach. The very mention of the word "compromise" suggests the surrender of some claim or principle. But modern orthodoxy is often more demanding than so-called right-wing approaches. It does not say that it will sanction the study of science by a few who will have to risk their souls so that society may have the physicians it needs.

It insists rather that science be properly understood so that it does not threaten the foundations of our faith and, therefore, that all Jews may study it. It does not want a few to be sacrificed for the benefit of the many. Nor does it say that everything that non-Jews have created is taboo, thus denying billions created in the image of God any respect or credibility whatever. It says, on the other hand, every group contributes to the sum total of human wisdom but one finds in the Torah the loftier standards by which to evaluate what comes forth from *all* mankind.

And the study of Torah in the search for values becomes a glorious spiritual enterprise. Moreover, modern orthodoxy is often stricter in religious observance than others: Only from them does one bear protests against resort to legal fiction in order to permit outrageous usury even in orthodox circles as well as against the use of the word *Dati* to describe one who observes ritual no matter how unscrupulous he is in matters other than ritual.

The modern orthodox are not indifferent to the traditional values of modesty and chastity in the area of sex. They are not yielding to the *Yetzer Ha-Ra* – to the human "id" – when they are more permissive or more candid in sex education. On the other hand, they are trying to fulfill the Torah's ultimate value – which involves ideal relationships between husbands and wives and parents and children, and perhaps in the society in which most Jews do in fact now live there may have to be a different approach if the proper attitudes cherished by the tradition itself are to be cultivated with better judgment in choosing a wife and even greater skills in relating to her.

Alas, even among those who isolate themselves from the modern world the situation of the family is not what it once was. The divorce rate is high, cruelty is on the increase as well as child abuse, alas, even venereal disease. The truth is hard to face but the modern orthodox know not only the good of modernity but its enormous evil which has invaded even the ghetto with the tallest walls.

In any event I continue to stand firm in my conviction that the modern orthodox are the standard bearers of the authentic tradition. They do not compromise it or falsify it. On the other hand, they are loyal to its letter and spirit and walk in the path of those who were the giants of Jewish history these past few thousand years.

The Bible Is a Guide to Mankind, Not to God

T he Bible can be read or studied in many ways. One way that I have found most helpful and meaningful is suggested in the writings of Samson Raphael Hirsch and Abraham Joshua Heschel. The latter encapsulates it by saying that the Bible should be viewed not as a guide for man's theology but rather as God's anthropology. I shall explain this and illustrate its importance, at least for me. Most often people search the pages of the Bible for insights about God. These are rare, if they exist at all. For reasons known best to Him, He denied us this information. Moses tried to elicit from Him more details, perhaps even certainty. He failed to get what he wanted. Therefore, we would do well not to regard the Bible as a textbook for man's theology. It was not given to us for that purpose.

Our theology will continue to be based on faith and details are about as conclusive as all guesswork. We will delineate attributes; we will argue for and against corporeality; we will try to rationalize the existence of evil – the so-called problem of the theodicy. However, no one – not even the greatest of men – has provided the ultimate answers. Apparently, God wanted not only Moses to be frustrated in this regard but all of mankind forever.

It may be intellectually challenging, even exciting, to philosophize and theologize, but let us reconcile ourselves to the one inescapable truth: God is beyond understanding. And the Bible was not given to us to solace Him within our understanding. Yes, to place Him within our reach but not within our conceptual grasp. Therefore, let us not use the Bible in a way that it was never intended to serve.

Wherefore, then, was the Bible given to us? Not that we might fathom how to view God but rather that we might fathom how God views us, how God views man.

In a conversation that it was my privilege to have had with (the late) Professor Heschel, I told him how much this insight meant to me – how many passages of the Torah it illuminated for me. He asked me to spell it out and I have the feeling that he was grateful to me for the specifics I provided.

Is the Bible clear on what God's design was for the trees in the Garden of Eden? Do the commentaries agree on any one position? Is there not much mystery about what God intended? Of course. But the Bible does not reveal. What does it reveal? Not what God had in His mind but rather how man reacted.

Adam had the perfect world. He was denied virtually nothing. Yet he would not be content and restrain himself. He had to flout God's will. This is how Adam – or all men – react in similar situations. The Bible is telling us how God sees us, how we behave. Our greed is simply our ruin. This the Bible wants us to know.

Then comes the second mystery. Why did God prefer the offering of Abel to that of Cain? Everything the commentaries say about this is based on the flimsiest evidence, on conjecture. These are trying to fill in where God chose to be silent. But again the Bible wants us to know how man reacts. Cain is the symbol of humanity. He cannot fight God; instead he kills his brother. The Bible is mirroring man. It is giving us a reflection of what we are like.

One turns similarly to the story of the flood and the Tower of Babel. Here God's behavior is made reasonably clear. But it is the behavior of man that remains the focal point of the story. God brought the flood because the race of man had became corrupt. Did man learn a lesson? Not at all. Instead of improving the social order and making it a just one, man seeks to build into the skies and frustrate God from repeating His performance.

The sins of Sodom and Gomorrah are also not clearly identified in the Bible. The rabbis tried to fill in the empty spaces. But how Abraham reacted to the news that God was about to destroy the cities is one of the most magnificent chapters of the Bible. The contrast between Noah and Abraham is dramatic; Noah, when told about the impending flood, is content to save himself and his loved ones. Abraham, on the other hand, challenges God in an attempt to save the cities. Again what the Bible is teaching principally is not how God operates but rather how man ought to react.

Especially was Professor Heschel pleased with what I had to say about one of the most difficult problems in Jewish philosophy. How could God have punished Pharaoh if God Himself had hardened Pharaoh's heart so that Pharaoh would not free his Hebrew slaves? Again the answer is: The hardening of the heart is simply a description of the typical human being – and a typical monarch – stubbornly resistant to God's message, unable to do what is good for his own subjects because his personal pride stands in the way.

All of this came to my mind this past summer as I continued to read and hear of the reactions of all of mankind to the significant, historic performance of the people of Israel in Lebanon. One must ponder the reactions and thereby learn much about human nature.

I know that I have learned much about the nature of my fellow men, the nature of many of my colleagues, the nature of the Jewish intelligentsia, and the nature of so-called liberal humanitarians and universalists.

One of Century's Great Jewish Teachers Is 80

This year world Jewry celebrates the eightieth birthday of one of the century's greatest teachers of Judaism – Talmudist, philosopher, educator and statesman Rabbi Joseph B. Soloveitchik. Many essays about him have already appeared in Jewish periodicals and undoubtedly several *Festschriften* will be published as well.

At least two universities will dedicate to him days of study and appreciation. And the American Jewish Year Book will feature a brilliant and lengthy analysis of those of his writings presently available to the public. By comparison with all of this, a columnist's tribute may not be very significant. Yet there are several points which will not receive attention in the more learned presentations and perhaps they are worthy of consideration.

He appeared upon the American scene more than 40 years ago and almost immediately was recognized as the most brilliant and lucid teacher of Talmud that this generation had ever beheld. He so surpassed all of those similarly engaged that no one could suggest who else might be put in his class. Indeed, one would be hard put today to be his equal, even though he has trained many in his method.

That alone would have made him the giant in Orthodox circles. And since he taught thousands at Yeshiva University and almost as many in the Boston area who flocked to him, especially from the local universities, it was to be expected that his role as the *Rov* without peer would be assured.

However, when he appeared upon the American scene years ago he was a dramatic phenomenon. He was not only the great Talmudist, he was also the master of Western thought – he knew science and philosophy, he had a profound understanding of literature and current events, and his gifts for expression and communication made the famous orators of the day seem like rank amateurs.

Indeed, here was a man! Many of the somewhat younger Orthodox spokesmen who in that period were struggling to accomplish what then seemed impossible recognized that he was virtually their savior. They were trying to achieve a synthesis between Torah tradition and modernity. They cherished their total heritage but they did not want to reject the new world of which they were a part. And in every area they had to cope with challenges – scientific, philosophical, psychological, sociological, anthropological, archaeological, and certainly social and economic.

Some had decided to return to the ghettos, intellectually speaking. Others had decided to acculturate and assimilate. Few were they who were intent upon the synthesis – the fusion of the new with the old – the dream of the late Chief Rabbi Kook. To these few the appearance of the *Rov* was tantamount to the coming of a redeemer.

Well do I remember the first time I listened to one of his lectures for almost seven hours. I missed all the trains to Long Island that I had hoped to board and my family at home could not fathom what had happened to me. And for 40 years – despite many differences and sometimes bitter ones and an occasional, momentary, disillusion – my sense of awe for him never departed.

But I was not the only one. To all of us who espouse what is now called "modern Orthodoxy" he was the model. (If Jews were not so allergic to idolatry, I would have said the idol.)

Yet that does not mean that his own personal synthesis – his way of living in his two backgrounds – that of Brisk where he became a great Talmudist, and that of Berlin where he became the great philosopher – of necessity became the way of those of us who revere him and cherish his every thought. He differed from many of us in that he was raised in Brisk and encountered Berlin at a later stage in his life.

In his intellectual development there was a period when there was a clash – a confrontation between two ways of life and modes of thought. For some of his admirers and disciples there was no such clash. They grew up in both cultures simultaneously and the synthesis they sought and achieved was a gradual achievement over a long period of time, virtually from elementary school days through graduate study.

What little they achieved was not born altogether from anguish but more by the slow natural process of mental and emotional maturation. That is why they often part with the master in whose thought existentialism plays the major role. Moreover, they are often less timid with regard to the correctness of their views because their sense of security would appear to be greater than his. Perhaps they merit criticism for experiencing less "fear and trembling." He is their *Rebbe* but unlike Hassidim, they are only deferential, not blindly obedient. Often that made him happy. They did what he would have liked to do but couldn't get himself to do.

Last but not least, he has a profound understanding not only of modern trends of thought but also of the practical problems of worldwide Jewry, everywhere, and especially in America and Israel. In this area he prefers to be unseen and unheard but his views became known to disciples who not only express them but also act upon them in those establishment circles in which they play leadership roles.

However, one cannot help but be amazed that unlike the emotion-ridden Soloveitchik the philosopher, Soloveitchik the statesman – like Soloveitchik the Halachist – is brilliantly rational and empirical. Unfortunately the non-Orthodox world knows him principally as the philosopher. But his Orthodox disciples have had the blessing of his many faceted genius.

May he, like Moses, have another 40 years in which he may continue to lead many of us through the wilderness, which contemporary civilization now appears to resemble.

Retirement:
The ages-old dilemma

It is a pity that what was once deemed a blessing for which man actually prayed is now deemed a curse or at least a serious problem, a situation to be feared or dreaded. I refer to old age and to the concern of governments and individuals because so many people are living longer that society finds it difficult to cope with the challenges of aging populations.

It is not only in the United States that social planners deal with the problem. In Israel, too, the concern is great, and many programs are projected not only to "add years to life" but "to add life to the years." The Brookdale Foundation, in cooperation with the government, the American Jewish Joint Distribution Committee and the universities, is rendering a historic service.

We must not forget that the Jewish people lost a million children who, if still alive, would now be middle-aged. Thus the average age of Israel's population would today have been considerably lower. Alas, that is not so.

Both the U.S. and Israel can learn much from each other in this area. The two countries can be partners not only in weaponry but in innovative social programs.

In Israel many government departments and businesses conduct seminars for employees on the eve of retirement. Here, too, we find a paradox. The overwhelming majority of people do not enjoy their work and look forward to the day when they can stop working and do whatever they please. Yet as that day approaches, they are worried. What will they do with their free time?

How will they adjust to the fact that there is nothing to get up for in the morning? Surveys show that people in the same age group who do not retire have fewer complaints about physical illness than those who do retire. But retirement is usually not voluntary; it is mandatory.

Pondering this and related problems, I decided to look at the Bible to see what guidelines it might offer. Unfortunately, source material is sparse.

From the Bible one learns that old age was meant to be the golden age, the time when one reaped the reward of one's labor. The Bible ordered reverence for the elderly. (*Leviticus* 19:32) This was virtually conclusive proof, however, that people generally did not behave that way. Otherwise, the Bible would not have had to mention it. It would, therefore, appear that God willed that his people should not behave as many pagans did. Pagans often abandoned their aged. Sometimes they even hastened their deaths.

The Bible wanted to insure not only the survival of the old but their honored role in society. To be deemed an elder was a compliment. The young had to apologize if, despite their youth, they offered advice. The old were thought to have a monopoly on wisdom and experience.

But does the Bible say anything about retirement? Yes. There are important references in several chapters of the Book of Numbers. (Chapter 4 especially)

The Levites, it would appear, were to begin five years of training for service in the Temple at age 25. From age 30 to 50, they were to be on duty. At 50, they retired, even though they continued to enjoy all the privileges of their status, such as they were.

Unfortunately, many see good and evil in this arrangement. The good is that in retirement one suffers no change of status. The evil is the compulsory retirement at what is now regarded as a comparatively young age.

A bit of additional research showed that the rabbis saw the Bible's mandate as one that was applicable only to the period when Jews were in the wilderness. Then the Levites were responsible for transporting the mobile sanctuary and all its contents. Once the Jews settled in the Promised Land and there were permanent shrines, the Levites' duties were changed; no one had to retire so long as he could do his job. His privileges were never affected. But the duty to work ended only when a man could function no longer. In Jewish law this rule also applied to judges.

This rabbinical limitation is quite a revelation. The Oral Law apparently did not approve of compulsory retirement. Yet we know that there is much to be said in its favor.

Compulsory retirement has a number of benefits. It permits the young to move up and assume positions of authority. It eliminates men who are not receptive to new ideas. And it prevents people from acquiring vested interests in positions that they hold until they die. By the same token, compulsory retirement is often devastating to able men who, despite their age, can still function with credit.

The conflicting claims were recently considered in Israel in connection with the election of the chief rabbis. Many wanted to see new faces in authority; many others argued that the incumbents should be permitted to stay on so long as they were still in their prime physically and intellectually. Those favoring change won, but the debate continues in other areas – in industry, in the civil service, in academia.

Is there no way to reconcile the conflicting claims? I believe that there is, but senior people will have to cultivate much more self-control if they want to continue to serve. Rotation in every sphere is important. Younger people must be given a chance to advance. They bring new ideas to all the programs. But if senior people could learn to surrender their authority graciously and be ready at all times to give new incumbents the benefit of their counsel and experience, employers would enjoy the best of all worlds. The trouble is that too often senior people are filled with resentments and want their successors to fail. Often they are given the status of consultants, but they do not know how to give advice without being demanding, imposing or authoritative.

Sometimes I feel that this should also be the role of grandparents toward children who are raising the grandchildren. They would be supportive with counsel when asked but never be the deciders.

Needless to say, Jewish literature has much more to teach us about the aging, but at least the status of the Levites is an interesting illustration of the ongoing tension between the wise requirement for compulsory retirement and the possible waste of valuable manpower that is its inevitable consequence.

Needed:
A Universal Jewish Family Law

The Reform rabbinate in the United States has made a decision which angered its Orthodox colleagues far more than any prior decision in at least half a century. Hereafter they will recognize as Jewish any child born to a Jewish father, even if the mother is not Jewish. They will require that the child be raised as a Jew, but they will no longer be bound by the time-honored definition that makes the Jewish mother the key to a person's Jewishness.

The reaction of many Orthodox rabbis was so negative that they wanted their Orthodox rabbinical organization to sever what minimal ties they had with the Reform rabbinate in such mixed Jewish groups as the Synagogue Council of America. In that body six organized rabbinic and congregational bodies are represented and deal with issues involving the total Jewish community, especially in its relationship to the non-Jewish world. All the council's actions must have the unanimous approval of the constituent organizations.

To prevent the Synagogue Council from taking any steps whatever in any matter that comes before it, the Orthodox need only exercise their right to veto. Therefore, withdrawal from the group of six was not a step which might have had practical significance. The group could be emasculated now by its existing mode of operation.

It was obvious that withdrawal was suggested only to demonstrate how far the Orthodox want to remove themselves from any association with rabbis who commit such a horrendous flouting of the tradition. It was to be an act symbolic of anger or disgust and a way of telling the world that the Orthodox do not want to be linked in any way with those who ride roughshod over virtually irreversible halachic rules.

At least one Orthodox rabbi suggested that the radical move of the Reform rabbinate was an expression of its own anger that the Orthodox continue to be so totally unresponsive to any proposal that comes from the more tradition-loving Reform rabbis to arrive at some understanding as to who is a Jew. To be more specific, this minority of Reform rabbis wants an understanding that all the requirements of the Halachah for conversion to Judaism must be fulfilled but that in the application of these requirements there should be a greater measure of flexibility. Such concessions are not without precedent, even among Orthodox rabbis in Israel and in America. But the Orthodox rabbinate was not sympathetic. Consequently, radical reformers in the Reform majority made their countermove.

Perhaps this analysis is correct. However, anger on neither side will rebound to the advantage of anyone, and hereafter children whose parents were married by Reform rabbis will have an even harder time when and if they want to marry into Orthodox or Conservative families. They will have to prove that they are Jews as well as legitimate. Not a very happy outlook. Yet I do not anticipate that the situation will be much worse than in the past. Hundreds of thousands will not be affected. Perhaps not even tens of thousands. What really concerns me is that while there are moves in Israel toward achieving one family law for all Jews, the anarchy in the Diaspora will be exacerbated. This may be the price that Jews must pay for an open society, but it is a high price. Even in modern Jewish history, we have had problems achieving status as Jews for Falashas and Jews from India. This recognition is still denied to Karaites, who are few. America will now contribute materially to the increase in the number of unrecognized Jews.

Recently I was invited to lecture before an assembly of distinguished Reform laymen on pluralism in Jewish history. I made the point that the Jews have always had internal differences. We are a thinking people, and a thinking people cannot be regimented to believe and act like a herd.

I also pointed out, however, that in Jewish history there was one area in which the rabbis were quite insistent that dissenters yield to the majority and become conformists. This area was the Jewish calendar – and especially the dates of Jewish holy days.

Even in Talmudic times there were differences of opinion as to
when a new moon appeared and consequently when the Day of
Atonement occurred. We are told that the head of the Sanhedrin
once ordered a colleague who dissented from the majority decision
to observe the Yom Kippur that the majority had fixed and to des-
ecrate the day that he held was the sacred one. (*Rosh Hashana*
25a) In the early medieval period there were disputes between
Babylonian scholars and those in the land of Israel with regard to
the calendar, and the rabbis who prevailed showed their strength.
There would today be bedlam in the Jewish world if there was anything other than total uniformity on the dates of holidays.

Once I was a pulpit rabbi. I can imagine how I would have reacted if a member of my congregation had come to me to tell me
that by his computation we were observing the wrong day as Yom
Kippur and that he wanted the cantor, the choir, and me to be on
duty for him on the day that he regarded as the Day of Atonement!
The Christian world has several calendars, and all their holidays
do not coincide. This could easily have happened to Jews, too. Indeed, the Reform rabbinate once wanted to move the Sabbath to
Sunday. I spent my youth in a city where this was Reform policy.
Fortunately, experience prompted the return to the tradition of
observing the Sabbath on Saturdays.

At the conference at which I spoke to Reform laymen, I expressed the hope that Jews will do with Jewish family law what
they did with the calendar – and there would be one law for all of
us. I referred to the fact that there were Reform rabbis – one of
whom is a revered friend and devoutly religious – who have reservations on ethical grounds with some points of Jewish law. On ethical grounds, they cannot reconcile themselves to being
conformists. Yet, I had hoped that they would find a way to give
greater consideration to the damage that the lack of conformity
would do to the total Jewish community by comparison with the
hurt that some ancient rules of law caused isolated individuals.
This point is not only mine. Some of their own colleagues raised it
before I did.

I want to add but one point. If all Jews will be committed to one
family law, I am sure that the desired liberalization in Jewish family law will be achieved. Then there will be no unethical situations

to give concern to those who are troubled by them. Ways will be found to help the deserted wife and the illegitimate child. Jewish law contains within itself this potential. The failure to realize the potential is due precisely to the fear that in the present climate no encouragement must be given to radical reformers. Orthodox reaction to radical reform is generally to put the Halachah into a deeper freeze.

Not too many years ago, the great Rabbi Moses Feinstein handed down a remarkably liberal decision permitting a woman to remarry without a Jewish divorce. I wrote enthusiastically about his courageous ruling. He was told by the more rigid and intransigent Orthodox that he merited the punishment of praise from one the likes of me. True, the number of such rigid Orthodox Jews is growing. But they will not be able to halt the creativity within Jewish law to cope with the just and ethical demands of the greater number of Jews who want one family law for all but a family law that in the future, as in the past, is one of the most progressive in the legal systems of all mankind.

Every move away from the applicability of one Jewish family law to all Jews delays the advent of that hoped for day.

Forgive the Germans,
But May They Never Forget

I write this column as I fly from Berlin to New York. It was my first trip to Berlin since 1946 when I saw it in ruins – razed to the ground with only the shells of buildings visible above. It is difficult to describe how I felt as I returned not only to meet with Holocaust survivors there and the leadership of the Jewish community but also with Axel Springer, the publisher who is not only Israel's great friend but also the man who hosted the event which I was to address.

I want to report on what I said to hundreds of outstanding German officials, none of whom 1 am sure, was ever a Nazi. As a matter of fact at least one was the son of a Hitler's victim and is presently the minister of finance of West Berlin.

I could not address this distinguished group of German statesmen and clergymen without telling them how a Jew like me feels in the land which spawned and implemented the "Final Solution." I told them that I cannot seek the punishment of anyone but former Nazis responsible for the annihilation of six million Jews. To warrant punishment one must himself have committed a crime. If one sinned only by acts of omission – by failing to resist – one may not be punished. Even Jewish law, which in some instances requires martyrdom, does not prescribe punishment of all Germans. But I did suggest that the German people, collectively and forever, must bear the shame or guilt of what was done by their people. Punishment, no; but a sense of guilt, yes.

What I said impressed many because I explained that in our Jewish tradition we still seek atonement for sins committed by our people thousands of years ago. We punish no one for these sins but we never allow ourselves to forget them. In our ritual for the High Holy Days we refer to atonement for the crime committed by

10 sons of Jacob who sold their brother Joseph into bondage. The special prayers for the penitential season are so structured that we may bring to mind the sin of the Golden Calf and the sin of the *Meraglim* – the scouts who betrayed Moses and caused a generation of the liberated slaves to die in the desert.

All of these sins were committed thousands of years ago. But the Jewish people must not forget them. As a people we bear the taint forever, even if we inflict no punishment on ourselves or others because of it.

By the same token I told my German audience that while I bear none of them any malice, I ask of them no more than I ask of Jews – to bear in mind their collective guilt so that all of us will never let evil triumph again.

One German official took issue with me. He could not accept my notion of collective guilt. He himself feels no guilt – he was born after the Holocaust and his father had been persecuted during Hitler's reign. Why should he sense what I wanted him to sense?

I met with him on the day following my presentation. I simply had to discuss the matter with him. I knew that he was typical of millions of Germans; among them are many who are fine, decent people. If I could reach him perhaps I could reach others – or at least he would.

My argument was a simple one. I asked him whether he was proud of the contribution of the German people to every area of human culture in the last few centuries. He could not deny that he was proud of what the German people had done in science and philosophy, in music and art, even in social legislation. I then asked him whether his pride was due to his own share in that achievement. Of course it was not. But he had the right – and I agreed with him – to be proud of what his people did collectively, those living and those dead.

However, if he deemed the German people collectively a real entity whose past gave him feelings of exaltation, how could he not deem the same people collectively responsible for a shameful chapter in their history – indeed, so shameful that he himself regarded it as the most evil thing to have happened in the annals of man. Call it guilt or shame, Jews feel that a people too must atone – and not only those who lived when it happened but even those who were born thereafter but deem themselves part of the one collective entity that did the damage.

The least he had to understand was that I was not relating to the German people in a manner that was inconsistent with the manner that Jews relate to themselves and their forbears.

Do we not pray on the High Holy Days for our sins and the sins of our fathers? And do we not ask on the Day of Atonement that God forgive us our sins – as individuals – and the sins of the "House of Israel," which is the Jewish people in their corporate entity separate and apart from the individuals who constitute it?

German lawyers especially must understand this for it is they who gave the world the "realist" theory of corporate existence as distinguished from the "fiction" theory of American jurists.

After our discussion he admitted that my point was well taken but he prefers the concept of collective shame to collective guilt. Since we were not thinking of anyone being punished for collective guilt, it was only a matter of semantics which term we would use. In our High Holy Day ritual we speak both of shame and sin. Perhaps Jews have a greater capacity than others for self-flagellation.

I cannot conclude without adding that for Axel Springer my position was "too mild and considerate." He will not rest until the world in general – and Germany in particular – atones for their collective guilt by securing the State of Israel forever, as minimum retribution for the collective guilt of the Holocaust. May his tribe multiply.

Self-Defense No Guarantee of Right to Violence

With regard to violence, Judaism appears to agree with Konrad Lorenz that to act aggressively is human. However, as with all instincts, whether for food, sex or recognition, Jewish law never seeks totally to repress. It seeks only to control, to regulate, to make constructive, to dignify, even to sanctify. That applies to the drive for violence or aggression. For this reason, it must be conceded that Judaism is not committed to pacifism.

It may be that there were rabbis in the third or fourth century who opposed violence as a means of ensuring Jewish survival, but theirs was decidedly a minority point of view. On the other hand, Rabbi Maurice Lamm, in his essay "Red or Dead," shows that the sources establish that pacifism is not a Jewish ideal. If pacifism is the pursuit of peace at any and all cost, then it was never an authoritative Jewish teaching.

Tolstoy rejected all violent resistance to evil in the social order, regardless of cause and circumstance, because an active revolution must fight evil with another evil, violence. He believed in passive, individual resistance and derived it from the New Testament, from Matthew: "resist not evil."

Gandhi also made it a strategy of politics and later attempted to make it a policy of state. Gandhi's proposal for Jews during the Holocaust was also passive resistance. Gandhi's passive resistance might have been effective against an England which had a conscience, but it would not have accomplished anything with Hitler. Quite the contrary, it was precisely what Hitler would have wanted.

But even in situations in which humans less beastly than Hitler are the enemy, passive resistance often has serious limitations. It either cannot be consistently maintained, or it results in the loss of the best manpower that a cause can possibly mobilize. One such situation in modern times is that of the Student Nonviolent Coordinating Committee, which played an important role in the black revolution in the United States during the '60s. Howard Zinn's "The New Abolitionists" questions how nonviolent a nonviolent direct action can be. He proves, for example, that in 1964 the group had to concede that it would not stop a Negro farmer in Mississippi from arming himself to defend his home against attack.

Judaism, therefore, is more concerned with regulating the circumstances which would permit the exercise of violence – by individuals, by groups, and by states – than it is with the elimination of violence at all costs. Violence is an important way both to destroy and to conserve one of the most important of the values system of Judaism – human life.

Violent action usually endangers the life of the aggressor as well as the lives of those against whom violence is directed. Generally, one's own life is regarded as having the highest priority. But if one is to engage in violence, it must be in accord with Jewish law and in behalf of the value of life or a value even higher than the value of life. Never is one to lose sight of the ultimate value to be achieved.

Thus, war for war's sake, which in Judaism is represented by Amalek, is the essence of evil. There can be no compromise in opposition to such a policy. Duels to vindicate one's honor are heinously sinful. Sadism and masochism are not to be tolerated. Even asceticism is frowned upon. It is held to be a form of violence against the self, except in the very special cases in which nothing less will help a person to overcome physically or spiritually self-destructive behavior.

It must be obvious that when one practices violence against an aggressor to save one's own life, one is committed to a value – the value of one's own life. One has a right to prefer one's own life to the life of the attacker. However, may one use an innocent bystander to protect oneself?

Or may one kill another, complying with the request of the attacker, in order to save one's own life? Jewish law in such cases says that it is morally wrong to do this, although one may not be punished for so doing except by God Himself.

Jewish law also held that if an enemy should demand that a city surrender to it one person – male or female – or face total destruction, it is better that all should die rather than save themselves by betraying an innocent human being. In Jewish history communities may have been saved by volunteers who martyred themselves. But to use the life of an innocent person for any purpose was absolutely forbidden, even if the purpose was to save many lives.

Are modern terrorists guided by such an ethic? I refer especially to terrorists who are killing their own people, not even enemies. They have no regard whatever for human life. And when they are the trainees of a foreign state who infiltrate another country to destroy it, they certainly are not guided by any regard for the value of human life.

What was so remarkable about the underground activity of Jews in Palestine before the establishment of the State of Israel was that they attacked principally military objectives, never civilians, and only rarely the military personnel of Britain. They were mindful of the sanctity of human life. How can one equate them with the terrorists of today!

During the Holocaust many Jews suffered martyrdom because they would not substitute someone else for themselves on the lists for the gas chambers. It also happened at other times in Jewish history that many a community refused to resist and kill Christian attackers because of the disastrous effect their resistance would have on Jews elsewhere.

A Moslem minority in a Christian country could always threaten assailants with reprisals against the Christian minorities in lands where Moslems were in the majority. Jews, however, even when they were in a position to deal a strong blow, found that they had to subordinate the destiny of their particular community to the welfare of Jews all over the world.

Thus, for example, the Jews of Tulczyn in 1648 refrained from attacking treacherous fellow combatants among the noblemen. They chose to die instead when their leaders exhorted them: "We are in exile among the nations. If you lay hands upon the nobles, then all the kings of Christianity will hear of it and take revenge on all our brethren in the dispersion, God forbid."

In our own century we had a tragic but eloquent example of what the Jews always dreaded, the bullet fired in 1938 by Herschel Grynzpan. At that time Poland was calling back all of its citizens, and Grynzpan's parents were caught in a vise. After receiving a letter from his parents describing their distress, he decided to take revenge by destroying some great Nazi officials. He made his way into an embassy in Paris and killed a third-rate bureaucrat of Nazidom. That shot was the pretext for the dreadful pogrom of November 1938, a reprisal against all the Jews in Germany.

Is the situation so different today? Self-defense may sometimes be helpful to one Jewish community, but Jews must always be terribly concerned about how it will affect Jewish communities elsewhere. Thus Jews in South Africa are concerned when the State of Israel exercises its sovereign right to vote in the United Nations in accordance with the dictates of its conscience against South Africa. And Jews of the Soviet Union are pawns in an international struggle with the U.S.

From all of this it appears that even in self-defense one must be mindful of values. Even in self-defense there is no absolute right to engage in violence. Thus, while Jewish law does not absolutely outlaw the right to rebel or resort to violence, it is preoccupied with the when, where and how. Perhaps this should apply to all rights.

Orthodoxy's Rift Must Be Healed

Modern Orthodoxy is very critical of itself. It also has the dubious blessing of hostile criticism from Jewish thinkers to the left and to the right.

From the right come the arguments that modern Orthodoxy has lost its "war" with the yeshiva world, which is equated with ultra-Orthodoxy; that modern Orthodoxy has few accomplishments to its credit, while the ultra-Orthodox have been phenomenally successful; that the cooperation of Orthodox rabbis with the non-Orthodox, as supported by the modern Orthodox, was prohibited by one who was considered the greatest Jew of his period, Rabbi Aaron Kotler, whose eloquent spokesman was the late Irving Bunim.

I believe it important that tens of thousands of Orthodox Jews who read The Jewish Week should know the facts and, instead of exacerbating hatreds, should contribute to amity and mutual respect in the Jewish community. At the same time non-Orthodox Jews should learn not to deem all Orthodox Jews as of one mind and certainly not to identify the overwhelming majority of Orthodox Jews with the tiny minority of stone-throwing and police-resisting zealots who are more considerate of dead bones than of living Jews.

Orthodox Jews do differ on many issues. Bunim adored his rabbis, as I do mine, including my saintly father who taught me differently. Moreover, Rabbi Kotler, of blessed memory, was the founder of the great Talmudical Academy of Lakewood. But his father-in-law, Rabbi Isar Zalman Meltzer, taught my father. My father was closer in spirit to his teacher than was the son-in-law, Rabbi Kotler, whose brothers-in-law were also of quite a different mind. I knew all of them well, worked with them and often heard them complain that the philosophy of separatism which was advocated by Rabbi Kotler was not one that they shared.

However, all of them are to be respected. They held what view they held with sincerity and often with self-sacrifice. The important fact to remember is that there are different points of view. If the modern Orthodox embraced one and not the other, it is not because they are brazen innovators who have no respect for spiritual giants. It is rather that they have their own giants for guidance and adoration.

What ought to impress everyone is that Rabbi Joseph B. Soloveitchik never approved of the separatism which Rabbi Kotler espoused. Nor did the late, lamented Dr. Samuel Belkin.

So much for separatism. As for the "war" between the modern Orthodox and the yeshiva world, let it be known that modern Orthodoxy gave, and still gives, enormous support to yeshivot, even to those with whose philosophy it does not necessarily agree. One should not confuse opposition to Rabbi Kotler's separatism with opposition to yeshivot. Readers of The Jewish Week know how often I have pleaded for the Israeli yeshivot to be accorded at least the support Israeli universities get. And Yeshiva University is one great achievement of modern Orthodoxy.

No one can deny that the renaissance of Orthodoxy in the Western Hemisphere is due to Yeshiva University. Yet the disciples of Rabbi Kotler never accorded it the respect, appreciation and support due it. And that too is a difference between the modern Orthodox and those who differ with them. The modern Orthodox are quite ecumenical – they also support yeshivot with whose ideology they are not very enthusiastic, including Rabbi Kotler's, while their opponents are as hostile to Yeshiva University as they are to non-Orthodox schools.

Modern Orthodoxy could rest its case on its establishment of Yeshiva and Bar-Ilan universities. These achievements of modern Orthodoxy dwarf the achievements of the Lakewood Yeshiva and others similarly minded. But even that is not the heart of modern Orthodoxy's case.

What modern Orthodoxy has insisted upon is that Orthodox Jews shall cope with the culture of the modern world. It seeks not only the brotherhood of all Jews but also the mastery of the natural and social sciences, philosophy, literature and the humanities. All the living Orthodox Jews who have made it in the modern world have achieved what they achieved because they ignored

Rabbi Kotler's counsel and attended a university. The doctors, the lawyers, the chemists, the physicists, the academics and the professionals are alumni of schools which Rabbi Kotler and many of his peers in America and in Israel would have placed out of bounds for them.

Thus all of that which prompts critics of modern Orthodoxy to be so happy with the state of Orthodoxy today is the result of defiance of the view of Rabbi Kotler. Therefore, I ask who won the "war?"

It is not pleasant to fault a saint and scholar like Rabbi Kotler, but I must try to convince more Orthodox Jews that, just as Rabbi Kotler erred with regard to his position on secular education, so he may have erred in his position on separatism. The Jewish people cannot afford internecine conflict. Soloveitchik has stated it better than I. When Jewish blood is shed – the enemy does not discriminate between Orthodox and non-Orthodox.

And while the Jewish situation is not as dark as it was in the 1940s, Israel's fate still hangs in the balance. Consequently, every divisive step is to be shunned. We are all one and must make every effort to remain one.

An Advocate of Integration
Without Assimilation

Intelligent modern Jews who cherish their heritage and want to understand it better owe it to themselves to become acquainted with the writings of Samson Raphael Hirsch, one of the ablest exponents of our faith in the last two centuries. Fortunately, much of what he wrote is available in English. Moreover, Yeshiva University, Bar-Ilan University, London's Jews' College and other institutions of learning will hold this year conferences which will deal with many aspects of his philosophy and teachings. My brief tribute will deal principally with his place in Jewish history.

When the walls of the ghetto crumbled in Central and Western Europe and Jews had to cope with the challenge of a new culture into which they wanted to be integrated, there were many different responses. One of the most important and most enduring was that of Hirsch, the rabbi of Frankfurt-am-Main and founder of a movement which made possible profound commitment to the beliefs and practices of Judaism, coupled with involvement with the general, preponderantly, non-Jewish society, and its economic, political, philosophical and aesthetic enterprise.

His approach was given the name *Torah lm Derech Eretz* – which means "Judaism combined with the way of the world." The least that the approach suggested and recommended was intercultural activity between Jews and their neighbors, at the same time that Jewish tradition was to be conserved and enriched. One can readily see why modern Orthodoxy deems Hirsch one of its spiritual giants, even though it also espouses approaches other than his.

Historians often refer to Hirsch as the founder of neo-Orthodoxy. I am not so sure that I like that designation for him. Neo-Or-

thodoxy conveys the impression that he did something new –
something his predecessors did not do. Of course, he was creative.
He interpreted Judaism with a view of the intellectual climate of
his day. But great Jews always did this.

Saadia and Maimonides did it with a view of the philosophical
doctrines that were current in their time. So did Yehuda Halevi
and Nachmanides. There always were intercultural reactions between the Jewish people and the people among whom they lived.
And the reaction was different in Christian countries than in
Moslem countries.

Hirsch is to be credited with the fact that he was able to cope
with the state of Western culture in the 19th century just as Rabbis Kook and Soloveitchik cope with it in the 20th. Judaism is a religion of life, and to be alive means that one continues to cope with
one's environment, physical and cultural – even in the face of
change.

Yet what always impressed me is that the way in which our spiritual giants reacted to the challenges of their time always added
something to the Jewish tradition which endured. Much of what
they said and wrote was timeless. It had meaning for generations
thereafter, despite the fact that originally it was a reaction to a
contemporary challenge or cultural phenomenon that did not last.

On the other hand, their contemporary situation stimulated
them to discover insights in the eternal Torah which remained
eternal. The philosophical doctrines of Hirsch's period may no
longer be in vogue, but they helped him to reveal insights of the
Torah which in another culture might not have been detected. And
these new insights are not dated because of their linkage to the
intellectual scene or period in which they were written. This was
true of his predecessors and his successors as well.

Soloveitchik may write in a world in which philosophical existentialism enjoys great popularity, but his encounter with existentialism has evolved the revelation of insights which will outlive
the particular philosophy to which it was a response. I am san-
guine enough to believe that the responses of some Orthodox rabbis today to the American philosophies of naturalism and
pragmatism will also outlive the outlooks that presently dominate
the American horizon.

In any event, every Jew owes it to himself to become familiar with Hirsch. Two more points I must make about him have special significance for some issues confronting us at present.

Hirsch helped Jews see that not every practice of East European Jews was necessarily irreversible. This applied to educational methods and content, as it did to daily habits and personal appearance.

In our day there is a tendency among many Orthodox Jews to sanctify much that has little or no basis in tradition, only because it was part of life in the shtetl.

Hirsch even created a stir when he walked beside his wife instead of having her walk behind him as was the case with most rabbis of Eastern Europe. Thus he helped Jews to see where there might be acculturation which would not result in assimilation. And those who were raised in his movement were more consistently traditional than those East European Jews who resisted acculturation and found that their offspring rejected Jewish tradition altogether.

Furthermore, Hirsch is usually regarded as the man who espoused Jewish separatism. Because he broke with the *Gemeinde*, the established community of his day, his example is cited to prove that Orthodox Jews should not become involved in mixed groups like the Synagogue Council of America in which Orthodox and non-Orthodox participate.

Perhaps I err but my reading of the case prompts me to believe that he broke with his Gemeinde because it was moving toward Reform. This is understandable. But it is no precedent whatever for our contemporary scene, which calls only for cooperation between totally independent groups for the common good.

Jewish Education Belongs in the Family Too

Jewish identity and Jewish education are, at one and the same time, causes and effects of each other. When one gives one's child a good Jewish education, one deepens the child's Jewish identity. When one has a strong sense of Jewish identity, one craves to know more about one's roots. This causes one to seek more information about one's Jewishness.

This thought is suggested to me by the Passover Seder service. The Seder was, and still is, for most Jews an educational experience as well as a culinary one. It always was a most effective way to transmit to the young a sense of Jewish identity. And because of that, I believe, more of these young, when they became parents, made an effort for the experience to be meaningful for their children. They read books in preparation for it, bought records, decorations and a great variety of illustrated Haggadot. In doing so, they themselves learned more about their past and its values.

It saddens me to think that we do not do this with regard to the Sabbath. If only each Jewish family could have a weekly experience comparable to the annual one on Passover, what a harvest of good we would reap! After 50 years in the American rabbinate, I fault myself for having expended more energy and ingenuity on synagogue services for the Sabbath than on home services.

True, a beautiful synagogue service and an inspiring, informative, sermon can contribute to Jewish identity and Jewish learning. But much more effective would have been a weekly family gathering around a table, with themes for discussion based upon the weekly Bible reading, with songs and special tales for the very young. Add to this a weekly television program a day or two before the Sabbath, demonstrating how heads of families might conduct the Sabbath meal for that particular week, and then ask yourself whether today we would have to worry as much as we do about the problem of intermarriage and assimilation.

198

And I write not only of the diaspora. How Israel could use such a program to combat juvenile delinquency, to create a sense of national unity, to educate many of its inhabitants and to induce pride in a historic way of life that helped to make us an eternal people.

For a moment let us ignore the Jewish component in what I have written thus far. Instead of considering Jewish education and Jewish identity, let us think only of the institution we call the family.

It is well known that the family today has many problems and because of these problems, it is not as effective as it once was in contributing to the mental health of its members and the transmittal of values to offspring. The amount of crime in urban centers would certainly be reduced if the family were as much of an influence for good as it once was. The longer I live, the more convinced I become that if we do not restore in the hearts of youth a love of kin and a desire not to shame those they love, we will not reduce the rate of crime.

In one of my classes I recently made a simple mathematical calculation. The probability in most of the world's cities that a criminal will be apprehended and punished is about one in eight. Thus, one has seven chances out of eight to succeed in a career in crime. The chances for success in a business or professional career are not even remotely as good. Why, then, should one not prefer the life of sin? The only answer is to be proud in one's commitment to morality, and it is the family that is the principal factor in creating moral commitment. As the family fails to fulfill its mission, the entire social organization suffers. And crime is the deadliest cancer of the social organism.

I wish that I were genius enough to have the solution to the problem. But I can propose at least one way that succeeded in the past, and that was the family tie – the love of family, loyalty to it, pride in it and a sense of horror that one might shame those one loved. Alas, today we do not have it. There are presently many parents who do not hesitate even to shame their children and their parents by behaving as immature adolescents as they sever family ties in pursuit of one or more infatuations.

For all mankind, it is imperative that we dedicate ourselves to the solution of the problem. The moral health of the family is the key to at least one major resolution of the problem of crime.

Justice Brandeis, as an undergraduate student at Harvard, once wrote an essay poking fun at Plato's "Republic" because Plato was so stupid as to think that society could raise perfect philosopher-kings outside the family circle, with the children never knowing who their parents are. From where would these perfectly trained rulers derive all the virtues they required to be perfect men if not from the family circle in which the virtues are taught and experienced?

That the family is central in Judaism is well known. The first commandment given to be observed by all Jews was the commandment with regard to the Passover. And that was to be a family celebration from its very inception. Remarkable it is that thousands of years of observance have not changed that aspect of the holiday.

People who must for one reason or another celebrate the holiday in synagogues or hotels feel the difference and are unhappy because of it. Even they try to retain the family dimension by having their loved ones at the same table with them or in a separate room. Suffice it to say it is a family holiday. As Jews helped to endow the festival with its unique character, so the festival helped to endow the Jewish people with the gift of eternity.

But again I ask why is it impossible to do this with the Sabbath and thus achieve many goals – the deepening of Jewish identity, the dissemination of Jewish information, the strengthening of family ties, the improvement of the moral tone of life and all the benign consequences that will flow from these gains?

The Jewish Agency and World Zionist Organization are trying to do something along these lines. The rabbinate should cooperate. The synagogues will gain and not lose. They will become the centers for study and worship attended by those more desirous than ever to come closer to God and the heritage that is ours.

Israeli Terrorism:
Reasons but no excuses

Despite the historic aversion of Jews and Judaism to violence and war, the worldwide Jewish community was shocked recently by the disclosure that scores of our people were actively engaged in terrorizing Arabs to stimulate their exodus from Israel. The shock came during that season of the year when three national observances were the focus of everyone's attention: The day for remembrance of the Holocaust, the day for the remembrance of the casualties of Israel's wars and the day commemorating Israel's declaration of independence.

No Jew could have failed to ask himself at the time. "Have we learned from our enemies to behave as they did and still do? Are we too developing a casual disregard for the sanctity of life? Are we incapable of prolonged commitment to the 'righteous use of weaponry' which once was the ideal of Israel's army? Can we still see ourselves as a beacon of light, morality and justice for all the nations?"

Perhaps the press exaggerated the number of those engaged in the outrageous planning of unadulterated murder. However, the fact that even a few were involved is enough to depress us. And we must give the matter our most careful consideration.

The reaction of some Israelis is that we ought to understand that in every society, and in every conflict, there will be some whose behavior will be criminal, anti-social, even self-destructive. And Jewish society is like all others: It too has its lunatic fringe. Yet in the past Jews always had a very low rate of crime, and what crime there was, was rarely violent crime. Therefore, one cannot help asking what there is in the modern world that caused this painfully horrifying development.

True, religious zeal was a factor. When a person becomes so committed to one ideal that he forgets that there are others equally compelling, he is prone to act fanatically for his own goals and flout others, even when those others are more sacred. The Jewish view of the sanctity of life is far greater than the sanctity of land. Yet somehow the misguided youths were ready to sacrifice the more important for the less important.

And who is to blame? Unfortunately, with all our love for Torah education, and all our concern for the establishment and growth of yeshivot, we failed to impart in them what is more important: *Menschlichkeit*. And that is why there is violence between different Hassidic groups, bitter incriminations and recriminations between yeshiva heads, an unprecedented splinterization of the religious parties in Israel so that instead of two or three party lists, they may have five in the next elections.

In the United States there is more concern as to how we can fault each other rather than respect each other, exacerbating the existing hostility among Jews and making for more divisiveness.

Well do I remember the words of the peerless Rabbi Joseph B. Soloveitchik many years ago with regard to what then was, and in many ways still is, the best Zionist youth movement in the world, the Bnai Akiva movement. He expressed concern even as he admired the movement's leaders and members.

His concern was that too much preoccupation with the notion of land, rather than Torah, could produce a new idolatry. I dismissed his words at that time in the belief that such a perversion could not come to pass. Alas, it did in the minds of some of the youths. They may be few, but few are too many.

And in other movements the perversion can be of another kind, such as the love of Torah replacing the love of man or the love of the rebbe replacing the love of Jews. Many of us simply lose our sense of proportion when we seize upon one Torah ideal and ignore the others. And in our religious education we have stressed ritual and not morality, rigid customs and not personal integrity.

But many secularists have been at fault too. They may rejoice that the Orthodox have produced many monstrously misguided fanatics. However, they cannot pretend that they bear no part of the guilt.

First, they did so much to alienate most of Israel's youth from the Jewish tradition that, as a reaction those youths committed to tradition swung to the opposite pole. As a matter of fact, I often ask myself why the intelligentsia among Israel's secularists have produced many who justly and righteously plead for more compassion for the Arabs but thus far have not produced a spokesman who pleads for the love of religious Jews whose outlook on Judaism is different from theirs? There was one such man – Ephraim Kishon. The secularist intelligentsia made him so uncomfortable in Israel that he moved out and settled in Europe.

Religious Jewry can proudly point to Rav Kook and a host of disciples who always pleaded for the love of all Jews, even those who were sinful. He and they have no counterparts in the secularist community.

Yet the picture would not be complete if, in addition to faulting religionists and secularists for the emergence of Jewish terrorists, we did not take account of the contribution of the Arab world to our shame. For 36 years Jews have patiently waited for them to produce leaders who will try to end hostilities and achieve coexistence for the greater happiness and security of all. But there is virtually no such leader on the horizon, and the patience of some Jews simply ran out.

I smile when some American Jews fault Israeli Jews for not finding Arabs with whom they can engage in dialogue to achieve peace. Are American Jews any more successful in the opening of meaningful dialogue with blacks in the United States to avoid what may yet become bloody confrontations?

The reasonable blacks are terrorized into silence. That happens to reasonable Arabs as well. In the United States the militant blacks run the show; so also the militant Arabs are in control in Israel.

As a matter of fact, in both countries Arab oil funds are financing obstacles to mutual understanding. In such a situation, resorting to terror, alas, appears to many a youth as the only road. Yet dissuade them we must. Little or no good can ever come from evil.

Progress Often Surprise Result
of the Bitterest Confrontations

Perhaps I ought to make it clear that even those Jews who want Jewish unity (among whom I count myself) do not necessarily insist on sameness. We recognize that inevitably there will be differences among Jews, because we are a people given to thinking. And a people that thinks usually generates challenges to old ideas and proposes new ones.

This was always true in Jewish history, and it is the sheerest folly to hope that in an age when there are so many well-educated Jews the situation will be different. The best we can hope for is mutual respect for differences and a consensus with regard to matters that make for survival.

As a matter of fact, what impresses me as I study the history of Jewish sects is that when these sects actually dominated the scene the feuding between them was intense – occasionally even violent. However, when the struggle between them is studied centuries thereafter, one finds that they influenced each other considerably. Later generations enjoyed the benefit of ideas which, when first advanced, were resisted bitterly.

Even today many Orthodox rabbis will admit that their understanding and appreciation of Judaism was enhanced by ideas which were advanced by non-Orthodox rabbis. The latter will also admit that they have learned much from the Orthodox. From the way the two groups presently relate to each other, one would never surmise that this is true. The general public gets the impression that these are warring groups like East and West on the world scene.

Yet the fact is that the differences have benign effects on both sides, even as they do some harm. The harm might be reduced if there could be mutually respectful dialogue instead of acrimony.

However, one can virtually prophesy that a century hence Judaism – even the most Torah-true Judaism – will have been enriched by some of the insights and challenges of those who presently are deemed dangerous heretics.

Recently, at Bar-Ilan University, a very stimulating lecture was delivered on some Hebrew literature published in the 18th and 19th centuries in Eastern Europe. That was the time when the so-called Enlightenment movement – known as *Haskala* – emerged. It was also the period when the Hassidic movement flowered. And, of course, it was a golden age for the deepening of Talmudic study.

The hostility among the three groups, as expressed in the literature, was enormous. The tone of the authors was vitriolic, saturated with irony and vilification. Yet, when the battle was over, and no one again tried to place any members of the opposition in jail, what did one find? The Enlightenment had very definitely yielded a Zionist idea and program – which though authentically traditional – would not have achieved a foothold in the Jewish world without the so-called heretics.

And many of the Hassidim and opponents of the yeshiva world embraced Zionism. Certainly the Hassidim upgraded their commitment to Talmudic study and the intellectual quality of their leaders, and the leaders of the yeshiva world began to appreciate the contribution of the Hassidim to the joy of Jewish living and the need for more Jewish fellowship and less arrogance on the part of scholars.

The Zionist secularists also learned from their devout and observant brethren how impossible Jewish survival is without that which the Hassidim and Mitnagdim (followers of the Enlightenment) contribute in basic commitment to Judaism.

If only they could have fought less with each other and listened more to each other. I suppose that if they had not fought as hard as they did, they would not have contributed as much. Is it, then, only through strife that mankind can advance? I hope the answer is no.

One might reply and say that those who feel strongly about an issue must inevitably fight hard for its acceptance; sometimes one's fervent commitment to a position prompts one to lose one's tolerance and even to become violent. This happens especially when it is as important a matter as one's faith. Consequently, if we want people to espouse causes with strong conviction, the price we must pay is the feuding – as mean and bitter as it may sometimes be. Thus, Jews who feel strongly about their Orthodoxy, Conservatism, Liberalism, Reconstructionism or secularist humanism must regard their opponents as enemies and enemies find it hard to relate to each other civilly or respectfully.

It is precisely in this connection that Rabbi Abraham Isaac Kook – with his insightful interpretation of the relevant Talmudic texts – made his brilliant distinction. Our ideas may be inimical to each other but not our persons. Therefore, Jews may hate each other's ideas but never each other. Therefore, the disputes, the debates, the confrontations, must be between loving brothers who bemoan the fact that those whom they love are on a course of error or heresy, and with love and understanding they must be helped to see where they err.

Kook believed deeply that they erred, but he expended more thought and feeling on trying to discern how they arrived at error than he did on castigating them.

It was for that reason – as I wrote several weeks ago – that he faulted his own Orthodox brethren for their contribution to the misunderstanding of Judaism by those who abandoned the faith and the tradition. Visualize how much Jewish brotherhood would be advanced if every Jewish group or sect spent time asking itself why others find it so difficult to accept their point of view.

Every group would then try to improve itself. As it improved itself, it would be more understanding and tolerant of its opponents, who would also try to improve themselves. The competition would then be between groups that try to edify their own perspective and program instead of competition as to who can outdo the other in abuse and calumny.

It is to such an ideal that Israel's celebration of its 36th birthday was dedicated. Everyone in Israel knows that in an election year Israelis are at their worst. The parties, the candidates, the media – all show their seamiest side. And those who say it is religion that breeds hatred and intolerance can discover in Israel that politics breeds more of it than religion ever did. Indeed, when religion and politics merge, the mixture may be impossible to bear.

That is why so many Israelis are worried about what their country will experience in these pre-election months.

I doubt that this soliloquy on the right and wrong way to deal with differences will do any good – as sermons seldom do. But one must sometimes pour out one's heart.

The Special, Two-Faceted Sensitivity of Jews

Simone Veil, the distinguished and highly respected political leader in France, is a survivor of the Holocaust. At times we Jews have reason to be critical of her views on Israeli policies. Yet no one denies that she is a Jew identified with her people and loved by thousands of them.

Recently she lectured at Bar-Ilan University. The occasion was the dedication of a chair in her honor. The chair was for research into the European resistance movements as reflected in European literature. And Veil spoke of herself as a survivor and the impact of the Holocaust on her psyche.

It was a most revealing talk. Too often survivors hesitate to open up. She did, and we were privileged to listen to what was virtually a confession. She described herself as a tormented, conflicted person for whom moments of peace of mind are rare indeed.

On one hand, she lives with people, gives the appearance of normality, enjoys what they enjoy and participates in all activities that are associated with her cultural environment – art, music, theater. One can hardly detect that she is not altogether at one with everyone around her and visibly be identified with all that is happening then and there.

Yet on the other hand, she is wondering: What is she doing there? Why is she alive? How, did she survive? Where are they with whom she once suffered? Was her concentration camp experience real or only a dream, a nightmare? The real world seems so unreal to her when she brings to mind the horrors which she endured. Guilt feelings also bear heavily upon her; from among all who were there, why is she among the few who lived to tell the tale?

No one who has heard survivors unburden themselves would have found her self-analysis unfamiliar. Yet I dared to respond by telling her that hers was the existential situation of every Jew, even those who did not experience the Hitler Holocaust. Of course, the experience of survivors of the Holocaust was infinitely more traumatic and perhaps it is improper to compare it to anything else.

Nonetheless, the Jew, by the very nature of his history and mission, is expected to be in such a perpetual state of tension. He is to be very much a part of this world, "living it" and enjoying it. The Jew is not allowed to dissociate himself from the normal activities of all mankind. At the same time, he cannot forget even for a moment that the world needs "mending"; that our history bears witness to the worst in human behavior; that we were slaves in Egypt: that, when we were helpless, we were attacked from behind by Amalekites; that in antiquity no great power permitted us to enjoy peace; that our forebears fought with lions in Roman stadiums, were massacred by Crusaders, were sent into exile from almost every country in Europe, were butchered by Cossacks, Chmielnickis, Petluras, Denikins and most recently by Hitler, his cohorts in Europe, and his spiritual successors in the Middle East.

At once the Jew is expected to enjoy Sabbaths and festivals, creative cultural enterprise of every kind, especially within his own heritage, raise families who will yield *nachas* and radiate the joy of being alive. Of course, for Holocaust survivors it is much harder to cope with the tension between what is and what was. But this is expected from all Jews – perhaps from all human beings who are sensitive to the fact that the world is not yet right, that the Kingdom of God is still not here.

This most people overlook. A sensitive person, Jewish or non-Jewish, must ever live in two worlds, the real and the one he wishes to make real. What he sees in the real world helps him to fathom what ought to be made real, and this knowledge drives him to achieve it. This is the polarity of one's existence as a sensitive human being. But for a Jew the polarity is more pronounced. The evil the Jew knows is the worst imaginable; the dream he dreams is the most visionary – universal peace and plenty, a perfect world, even resurrection of the dead. He always veers between these two widely separated poles.

Jews who have been denied their birthright and are ignorant of their past may not feel this way. But they are to be pitied. They are to be compared to orphans. This was how the late Prof. Uriel Tal spoke of them. For there are those who are orphans because they suffer the loss of their heritage. The knowledge of their past could help them maintain a veering between the real and the visionary; this veering helps to safeguard one's sanity and healthy psyche, if one is a sensitive person.

However, Holocaust survivors have lived the most horrendous history which most of us know only from books. Perhaps that is why so many of them are doing so much to hasten the realization of the messianic dream. But many also find it hard to rediscover the art of veering between the poles that lessens the inescapable turbulence within the Jewish soul.

It was this that Simone Veil was describing. And I tried to help her see that her bifurcated consciousness was only an aggravated instance of what is typical Jewish living, even as it is found among non-Jews who are sensitive to the potential of the human species both for the most lofty and the most depraved in human performance.

There is one difference, however, between the Jew and the non-Jew. For the Jew the tension is not only his lot but the lot of his people. It is the raison d'etre of their national existence. The founding Covenant so provided, for that is the meaning of their becoming a "holy people and a kingdom of priests." (*Exodus* 19:6) They committed themselves from the beginning to be a part of the world and yet "holy," separate and committed. Other peoples can choose to be that, but they do not conceive of their very conception and birth that way.

One last thought, one that is relevant to observance of the Day of Atonement. What is more appropriate on such a day than that every Jew should think of himself as he is and at the same time think of himself as he might be. It is a painful thought but also challenging. And one ought to act before what is is irreversible, before it is too late.

When Extremism Is Sin, When It's a Virtue

From the teachings of the ancients and from our own experience, we know that the middle of the road is generally the better course for a human to follow. We call it the golden mean. One should avoid extremes. Too much of anything is usually harmful.

However, Maimonides recommended that occasionally one ought to practice going to one extreme if that will help one from going to the opposite extreme. In this way one may be restored to the middle of the road again. (*Holchot De'ot* 1-4) The Bible provides a simple illustration. (*Numbers* 6:1-21)

From the Bible it appears that he who vows not to drink alcoholic beverages is a sinner. Certainly the Bible did not mean to encourage the use of wine and liquor. What the Bible wanted is that, as with most beverages, both should be used in moderation. And the average person should not require a vow of total abstinence to prevent intoxication and the ugly behavior that follows.

The sin, therefore, is that the vower feels constrained to resort to a vow to control himself and thus he adds a prohibition on himself when he should be able to manage without it. He should not have to prohibit what the Bible permits. Yet, if the same person knows that his use of wine may lead him to sexual promiscuity, then he should make the vow. Under such circumstances, making the vow and its fulfillment are encouraged.

Alcoholics Anonymous teaches the same lesson. When one wants to overcome the disease of alcoholism – and a disease it is – one must resolve totally to avoid liquor. Going to an extreme is the corrective for a failure to adhere to the middle of the road – the golden mean.

By now readers must know that I subscribe to the wisdom of the ancients. I am allergic to extremism and extremists. However, the insight that Maimonides expounded can help us understand why we are encountering so much extremism in our day. In many instances, people are embracing extreme positions and adopting extreme measures as a reaction to, or preventive of, the opposite extreme.

One notices, for example, that among the Jews who are returning to the fold – those who never were a part of it, and those who are being "reborn" – there is a great deal of extremism. Frequently, the "returnees" take on disciplines and commitments which are not expected of even the most pious among us. Sometimes it is their ignorance of our tradition that makes it difficult for them to discern what is really important and what is peripheral. However, more often it is their firm resolve to get as far away from their earlier life patterns as they can. To avoid reversion to what they have rejected, they go to the opposite extreme. This may disturb those who were always committed and observant Jews. But it should be understood and not resented.

I find a similar situation prevailing with regard to the status of women in Orthodox Jewish circles. At one time separate seating in synagogues was the norm to be conserved. Now it is also separate seating at all functions, separate beaches, no mixed swimming in pools, no mixed choral groups, etc.

Much that involves women's attire has also changed. Orthodox mothers are being outdone by their daughters in the modesty of their appearance – covered heads, long sleeves, etc. Yet, if in the last few decades the environment in which we live has so changed that stimuli to sexual thought and fantasy are omnipresent – virtually nothing can be sold today without seductive, sexually suggestive ads – then one should have expected a reaction from some quarters.

It is not Khomeniism, as in Iran. No one is coercing the Jewish woman to resist the trend to permissiveness. Those who do so are acting of their own free will. But the trend to one extreme has evoked a reaction to the opposite extreme. And this too should be understood and not resented.

One might here add with appreciation the fact that so many young Orthodox Jewish women do not mind being pregnant for so much of their lives and bearing 10 or 12 children. They are compensating for the opposite extreme – the minus-zero population growth of most Jewish families.

Especially in the sphere of Jewish education, there is movement away from the middle of the road.

Only 30 years ago one of Israel's most learned rabbis – and a highly respected member of the chief rabbi's council – gave a course to high school students in one of Israel's most prestigious secondary schools. In it he taught with considerable detail the so-called "Higher Criticism" of the Bible which is still the greatest challenge to the creed of Orthodox Jews. He did not fear to cope with the challenge of heretical views. At the present time he and his colleagues would probably oppose giving such a course, even to university students. Why?

Again it is a deliberate movement to an extreme to avoid the opposite extreme. In Israeli universities it was difficult to be hired as a Bible teacher unless one accepted "Higher Criticism" as truth. Israel's most beloved teacher of Bible, Nehama Leibowitz, experienced this difficulty. When her worldwide popularity reached its zenith, she was given the position to teach not Bible but biblical commentaries.

Thus in so many areas, we find the middle of the road abandoned. Instead there is movement in the direction of one extreme or another only to prevent movement in the opposite direction.

Yet that does not mean that the middle of the road should be surrendered as an ideal and extremism substituted for it. In individual situations – as with the alcoholic – it may be necessary to take extreme positions or measures.

Alas, what is happening in Israel is that in almost every area there is only polarization and a reluctance to steer a middle course, with respectful accommodations between polarized views.

Paradoxes for Committed Jews
in a Secular World

There is some basis in fact for the fears of Orthodox Jews that they and their offspring may become alienated from Jewish tradition as a result of their proximity to non-Orthodox Jews and their exposure to alien cultures. The fears are justified. Yet must the response be separatism – detachment from fellow Jews and rejection of advanced secular studies?

Every Jew must consider this question for himself. And his answer will depend upon how he feels about placing himself in danger for a worthy cause which warrants taking risks. Of course, not all of us are endowed with the faculties of heart and mind that the risk may require. But if one has those faculties, perhaps it is one's duty not to play it safe, but rather – as Joseph the son of Jacob did – perform one of God's missions that may be no less worthy than the security of one's soul.

Sometimes the best-made plans to achieve the security of one's soul backfire. I have in mind, for example, a man I met 50 years ago. He was deeply religious and observed the commandments with matchless fervor. He did not want his children to think that Jews could be otherwise. Therefore, he decided to raise them in communities where they would not know non-observant Jews existed. The communities were exclusively Christian. Interestingly enough, the Christians received and respected him. But how long could he hide his children from the facts of life?

If Manhasset, L.I., at that time had no Jews other than his family, how far away was Great Neck or New York? And even in Manhasset how could he have hoped to exclude the media – to stop his loved ones from reading or listening to radio or viewing television? I have followed the career of his son, now one of America's most distinguished actors but a Jew minimally involved in anything

Jewish and certainly not religious. As a matter of fact, I often wonder how positive his feelings are with regard to his Jewish identity.

By contrast, there are Jews who want to raise their families in
a mixed Jewish community precisely because they fear that if their
children spend the first 20 years of their lives only in Orthodox
environments, they will never know how to cope with the world
outside when they enter it.

They know how many persons raised in Orthodox families leave
the fold even after they marry within the Orthodox community –
even when the bride and groom are products of a sheltered up-
bringing. Therefore, these parents prefer to raise their children
by making them aware from their earliest childhood of the differences among Jews and by impressing them with the love of and
tolerance for all and with the feeling that those privileged to be
loyal to tradition have a sacred mission to win back the others with
respect and compassion. This may be a risky course, but it is the
only way that is safe if one wants to produce Jews who will not
turn out to be the zealots who hate all who are not like them.

Nonetheless, it will be argued with some success that the safest
course is to live all one's life in a closed Orthodox community.
There are tens of thousands of such people all over the world.
Their risks are few. They can save their souls. But how can they
live with their consciences when one of the most fundamental
mandates of Judaism is that we act with responsibility for each
other? Indeed, according to Jewish philosophers, no Jew has properly performed any mitzvah until all Jews have performed it. What
will these separatists say to God on Judgment Day? How will they
explain their failure to fulfill this major obligation of their religious burden?

I have said enough to justify the conclusion that the problems
posed have no simple answers. With regard to secular education,
I can understand the reluctance of some Orthodox Jews to expose
themselves and their offspring to it. However, I am less tolerant of
Orthodox rabbis who fear it and sometimes not only fear it but ar-
rogate to themselves the feeling that they are holier than others
because, unlike Joseph, they fear to take a risk for a worthy cause.
That is the cause of saving Torah from the insulting suggestion
that it cannot cope with challenges from any source. It is as though

they feel that God and Torah need protection against an onslaught that could defeat them.

Recently I heard a charming story about a Hassidic rebbe who opposed secular education for himself and for his followers. One day one of his admirers walked with him from his home in Williamsburg to the Brooklyn Bridge. They stopped to admire the bridge and talked about its importance in linking Brooklyn with Manhattan. The young admirer of the rebbe then tried to convince the rebbe how important secular education is. "Rebbe," he said, "this bridge could not have been built without the knowledge that comes from a secular education." One wonders how that argument could have been refuted. But the rebbe had an answer. "But we already have the bridge," he responded.

Perhaps not all who oppose exposure to secular education are equally naive. But all of them, for their own longevity want natural sciences to be advanced, and with natural sciences come methods of inquiry and intellectual states, which are inseparable from research and which may challenge religious convictions. Is it fair for a rabbi to want the services of a doctor who had to risk his soul to become a doctor in order to cure or save the life of a rabbi who feared to do the same?

Fortunately for the rabbis who were not or are not enthusiastic about Yeshiva or Bar-Ilan universities there are braver souls than they who do act like Joseph. They risk. And many of them must be greater heroes in God's eyes than those who do not risk. They prove that God and His Torah have nothing to fear from the world's cultures. On the other hand, exposure to alien cultures only deepens one's understanding and appreciation of the Jewish heritage.

But alas, in a polarized Jewish world, this is being overlooked. Even the present chief rabbis of Israel – though carefully selected by the religious Zionist leadership – do not have the courage of some of their predecessors to speak up for the point of view of Hirsch and Reines in an earlier period and of other giants in our own day. I am far from being a giant – but I can choose the giants with whom I prefer to be identified.

And when I am asked to name these giants with whom I identify and I name them, I am told that they have disqualified themselves automatically from being Torah sages, because they have earned doctorates in a university. With a Ph.D., I am informed, one no longer has the pure *daas Torah* – an unsullied, untainted, Torah point of view.

Alas, these rabbis cannot be their own counsel and champions. At least I can render them that service, even if I incur the wrath of many. It is good to assume risks in a good cause.

Why Good Deeds Don't Guarantee Rewards
— and Vice Versa

From time immemorial the question has been asked: Why did a presumably good God create evil and why does evil befall people who deserve a better deal from the Judge of all the earth?

Lest any reader assume that I can answer these questions, let me state at the outset that I have no answers. I wish that I did. I would be able to share them with everyone and become immortal. In fact, I was challenged many years ago – when one of my books was first published – why I dealt so minimally with the Holocaust, and all that I could say was that I usually write when I have a solution to a problem that distresses me. When I have only questions, I prefer to be silent.

And I have no way to account for the most inexplicable happening in recorded history – the premeditated organized murder of six million Jews within a few years. Similarly, I have no way to solve what is known as the problem of the theodicy – why do evil men thrive while good men suffer. Yet, while I cannot explain why God does precisely what He does – why He tries some and others are spared — I do want to make it clear that I do understand why there is no connection, at least in this world, between a person's righteousness and God's behavior toward him.

If anyone of us were God, he or she could not act differently than does God, who must so confuse the picture that no one can detect any connection between being good and a reward that is visible on earth. And the picture must be confusing.

In the biblical Book of Job, we find that his friends tried to argue that this was not the case. But we do not require Job's denial to dismiss the contention ourselves. We see it almost daily in

218

human society. There is no connection between being righteous and enjoying rewards for good deeds.

And this must be the case. Otherwise, God would have destroyed the possibility that men could do good solely because it is good without thought of reward. If good deeds produced a reward – other than the satisfaction of having done the good – then all people would be good because of the blessings such behavior entailed. It is obvious that this must be the proper way to educate and motivate children.

Adults, however, must do good because it *is* good – and that is all there is to it. The absence of any this-worldly reward eliminates the pursuit of good for any other purpose. True, the promise of another-worldly reward helps many to behave well, but our sages preferred performance of a mitzvah. They wanted to achieve the perfect performance of the mitzvah by detaching it completely from the anticipation of reward.

If they rationally believed that there is another world in which the good are rewarded, it was because their belief in God's justice required them to hold that God himself would ultimately do the right thing by those who were faithful to Him. However, they encouraged faithfulness to him exclusively for its own sake.

I repeat: I do not know why God deports Himself as He does. His wisdom is beyond me, and I cannot account for the manner in which He blesses and curses. But I can understand why He must deny me any knowledge of His behavior in this matter. I must seek the good "even if he slay me" because it is good. And to insure that human beings so behave, God permits no one to see a connection between righteousness and a reward.

What then, one will ask, are the biblical promises to reward Israel if it creates a just society in God's service in the Promised Land? The answer is simple. The promises are to the nation, and a nation cannot long endure if it is not founded on the principles of justice and mercy and the ideals which the Torah mandates.

There is a causal connection between a righteous society and its longevity. And many psychiatrists are now discovering a causal connection between righteousness and mental health. But this proves only that righteousness may be part of the natural law for societies and individuals.

However, God's ways are still beyond our comprehension. We simply cannot fathom them, and I do not know that we ever will. But we can comprehend why there must be no connection for mature people between doing good and expecting a reward.

Questioning or Accepting Reasons for Commandments

Recently I overheard a brief exchange of views between two Jews, both learned in Jewish law. One suggested a reason why the Bible may have forbidden priests to marry divorcees. The other appeared to be impatient with the attempt to rationalize a divine commandment and emphatically stated that a Jew must obey without seeking explanations. Using a sophisticated term which may give the appearance of pedantry, one calls the latter view deontological.

I did not become involved in the dispute because the two men represented two well-known attitudes that Jewish scholars have maintained through the centuries. Both views are authentic in the sense that among the greatest Jewish thinkers – our luminaries of the past – one finds some committed to one view while others were committed to the other, and, therefore, one cannot say either view has no support in our tradition. Neither view is unorthodox. However, one is likely to find modern Orthodox Jews searching for explanations, while those who are opposed to modern Orthodoxy prefer blind obedience. And both groups believe as they do for reasons they consider adequate.

The group that prefers blind obedience is fearful that if one is prone to seek explanations for all the laws, then when an explanation is not readily forthcoming, one may be tempted not to obey the law. Or if an explanation is available but it is no longer relevant because of changed circumstances, one may dismiss it as no longer obligatory. The law is deemed obsolescent. Or one may feel that the explanation one has discovered requires most Jews to obey it but not those who are superior intellectually or spiritually.

Indeed, the Talmud cites one interesting illustration in support of the view that the search for explanations can yield undesirable results. (*Sanhedrin* 21b) The Bible tells us specifically why kings are prohibited from marrying certain women.

Many of these may be idolaters of foreign birth, and they will influence the king to forsake the ancestral faith. King Solomon, wisest of all men, held that the law was inapplicable to him – he was too wise to be misguided by the fairer sex. Unfortunately, he did not obey the law, and what the Torah predicted came to pass even for him. Therefore, it was best that the Torah withhold giving us more than the law itself. If the reasons had been revealed as well, the consequences might be as disastrous as they were in the case of Solomon.

In addition to this reason, there is another that is not articulated as often. The test of one's faith is one's readiness to obey God's wish, even if one cannot understand why He commanded what He did. To paraphrase Tennyson, "Ours not to reason why, ours but to do and die." If there were good reason for doing what we were asked to do, then the stimulus to obedience would be reason and not faith. And those who see in faithful service to God the ultimate for man prefer that the compulsion come from faith and not from self-propelling understanding.

Among Christians this approach was so central that some of their theologians felt that even with doctrines of the faith, reason ought to play no part, and the more irrational and the more unreasonable the doctrine the better. In that way one proves how faithful one is – one is prepared to believe even the absurd, if God so willed it. This approach helped them accept that three can be one. I cannot recall any Jewish philosopher who was so extreme in his position, but there were many who did not want to rationalize the commandments.

The modern Orthodox are generally committed to the opposite point of view. They agree with Maimonides that God would not have commanded anything what was without reason and not for the good of man. Thus they want to reveal what God concealed. They know that their own intellectual powers are faulty, that they may search in vain for the reason and, even if they find one, it may be far from the truth. That explains why they rarely modify their performance of the commandment because of their hypotheses with regard to the commandments' reasons. But they cannot repress their desire to understand the whys and wherefores of God. It is human to want explanations. Moreover, a good explanation makes observance of the commandments more exciting. Life without meaning is hardly worthwhile. And a commandment without meaning can become perfunctory.

In rare instances the discovery of a meaning may influence the development of the law and its application. The rabbis debated this in the Talmud, and there were differences of opinion. The majority held that one should not use the presumed rationale for a law to justify exceptions if the law itself did not make the exceptions. Yet one often finds that the presumed rationale was responsible not only for exceptions but also for its obsolescence. This was especially the case in connection with rabbinic legislation.

This is not the proper forum for a full analysis of the theme. For my purpose it is adequate to state that there are two views and the men who argued the propriety of explaining why priests may not marry divorcees had intellectual ancestors on whom they relied.

Needless to say, in an age of reason the modern Orthodox are more in accord with the times and search for reasons. In an age when the pursuit of the occult is in vogue, the pursuit of reason is less popular. But both approaches have their roots in our tradition, and Jews can choose one or the other.

It is when they become intolerant of each other that they reveal how remote they are from understanding that our tradition is non-monolithic and how much they must learn not only about the love of all Jews but also about the tradition itself.

An Optimist Sees Pessimism in Ecclesiastes

Jews have one major festival dedicated to the theme of happiness. This may come as a surprise to many. Is there a human being "with heart so dead" that he requires a special day to remind him how important happiness is? The answer is that most people do require it. True, they crave the blessing of joy but they do not always fathom what is the best way to achieve it. And among those seeking answers to this question were philosophers and kings and those who were both philosophers and kings.

Such a man was King Solomon who tradition credits with the authorship of the Book of Ecclesiastes, one of the writings of the Bible. And it is that book that tradition bids us to read precisely on the festival of Tabernacles (Sukkot) which is the season for our "happiness" and the time for pondering what happiness is.

Many reasons are given for our reading the book in connection with the joyous holiday. However, on its face, it would appear that it is the worst possible choice. The book is the most pessimistic of all the sacred writings. It describes a man who had everything but, in fact, it was all as nothing in his eyes. He appears to have tasted of all the pleasures but ultimately delighted in none. Do we read the book on Sukkot only to put a damper on our celebration? To urge us not to indulge in excesses? To remind us that happiness is an unattainable goal? Were our sages capricious or sadistic – to prescribe a holiday dedicated to happiness and to pinpoint its pointlessness?

I dared to give my own answer to the question on my 75th birthday – a milestone in one's life when one inevitably becomes philosophical. Many experts have dealt with the issue, I am not such an expert. But my answer has its source in my personal experience as a human being and not in any expertise as a scholar.

It seems to me that King Solomon wrote as pessimistically as he did because he completely failed to discover the three principal sources of meaningful happiness. The book of Ecclesiastes fails to make any mention whatever of what to me – the congenital optimist – are the greatest blessings a human being ought to crave. These are the love of family, the capacity for genuine friendship, and the ability to perform good deeds and bring happiness to others.

Perhaps I err. Yet, whenever I read the Book of Ecclesiastes I have the feeling that the author could not even enjoy the thought that the wealth he acquired would be enjoyed by his heirs – his family – his progeny. It were as if he begrudged them what he had bothered to accumulate. Many of us – by contrast – feel that one of the main drives that prompt us to achieve is that we may thereby bless those of our loved ones who survive. The Book clearly expresses the author's resentment that others will enjoy the fruit of his toil and there is no suggestion that these others may include those whom he ought to have loved – if, indeed he loved anyone.

Second, there is no reference in the Book to the blessing of friendship. Needless to say, there are many kinds of friendship and not all of them are of equal value. Maimonides – a greater philosopher than King Solomon – distinguished between three types of friendship. (*See Avot* 5:15)

There are people who seek the friendship of others in order to exploit them. This goal is not an ethical one and is hardly recommended. We ought to never exploit one created in the divine image. Then there are people who seek the friendship of others in order to dispel loneliness and enjoy the companionship of fellow-men. This goal is a worthy one but hardly the sublimest of all possible impulses. It is not unethical for it does not really involve the exploitation of others. One rather seeks in it sharing – the sharing of life's experiences and perhaps even the sharing of worldly goods. But the highest type of friendship is the friendship that two or more persons enjoy because in their togetherness they want to achieve the loftiest values of the human heart – sharing not only the facts and things of their lives but the aspirations that motivate them, the dreams that they dream and the deeds they perform as one to fulfill the dreams.

There is not the remotest suggestion of this yearning or blessing in the Book of Ecclesiastes. Thus, without the love of family or friends, how could King Solomon have achieved happiness? It is no wonder that he wrote as he did.

Yet, the greatest of all sources of happiness is the ability to bring happiness to others. Nothing ought to make a person as happy as his making others happy. This is other-directed happiness rather than self-centered happiness and one can never feel satiated with it. That is what the Torah orders in connection with all the major holidays. Enjoy them! How? Bring happiness to the widow and the orphan – to the expropriated Levite and the poor. And King Solomon, with all of his wealth, did not know this use of wealth. And he probably did not try it. Otherwise, he would have referred to it. He discusses all that he did – and all that he tried. But this very simple answer to his search is that he did not try.

That is why for me the book is a classic, made holy, because it is a documentary as to how one can best achieve the state of misery – depression, disillusion, pessimism. And if one wants to avoid such despair then one ought to abandon self-centeredness and focus on the happiness of others rather than one's own. It may not be easy to achieve such a goal in the fullest measure but it is certainly worth the try.

Saints did not achieve happiness this way. Whether in the love of God or the love of human beings they transcended their love of themselves and instead of maintaining a pessimistic view of life theirs was an optimistic one. "God's law was perfect and refresheth the soul."

Judaism's Special Sensitivity in Human Relations

Aperson who is insensitive to the feelings of others does not merit the gift of life. I know of no tradition that makes this point as strongly as does the Jewish tradition. The more one studies Torah, the more one realizes how true this is.

It may be impossible to love one's neighbor as one loves one's self. It may be difficult to wish for one's neighbor what one wishes for one's self. But it is imperative that one spare the feelings of one's fellow men and not cause them hurt. A decent human being never forgets this and exercises maximum self-control not to be guilty of embarrassing another.

One well-known Talmudic text tells us that one should even opt for suicide rather than humiliate another in public. (*Berachot* 43b) But sensitivity to the feelings of others was not a rabbinic invention. The Bible is also rich with illustrations.

For example, the Bible commands farmers not to harvest all their crops. They must leave a share on the edge of the field for the poor to come and take. (*Leviticus* 19:9; *ibid.* 23:22) The rabbis noted that the order was to leave that share uncut.

One might have expected that the farmer would be accommodating the poor if he completed harvesting what was available for the poor and then handed it to them. Nay, said the rabbis. The Bible ordered him "to leave" that share – to leave it and let the poor come and take it themselves.

The poor take what God gave them, not what the owner of the field dispensed. The owner may not even choose the poor whom he wants to favor with what he has made available. He is not the owner of that share, and he has no power whatever over its disposition. This was sensitivity for the feelings of those who had to live on "leavings"!

Another command in the Bible involves the sensitivity of the hired man who helps the owner during the harvest. (*Deuteronomy* 23:25-26) As he works, he can eat as much of the crop as he wishes. Of course, he can take none home with him, but as he works, he cannot be told by the owner to keep hands off the grain or the fruit because they are not his.

If an ox may not be muzzled as it threshes the wheat, so the worker cannot be muzzled on the job. (*Deuteronomy* 25:4) This would be cruel and demeaning, and the Bible prohibits such behavior. It would make the employee feel so much more disadvantaged than the employer, and this would be foul.

There is only one reference in the Five Books of Moses to road maintenance and directional signs. If a man kills another accidentally, he has a way to escape the wrath of the victim's kin. He can flee to a city of refuge. The roads to the many cities so provided were to be kept in good condition, with signs at crossroads to indicate where to go. (*Makkot* 10b) But the obvious question is why were similar provisions not made for the Jews who thrice a year were ordered to go to Jerusalem. Why the concern only for those responsible for a homicide?

The answer, too, must be obvious. If a pilgrim en route to Jerusalem should lose his way, who would not help him find it? He could ask, and his fellow Jews would be delighted to assist him. But if a fugitive asks about a city of refuge, he may frighten people away. They will know he is a killer. Doors may be locked in his face. In any event, he must be spared confessing to the misdeed. It would be terribly embarrassing to him. And this the Torah sought to avoid. Again, concern for the sensitivity of a human being.

When there was a Temple in Jerusalem, Jews would bring many kinds of offerings, especially offerings to atone for sins, usually for sins against God. But the Bible prescribed that none other than the sinner and the priest were to know the character of the offering. A sinner did not have to share his awareness of guilt with others in the Temple. This too was sparing him embarrassment and humiliation.

I could go on and on. However, my purpose is simply to query why it is that in the study of Talmud – wherever it is taught – so little attention is given to the Jewish tradition's concern for the sensibilities of others and its centrality in the texts themselves. Why are teachers of Talmud preoccupied with communicating the unique jargon of the texts, the methods of exegesis, the reconciling of contradictory passages and other elements which one must master if one is to become a master of Talmudic discourse, but which cause one to lose sight of the law's real objectives? They are the cultivation of a saintly personality constantly aware of God and His will. This I call the teleology of the law, the law's purpose, the law's ultimate. To fathom this does not require the genius and concentration which the other goals require.

Most beginners in Talmud study are now required to master a few pages dealing with lost property. (*Bava Metzia* Chapter 2) They are difficult pages. They involve concepts with which sophisticated lawyers deal, such as title to property, passage of title, abandonment or divesting of ownership, etc.

Perhaps I would not be competent to study Talmud now if I had not been exposed to these abstruse analyses early in life. But I was already a teacher of law in a college before I realized the purpose of the analysis which I had been expected to master as a child. It was to communicate the idea that, according to Jewish law, he who finds property had better exert himself to the maximum to return it to his owner. He should not indulge himself the illusion that he may be able to keep it for himself. It would be almost impossible for him to retain it for himself even if the owner could never be ascertained. Perhaps he would have to store it until the Messiah came. For what good reason should one assume that responsibility?

To the child student, however, that idea was never presented. Is it any wonder then that one does not often see a correlation between Talmudic learning and ethical behavior in matters pertaining to man's relationship with his fellowmen?

I do not demean the importance of other ways of studying Talmud. Without the other ways, there would be few who would be masters of Talmudic wisdom. But for the overwhelming majority of Jews, Talmud should be taught to reveal its concern for the welfare of human beings, and that is the better way. It will attract rather than alienate students and perhaps even change them for the better.

Orthodoxy's Champion of Sacred and Secular Synthesis

Altogether too often a nation fails to remember the people who were truly responsible for major achievements and breakthroughs in different areas of thought and action. Instead, it gives all the credit to those who come after and spectacularly capitalize on what was done earlier by the almost-forgotten persons.

Therefore, I am delighted that at long last greater recognition is being given the contribution of Rabbi Bernard Revel to the successful transplanting of Judaism to the Western Hemisphere. Others may have broadened the scope of his undertaking; still others may have defined and refined the conceptions which he advanced. But he was the pioneer, the innovator, who gave his life for what he believed; and he did so well that a cause deemed hopeless by most of his contemporaries became a spiritual force which no one can now ignore.

Dr. Revel was the founder of Yeshiva University and the man who appointed a dean of that institution who subsequently founded a sister institution in Israel, Bar-Ilan University. He was the dreamer who kept the faith that traditional Judaism can cope with the modern world and the challenges of the natural and social sciences.

Rabbis who hold that this is impossible and that Judaism can only survive if Jews isolate themselves in physical or spiritual ghettos still abound, but they too cannot deny that Revel's dream is being fulfilled and that they too have gained by his vision. Revel paved the way for their institutions to come into being and to enjoy status in America's open society without following the pattern of the Amish.

Revel was comparatively young when he died, and those of us who were privileged to be close to him in the '20s and '30s are now relatively few. His biography has been written and deserves a wider reading public. For those who may not read the biography, I want to record some impressions of his life and career and add my voice to the tribute being paid him as Yeshiva University celebrates the 100th anniversary of its establishment. For this milestone, the U.S. postal authorities approved a commemorative stamp for Revel.

He was the first man in modern times to insist on the introduction of secular studies into yeshiva programs. His was a revolutionary step and evoked the wrath of many Orthodox contemporaries, as it still evokes the resistance of heads of yeshivot in Israel and the United States.

Revel knew that if an iron curtain continued between sacred and secular studies, the tradition would not have spokesmen able to cope with modernity. He held fast and made possible not only a secondary school education for his students in a high school of incomparable excellence – with a greater percentage of students winning Regents' scholarships than any ether high school in New York State – but also an undergraduate college. His successor, Dr. Samuel Belkin, then added professional schools and a number of departments for graduate study.

Belkin expanded the scope of the university principally to enhance its image and its contribution to higher education and research. For Revel, however, the goal was an ideological "synthesis" – his favorite word. He insisted that modern spokesmen for Orthodoxy be masters of natural and social science. Otherwise, they would hardly be able to communicate with moderns and expound the tradition. In addition to mastery of sciences, they must be able to achieve the sanctification of the secular, the integration of the best that humanity has achieved with the eternal truths of Judaism, the greater appreciation of Judaism because of its differences with other religions and cultures, and the reformulation of' the cherished concepts and practices of Judaism and their rationalization in modern terms.

Until this day, Yeshiva students dream of the goal of "synthesis" associated with Revel's name. Belkin redefined "synthesis," but many old-timers and many of the Orthodox "intelligentsia" still prefer Revel's original notion.

However, Revel was concerned not only with creation of an Orthodox intelligentsia. He also wanted to train rabbis who would be more than halachic experts. He wanted rabbis trained for the kind of spiritual leadership they must now exercise. And he introduced into the rabbinical training program subjects that ancient yeshivot never considered – Jewish history, Jewish philosophy, pedagogy, even public speaking and homiletics.

Yeshiva students still frown upon the requirement to study these subjects; they make Torah study seem like preparation for a professional career. But Revel knew better, and because of his initiative, the great orators and communal leaders of American Orthodoxy achieved the status that they have. I mention only two of those deceased, Rabbis Joseph H. Lookstein and Irving Miller.

A few words about the man. In a brief career in the oil business with his wife's family, he invented a device which made him financially independent for many years. He, therefore, not only served Yeshiva University for a nominal salary, but spent many times that sum to feed and clothe poor students. I remember how often I called to his attention the need of students for winter overcoats, which he bought and for which he paid..

He knew the names of every one of the several hundred students; his memory was phenomenal. But what is more, he knew their travail. He knew when a student was struggling with doubt, and he undertook to give moral support. He never encouraged blind faith, but he also disliked iconoclasm. I remember that one day he encountered a student who was an avid reader of H.L. Mencken's American Mercury – the organ of skepticism and satire with a green cover – and Revel noticed that the student was carrying an issue of Harper's magazine, with a red cover. Revel charmingly congratulated him on moving "from the green to the red."

I think of him very often. He is responsible for so much I have tried to do with my life, and this tribute is my inadequate way of thanking him and blessing his memory.

Think Before Acting:
A godlike life requires discipline
and unrelenting thoughtfulness

One of the major goals of education is to enhance the self-control of the students. There can be no enduring family society or nation unless individuals exercise some measure of restraint in that which they do or even say.

In Judaism this function of education is of paramount importance. Committed Jews are expected to control themselves in such matters as food and sex, their occupations and their speech, their resort to violence and war, even their thoughts – virtually impossible for most of us.

Perhaps no aspect of Judaism has alienated more from the faith and its legal tradition than this self-control in one's personal performance as a Jew. Yet, Orthodox Jews will not abandon their focus on the law. They are not always successful in inducing the control that the law mandates, and often self-control in one area does not necessarily make for self-control in others. But no one has yet suggested a better way.

One celebrated author on traditional Judaism, Aron Barth, has suggested that what Jewish law forces a religiously observant Jew to do is always to ask – before he acts – is the act permissible or is it prohibited? Is the food he is about to eat a permitted food? Is the sexual urge one that he is allowed to gratify with the person in mind, and when and how? In short, impulsive action is to be replaced with disciplined, ofttimes inhibited behavior.

Leo Baeck was even more emphatic. He wrote that the real godlessness on the part of a human being is "thoughtlessness" – to act without forethought. And thus a godlike life requires unrelenting thoughtfulness.

What a wonderful world this would be if we could count on all human beings to be in control of what they do or say in every situation confronting them.

One related item I found recently in Talmudic literature warrants celebration. At the beginning of a meal, one is expected to seize the bread on which the blessing (the Motzi) is about to be pronounced with all 10 fingers and then recite the well-known words. Why? This is to suggest to the one about to give thanks to God for the food before him that he must ponder whether or not he fulfilled the Ten commandments which the Torah requires of him before he partakes of God's bounty. (*Jerusalem Talmud Challah* Chapter 1)

This point is made in the Jerusalem Talmud. There is a difference of opinion as to what these Ten commandments are. One version of the text lists Ten commandments that begin with the planting of the grain. Was the plough pulled by two animals that should not have been joined together? Did the seed contain a forbidden mixture? Did the farmer leave the required amount for the poor to harvest for themselves? Did the priests, Levites and poor get their share?

Another version finds all Ten commandments involved in the distribution to the needy that the owner must make. In any event, the point is simple and clear. You may not eat or pronounce a blessing if the food was produced in sin and the product was not duly shared with those whom the Torah has made partial beneficiaries of God's goodness.

Is this not thoughtfulness to an extreme degree? Imagine how blessed mankind would be if every time one spent money on himself or his loved ones he would pause to ask simple questions.

Did I acquire the money lawfully? Did I hurt anyone in the process of acquiring it? Did the poor get the share to which they are entitled? Am I mindful of the waste of mother earth that the acquisition involves? Will I use the property without causing suffering to anyone?

Most people to whom I would make these suggestions probably would reply, "Stop it. You are making me as neurotic as you are. You are taking the joy out of life."

Perhaps the law does go too far. Yet how wonderful is the message it conveys: Don't utter God's name when making a blessing if you have not made Him happy with what you are presently doing.

Now, I turn to Washington.

Messrs. Bush and Baker: How much advance thought do you give to what you are about to say before you say it? And how carefully do you control your pique with Israel when you act on matters involving Israel? And how much thought do you give to people for whose welfare you are responsible even if they may not have voted for you?

The one person for whom you do exercise restraint is Mr. Buchanan. Can it be his ideas and your ideas have so much in common?

Plea for Mercy:
"Miscarriage of justice" against Pollard begs for commuted sentence

It is not easy writing about Jonathan Pollard and his case without becoming emotional. I spent almost five hours with him in a federal maximum security prison, and find it difficult to subdue my anger that such a gifted man should be kept inert. Five days after that visit, his appeal for a new trial was denied by two federal judges, while one dissented, saying Pollard had suffered a "miscarriage of justice."

Nonetheless, he has no relief while the character of his incarceration evokes indescribable sympathy and even moments of horror. Yet both Israel and the Jewish establishment in the United States are blind to his plight and deaf to his plea.

These thoughts I must repress because I know that my anger will get him nowhere. Instead I must exercise all the influence and persuasion that I can to get the groups hostile to his cause to join in a respectful request for the commutation of his sentence to the time already served. If a federal appellate judge described what has happened until now as a "miscarriage of justice," who can possibly deny a modest plea for mercy without reopening, reviewing or erasing the past?

Several months ago I appealed in this column to those involved in the matter to respect the feelings of what I held to be the overwhelming majority of the world's Jews that there was anti-Semitism in the conviction and sentence of Pollard. For the purpose of this new plea I will assume for the sake of argument, and notwithstanding the mischief of Caspar Weinberger, that there was no such anti-Semitism. No one has argued that position more effectively than did Judge Abraham Sofaer in a debate with Alan Dershowitz. And he confirmed the Anti-Defamation League decision to avoid involvement in the matter.

Nonetheless, even Judge Sofaer, who argued that there was guilt and a basis for the unbelievably severe sentence, supported a call for *rachmones*, compassion. In his own words: "If you want to call for rachmones, how am I going to say no? How should anyone say no? Compassion? Find an appropriate basis for it and express it in appropriate terms after appropriately condemning this man, after appropriately condemning what the government of Israel did, and I have no difficulty with compassion." (The outstanding federal appellate judge David Bazelon was wont to call this a "writ of rachmones.")

In Judge Sofaer's argument he faults Israel more than the accused. If he is correct, then Israel's cabinet should take an active part in getting Pollard out of jail. The prisoner himself deserves compassion not only for having already been subjected to six years of the most harrowing prison experience, but also for his great contribution to humanity in having prevented a disaster during the Persian Gulf war. One dreads to imagine what might have happened if Israel had not had the information from Pollard's unlawful but overwhelmingly benign and heroic act.

In great measure, Judge Sofaer's presentation to the Anti-Defamation League influenced that organization, as it did other groups similarly minded, to leave to the courts to decide whether an injustice is being committed. Fine. The court has now decided. Must Pollard try against odds for an appeal to the U.S. Supreme Court to get the dissent upheld? Has not one federal judge already provided the "basis" for the commutation of Pollard's sentence to time served?

True, two judges disagreed. But why should it take a unanimous jury to convict an offender, while the opinion of one judge that there has been a "miscarriage of justice" is inconsequential to get a convicted felon out of jail after he had served for six years, most of them in solitary confinement?

My earlier plea to the Jewish establishment was to no avail. But now my plea is not for a new trial but only for the commutation of sentence. And if to that Judge Sofaer says, "How should anyone say no," why should there not be a unanimous Jewish community joining in a plea for a result that can please all?

If the strong words of the dissenting judge are not enough of a basis for commuting Pollard's sentence, let me offer two others that are found in the reasoning of the two judges who denied the appeal.

Why did they do so? For technical reasons. Do such reasons justify leaving a man in solitary confinement when many acknowledge his case has merit?

These two judges declined to offer an opinion on the life sentence. Yet it was the sentence that has aroused the ire of many. Must one be denied justice because of consideration for the honor of a fellow judge and a government official in high places? The second excuse is unbelievable – it is alleged the case should have been brought sooner. Must one languish in jail because he was too poor to appeal with haste?

"God of Abraham!" I must scream. Why did our sages use this phrase when they felt outraged? I now know why. Because it was Abraham who screamed even at God, saying, "Will the judge of all the earth not do justice?" (*Genesis* 18:25)

To judges of the earth I make my appeal. God yielded to Abraham's challenge. I pray that President Bush will yield to yours and ours no matter how he feels about Jews not voting for him.

Pollard stands convicted. He admits his guilt. He has expressed his remorse. He has suffered an unusual punishment. No organization need admit that it did wrong. They can all unite on one prayer – the commutation of the sentence to time spent. And an anguished Jewish community can put to rest at least one cause for internal strife.

Policy of Separation:
Government works best when the secular and spiritual coexist

For half a century I have tried to convince my co-religionists that Jewish tradition does not call for a Jewish state to be a theocracy if that means a state whose head of government is a cleric – Jewish, Christian or Muslim – and whose officials are members of the clergy.

I tried to make it clear that the Jewish tradition requires precisely the opposite – a separation between the spiritual and temporal authority. The two should coexist, but the vesting of both authorities in one person or group is disastrous, as it was in the time of the Maccabees.

I write about this because I was delighted to read in a Yeshiva University publication that one of the greatest luminaries in the Jewish world today, the renowned Rabbi Aharon Lichtenstein, head of Yeshivat Gush Etzion in Israel, has expressed the same view.

"*A priori,* one can postulate three primary positions," Lichtenstein wrote. "Civil and religious authority may virtually coincide, power being concentrated in the hands of a king-priest or curia, as in numerous primitive societies or in some instances in contemporary Islam. At the other extreme, the two may be theoretically totally separated, as in the United States. Intermediately, there may be some blend of difference and association, this being the prevalent pattern in most modem European countries.

"With respect to this cardinal issue, there can be little doubt about the classical Jewish position. Traditional Judaism has thoroughly rejected the fusion of secular and religious authority. Confrontations between prophets and monarchs were a hallmark of the First Commonwealth. Even as regards the relatively more mundane institution of priesthood, Nachmanides states that its members are halachically enjoined from assuming the throne, and goes so far as to suggest that the Hasmonean dynasty was divinely punished to the point of extinction because its scions, as priests, should not have ruled but only labored in the service of God (Comm. on Gen. 49:10).

"On the other hand, radical severance has been equally out of the question. A people defined as a kingdom of priests and a holy nations (Ex. 19:6) is hardly prone to divorce its political from its religious institutions."

Rabbi Lichtenstein cites only the instance of the Hasmonean dynasty. I have maintained that the policy of separation was initiated by Moses himself, who divided between the two authorities and bequeathed them to a high priest on one hand and a commanding general on the other. Augustine held the view that Jesus was entitled to have both powers – in him the two authorities were vested as they were in Moses. And it was only a millennium later that a Christian pope arrogated the same power to himself alone. Thus the talk about theocracy began.

Yet that was not the original meaning of the term coined by the historian Josephus. Josephus tried to explain the Jewish view to the Greeks and Romans, using the word theocracy to describe a state ruled by a law given by God. It would have been more correct to say "monocracy." But Judaism should not be demeaned because Josephus made a mistake and a pope took advantage.

The coexistence of the temporal and religious authorities is the ideal. But not always is it possible to avoid conflicts. For many centuries Jewish communities were fairly homogenous and clashes were few. In the contemporary heterogeneous Jewish state, however, there is likely to be ceaseless tension.

Many are the practical consequences of Judaism's approach. The principal one may be the very principle of separation of church and state, which I have deemed of Jewish origin. But there were other consequences as well.

A major one is the fact that political and economic power was never to be in the hands of the clergy. They had to rely on precept and example to influence the benign exercise of political and economic power by the secular authority. That priests and rabbis among Jews – and priests in the other faiths – managed to do the opposite of what God had wished does not disprove my thesis. But in the new state that we Jews have, it would be well to clarify what the ideal is and how we can fulfill it.

Certainly the religious parties are not to be credited with such an effort. In Israel's last election, a political party for which I voted and which had among its leaders Rabbanit Tova Lichtenstein, tried to restore the spiritual authority on course. It did receive support from tens of thousand of Jews, but not enough to elect a member of Knesset. But the ideal is still one to which these thousands plus many others are committed.

The Charedi parties in Israel see the Jewish tradition as the popes did and would delight in a state run by its "great Torah sages." But the religious Zionist parties are more loyal to the authentic Jewish tradition. Perhaps only the daring among them will assert this. But so it is.

The function of religious parties is to help the spiritual authority to generate values and influence the citizens and the rulers by persuasion to exercise the temporal authority in fulfillment of those values, but never to usurp the temporal authority unto themselves.

The most eloquent illustration of the difference can be seen in one striking fact.

The State of Israel does not have a law that coerces parents to circumcise all males born to Jewish mothers. Parents are free to do as they please. Yet almost all obey the mandate of the spiritual authority. There is no conflict. There is no coercion. What the spiritual authority mandates is fulfilled without the force of the temporal authority.

With regard to family law, however, the situation is exactly the opposite. The spiritual authority enjoys a monopoly on domestic relations. The result is disastrous. The law is hated; those in charge of the law are hated; the Torah is maligned; extortion and blackmail are rampant.

For 50 years I tried my best to defend the system in the interest of Jewish unity. But I now find the price is too great. And the cause of unity is not advanced.

Before it is too late, the situation must be given another look. A full revision is in order. The spiritual authority owes it to its own principles to make it.

Value of Non-Orthodoxy:
New ideas, once condemned,
sustain or advance Judaism

For me, the oneness of the Jewish people is a basic value that dominates much of my thought and action. From my father, of blessed memory, I learned that one must never "give up" on a fellow Jew.

Therefore, it pains me that presently this value is being challenged, and by none other than some Orthodox Jewish academicians — not necessarily the most learned or pious, but Orthodox nonetheless. Their argument is that a loyal Jew cannot "unite" with one who does not believe that the Torah is from God.

If these separatists mean that on projects involving the propagation of the faith, Orthodox Jews can work only with those who share the same beliefs, they may have a point — but not necessarily. They could still work together on those elements of the faith that all share.

However, apart from the faith there is much activity — many problems and many programs — in which there can be joint effort with all who are Jewish. That is why I have always supported cooperation between all groups of Jews that have some shared goals.

This for me is basic Judaism while the separatists are truly rebels, seeking to revise what was always basic. In the past, when Jews had to fight for survival, they did not examine the religiosity of those who fought with them; no one was cross-examined about his beliefs or practice.

In Orthodox circles I have often been subjected to harassment by these rebels. But that does not matter. What does matter is that the rebels fail to see that virtually every approach to Judaism which deviated at one time or another from the then-prevailing majority view, usually made some contribution to the survival of our people and our religious heritage.

When the Reform movement celebrated the 100th anniversary of its founding in the United States I was asked to write an essay for a Jewish scholarly periodical on the contributions of Reform Judaism even to Orthodoxy. I wrote the essay, listing several such contributions. However, because I was then very much under siege in Orthodox circles for my commitment to the unity of the Jewish people, my close friends pleaded with me not to exacerbate the hostility of my opponents. Now I am ashamed of myself that I yielded to their importuning.

Yet, it is a fact that almost every new movement of the last few centuries is to be credited with some good, though in its inception it was resisted by the establishment.

The Chasidic movement is the most eloquent example. Its role in the survival of Judaism is simply overwhelming.

By contrast, even the secular Yiddishist movement was remarkably successful: The alumni of its educational system display Jewish identity and loyalty at least as intense as that which one finds in most graduates of Orthodox afternoon schools or day schools.

The Zionist movement, in turn, was the faith of millions of Jews who refused to assimilate and it gave us the most important instrument for Jewish survival that we have had in two millennia.

This is also true of the non-Orthodox movements. At least they slowed up the process of acculturation and assimilation. Now, from among those who did not assimilate, Jews have a greater reservoir of young people who are being reached to retrieve much of the Judaism that their parents and grandparents abandoned.

The "revisionists" against Jewish unity argue that if there were no non-Orthodoxy all Jews would now be Orthodox. How naive can they be! Is not the situation in Israel proof enough that in a free world, in the absence of Zionism or non-Orthodoxy, most Jews would opt for secularism or assimilation?

The situation in Latin America provides additional proof. In the absence of non-Orthodoxy there, assimilation and intermarriage proceeded at a faster rate than in countries which had non-Orthodox movements.

However, it cannot be denied that there are also positive contributions by non-Orthodox movements beyond what they did to provide an alternative to Orthodoxy and the retention of Jewish identity for one or two generations beyond the immigrant generation.

Who can deny that they made all Jews aware of the need to further emancipate the Jewish woman, to give her birth and her maturation some recognition, and to enable her to receive a good education in both the Oral and Written Law! They also helped to make a significant Jewish contribution to the battle for human rights and economic as well as political democracy for the greater happiness of all Jews and all mankind.

There is one area in particular in which they rendered a great service to Orthodox Jews: Their challenge to Orthodoxy made Orthodox rabbis deepen their understanding of Judaism in order to cope with the challenges. This was no mean contribution. And Orthodoxy is coping as never before with virtually all the intellectual, emotional, institutional, and administrative challenges that helped Orthodoxy to experience a remarkable revival.

Non-Orthodoxy helped to restore to all Jews their historic sense of history. Orthodox Jews were forgetting that history is not only very much a part of the faith and practice but also an aid to our understanding and appreciation of Jewish law.

Of this I will yet write at greater length. I will do so not only because of the theme's importance, but also because I detect a tendency in some Jewish circles to falsify our history in order to sustain a position. And this is palpably unconscionable.

Keep Criticism Constructive:
When faulting Israel,
one should deliver the message "lovingly"

Of the many international meetings of import held in Israel this summer, perhaps those of Tikkun magazine received the most media attention. Michael Lerner, the editor, brought together almost all the parties and movements that have been bashing either Israel or its present government or both.

Ostensibly, it was a get-together of the liberals, progressives and peace-seekers. To most observers of the Israeli scene, it was a get-together of those in the opposition, the dispossessed, the disenfranchised, the malcontents.

Many writers in the Jerusalem Post dealt with the conference, some with respect, others with derision, still others with malice. Lerner was personally attacked for his affiliation with the Communist Party several decades ago and for his bitter attacks on Jews for persecuting blacks. He was defended by a Reform rabbi and portrayed as one who atoned for the sins of his youth.

Participants who had an Ashkenazic background discovered that like those in the Israeli establishment, they were guilty of discrimination against the Sephardim – their alleged liberalism was hardly what they professed it to be. And the Sephardim seemed to be less interested in the universal values of the progressives than they were in gaining recognition for themselves in the ranks of the objectors.

My problem is with Lerner and with the constituents of his conference, whether they represented organized parties and movements or only themselves. As much as any one of them, I want to make changes in Israel's political democracy, religious situation, economic system, manners and values. But I cannot possibly identify with the anger – simple, rudimentary anger – that comes through in the approach of so many of those who were part of the conference. And I ask myself: What prevents me from joining hands with most of those who engaged in the deliberations of the Tikkun conference, despite my agreement with so much of what they would like to achieve?

Anger by itself would not keep me distant. One should be angry when things are done badly or cause hurt to others.

To join anyone in an attempt to make Israel a more perfect state and Jews a more perfect society, I must detect in those I join the capacity to be "lovingly critical." This is basic to me.

Perhaps I err. However, I have been guided by one rule all my life: The best way to judge whether one likes or dislikes the object of one's criticism is to see whether the criticism is preceded by a complimentary comment and the complimentary comment is truly and deeply felt. Everyone knows the criticism of a child by a parent will achieve the best results when the child senses the criticism is born of love. This also applies to the criticism of spouses by each other.

I am very critical of the state of Jewish family law today, but even those who fault me for being so critical know that I love Jewish family law and sing its praises even when I fault it. I admire its millennial development and only regret that somehow that development stopped at the wrong time and in the wrong place. And anyone who speaks of the faults of Israel with no expression of love and admiration for its achievements in every area makes me hesitate to be at one with him.

I feel that way even more bitterly when Orthodox or non-Orthodox rabbis are critical of Israel. Are they "lovingly critical" or angry men? Rabbis who cherished the Zionist dream all their lives and were privileged to see it fulfilled in so few years in their own lifetimes could not possibly express themselves as some rabbis now do. Of course, it is the privilege of every Jew not to admire the government, despite the great things it accomplishes. One may focus only on the wrongs. But from a beloved, one expects a different tone, unless one feels that, like Jeremiah, God has given the mandate to blast.

Every day in Israel I see one achievement after another. Because of the failures or even the inequities, should I bury my love and my enthusiasm and harp only on what is bad?

Thus, I am allergic to anyone who is not "lovingly critical" of Israel. And I pray they will learn to appreciate the miracles God has wrought for us and bless Him daily for them.

Democracy in Judaism:
"Majority rule" is biblical;
dissent always was protected

Few people anger me as much as they who allege that Judaism and democracy are incompatible. Indeed, as I have argued many times, Judaism may not indulge the individual unbridled freedom. But neither does any democratic government.

However, freedom of thought and expression are remarkably well protected in Jewish law. The silencing or punishment of dissenters is sought only by fanatics and zealots who feel they are possessed of absolute truth and admit of no possibility of error in their views.

Not so long ago there were reports in The Jewish Week that in the Rabbinical Council of America there was a "witch hunt," some members being charged with heretical views. Rabbi Milton Polin, then the organization's president, ruled that members were held accountable only for their deeds or behavior when it constituted rejection of Halacha, but not for their theological views in which Judaism long tolerated a remarkable diversity.

The classic example is the dispute between two giants in the Middle Ages, one insisting that God is incorporeal, the other holding that even the opposite view is not heresy.

Recently I read an essay by Dr. Zorach Wahrhaftig, a winner of the coveted Israel Prize for his service to Hebrew law. It dealt with one fundamental feature of democracy: majority rule. The essay analyzed every aspect of that principle, and it was a pleasant surprise to learn that the Bible is the earliest source for its articulation.

In antiquity one person made the legal decisions – the king or the head of the clan. Even when several people might have participated in the trial or the deliberations, respect for the ruling decisor required that his view prevail. And it is in the Book of Exodus that we find the unequivocal mandate – decide by majority vote (*Exodus* 23:2) – and, in voting, do not feel bound by any superiors voting at the same time.

Yet that did not mean a majority is always right or that those who differed with the majority could not dissent. If the vote in a three-judge court was 2 to 1, then the dissenter was not privileged to identify who he was because that would cause the party who lost the case to honor him and hate his colleagues. The majority decision became the decision of all three, and all had to uphold it.

Yet, if a judge was overruled by the highest court in Jerusalem, he was obligated to abide by the decision of the higher authority and act accordingly. But that did not preclude him from arguing forever that the reversal was an error. In his official capacity he could not apply the rule his superiors had reversed, but he was free to say – even to teach – that his superiors had erred.

In this way freedom of dissent was protected for judges. But what of a minority that disagrees with the majority in other matters? Can it be coerced to accept the will of the majority? In this connection Dr. Wahrhaftig cites the rules, and they gladden the heart and make Rabbi Polin's stand authentic Halacha.

There are limitations on the majority: Its decision is binding on the minority in many matters, but not in all.

The most important exception for us today is the exclusion of matters of the spirit – one's faith, beliefs, thoughts. If they lead to deviationist behavior or subversion, then the majority might take action to protect its views. But the majority could not inhibit the expression of opposing views.

Dr. Wahrhaftig even cites an actual case that involved a rabbi whose sermons included some questionable statements. But because they led to no action unacceptable halachically, they were not actionable.

I do think a group may organize for the propagation of doctrines they share, and a rabbinical group may demand of those who are members that they do not subvert those doctrines in the instruction they give their members or students. But even Orthodox Judaism permits of such a wide range in doctrines, and even in practice, that "witch hunts" are certainly not in order.

The majority rule, however, plays its role in government and in virtually every aspect of social and economic organization. In the Middle Ages there were many conflicts about the power of the majority to impose taxes on the minority. But there was no difficulty, for example, in empowering a majority of residents in a common court to impose its will upon a minority to share the cost of improvements.

The one great exception was in the spiritual realm. If the majority rule were to apply there, then, alas, Jews might have to say that a majority of non-Jews could impose its will upon the Jews. And this was unthinkable.

The Torah had said, in fact, that we were chosen not because we were many; on the contrary, we were the smallest of all peoples. (*Deuteronomy* 7:6-8) Thus we, too, learned not to flee our minority status but to hold that what is right and wrong is not determined by a vote of the majority.

The Big Lie:
U.S. Jews must act to stop the misnomer "occupied territories"

R epeat a lie often enough and ultimately it is accepted as the truth. The Nazis used the technique. Now Washington and the media employ it.

The territories Israel liberated in 1967 are called "occupied." It's a lie, one nearly impossible to stop. Since the lie is considered truth by virtue of repetition, the "settlements" are concluded to be "illegal." Thus, one falsehood generates another. And a loan guarantee Israel needs for humanitarian purposes hangs in the balance.

Where are American Jews to kill this vicious cycle? Must one place a bomb under them to get action?

Let's start with some of the lesser media before taking on the giants. Cynthia Ozick, a brilliant author and committed champion of Jewish survival, has begun with a letter to the executive producer of the MacNeil-Lehrer News Hour of public television. She protested the reference to the land west of the Jordan as "occupied" as if this is axiomatic when in fact it is "entirely without historical foundation."

"Before the 1967 war," she wrote, "a war begun by Arab states with the intent to annihilate Israel, the territories west of the Jordan River had no internationally legitimate or historically recognized sovereign government, though they had been under Jordanian control for 19 years. Jordan, then known as Trans-Jordan, had seized those lands during the 1947 war, again a war begun by Arab states with the intent to annihilate Israel.

"Except for Britain and Pakistan, Jordan's control was not internationally recognized. Not a single Arab state recognized the legitimacy of that Arab takeover.

"Prior to Jordan's seizure of the lands west of the Jordan River in 1947, the territories in question were under the British Mandate, precisely for the reason that ownership of those territories was as yet unresolved under international law. The fact is that since the dissolution of the Ottoman Empire, there has never been an internationally recognized claimant to these territories, precisely because there has never been any internationally recognized sovereignty over them.

"Since ownership of the lands west of the Jordan River has remained unresolved from the end of the Ottoman Empire until this moment, a non-polemical, non-politicized, non-tendentious, non-Israeli, non-Arab and entirely accurate name for the lands in question would be 'disputed territories.'

"When – glibly, axiomatically and apparently without self-consciousness – you continue to say 'occupied,' you are willy-nilly, pandering to the PLO narrative and working to legitimate it."

It is on the lie so clearly and eloquently exposed by Ozick that the illegality of the settlements is based. And that is axiomatic for President Bush and Secretary of State James Baker – a lie based on a lie.

I suggest, to begin with, a test case for future action against newscasters. If on public TV the lie is still used, the time has come to withhold financial support and resign from membership. Letters to Bush and congressman are of little avail in comparison with the loss of funds. All public television need do to retain its devotees is to announce that hereafter the lie will not be uttered again.

Is that an infringement of its freedom of speech? Since when is the freedom to lie protected by the Constitution?

Would freedom of speech be extended to anyone denying that there was a Holocaust? If our enemies can lie with impunity on one major issue, they will do so on others as well,

And after we have succeeded with one transmitter that depends more on public support than others, we can proceed to do the same with other stations and their advertisers.

There have been other times when the negative attitude of public television to Jews and Jewish causes irritated me, and I would express my sentiments to friends. Their usual response was that one must indulge them because their musical and cultural programs are of such a high quality.

The response always made me think of the German generals who loved music so much they listened to symphony orchestras as Jews were burning nearby in their ovens.

If there is need for an adjective to be linked with the word "territories," neither occupied nor captured is correct. Call them "liberated" – then you have the truth!

Finally, apart from the legality of the settlements, which is attested to by no less an authority than Eugene Rostow, formerly of the State Department, there are other considerations. We do not stop Jews in New York from settling in Harlem or Crown Heights if they wish. Why should we stop Jews from settling in any part of the Holy Land whose rocky soil they want to redeem with their blood, sweat and tears?

Not only does Israeli Prime Minister Yitzchak Shamir speak sense, but Jews ought to also hear what Housing Minister Ariel Sharon is saying. You may not agree with all of it and may dislike his flamboyant manner, but he makes sense. He understands the Middle East better than anyone in power in Washington.

If Washington really wants peace in the area, Sharon may have the right formula. It is based on the assumption that the existence of Israel in the Middle East is not the cause of Arab strife and the disappearance of Israel will bring no peace. Therefore, a strong Israel is still the best bet of the democratic world.

Revel in Repetition:
Excitement and wonder can be found
in life's everyday experiences

In the 15 years I have been living in Israel and the United States, I have made the round trip at least six times each year. Many tell me that no human being – except perhaps airlines personnel – should do so much. But they do not fathom how thrilling it is on every such trip to view from the air the Statue of Liberty here or Israel's shoreline on the Mediterranean. It is as if every such view is my first.

More people owe it to themselves to learn that in many matters of great importance, the repetition of an experience ought not to make them blasé but rather should give them a deepened sense of the mysterious, the glorious, the historic, the eternal.

Perhaps an illustration will help one to understand this.

So many marriages fail because the spouses lose their sense of excitement with simply being with each other as if every day of their union was like the day they first fell in love.

I know that only the rarest couples can recapture that feeling every day – and every moment of each day. Most couples, however, do not know what it is to look at each other and feel how blessed they are. All kinds of problems – financial and familial – obsess them. And in their frustration they blame each other and often seek gratification in places other than home.

Most of us do not lose our sense of wonder when we view a beautiful sunrise or sunset. Why do we fail to see the miracle of human togetherness, the miracle of parenthood, the ecstasy of sexuality? Why is it we become so preoccupied with the problems of existence that we miss the joy of pondering the blessings we have? One says that such is human nature. We take too lightly that to which we become accustomed. But is it impossible to change one's perspective at least occasionally?

The late Dr. Leo Jung, one of America's greatest teachers of Judaism, was wont to say that Jewish law mandates for all married couples no sensuous contact with each other for fixed periods every month. They are to be followed by a renewal of the nuptials, virtually a monthly honeymoon. This is the prescription of the Halacha for the sense of excitement about which I write.

With each trip I make to Israel and the States I experience the thrill of renewing my deep ties with each country. As we fly over New York Harbor and I see the Statue of Liberty, I do not visualize the problems of racism and homelessness nor the poverty and depression of multitudes but the vision of the founding fathers, the Declaration of Independence, the Bill of Rights. I am no less committed to the elimination of the evils, but I ponder for an inspired interval the dream, the vision of great men for the New World they thought they were building.

The experience helps me to commit myself the more to the betterment of the society that gave me so much and with which I identify so emotionally.

And when I fly over Israel's coast on the Mediterranean I am not unaware of its problems, which are not due exclusively to its enemies but also to the shortcomings of its citizens. Yet I ponder for an inspired interval the dream and the vision of the founders of Zionism. Before my eyes I see the faces of Chief Rabbis Kook and Herzog and how they visualized the religious revival of Jews in their homeland, and I commit myself to their ideology – even if it appears now like it is a lost cause. The thought of what they were and what they stood for comes to mind as I see the waters of the sea touch upon the shores - the sea becomes the sea of the Talmud and the shores are the shores of the land made holy for Jews unto eternity.

Neither the failures of the United States nor the failures of the State of Israel are forgotten. But for at least precious moments I think of the hopes that I must help fulfill, which like the hopes and dreams of brides and grooms need refreshing from time to time.

This helps to make the round trips easier to take and significant in and of themselves. And I recommend it to all Jews. For a Jew to be a tourist to Israel must be different from being a tourist to any other country – if only one has a Jewish heart. And one should then do it often.

Yet the sense of excitement of which I write applies to many other areas. Students of Torah speak of it in connection with their love, which is the word of God and the insights of His sages and scholars. One would imagine that those who have celebrated Passover Seders for 30, 40 or 50 years would not find it exciting anymore. The text they can already recite from memory. Yet, each year there are new questions and new answers as I sit with my loved ones until after midnight with a sense of excitement. And the daily prayers one recites almost by rote can yield similar moments if only we give it the time we give the Seder.

Jews cherish exciting lives. And living can be exciting if only one chooses the right areas. Jews have ever found it in their family life and Torah study. Perhaps these were the only two areas available to them. But they certainly yielded many opportunities for the joys I have been describing.

The Beauty of Legal Loopholes:
Rabbinic fictions make for good reading
and better memory

Many Jews who practice and respect Jewish law have complained that the use of legal fictions impugns the integrity of that law. If a law cannot cope with a new situation, it should be changed, annulled, even dismissed as obsolete. The resort to fictions makes one feel that one is being evasive, even dishonest – not a pleasant feeling about a God-given law.

For example, if we are forbidden to engage in loan transactions that involve the payment of interest, we should either respect the prohibition or repeal it without seeking a way to avoid its application.

Jews once observed the law meticulously. Then for many centuries, under the pressure of capitalistic economic systems, they became money lenders on a grand scale. And when Jews dealt with fellow Jews, they resorted to a legal fiction. The money loaned was deemed a guaranteed investment on which the borrower paid a fixed profit. The document is used even now by many Jews.

Now, one asks, should the prohibition against interest have been made obsolete? For Jews who hold that the prohibition is from God, as are the prohibitions in the Ten Commandments, such a thing is unthinkable. But is it not wiser to help Jews survive economically in a capitalistic world, and at the time remember the fact that in a better day the law may be observed as it was first intended?

The Torah addressed itself to the Jewish people, all of whom are brothers, members of the same family. They ought to relate to each other as such. And when a brother needs financial assistance, should one come to the rescue, then seek a profit for having done so? Isn't that immoral?

To avoid this, Jews developed the free-loan societies as few others did, and the concept is still among the most highly rated in the Jewish hierarchy of mitzvot.

I cannot be sure that the great philosopher Plato ever saw our Bible. Yet in one of his dialogues he proposes laws for the ideal state of Athens, and one contains the prohibition against the giving or taking of interest. With each other, Athenians were to act as brothers. To foreigners one could give interest and one could take it from them. But within the extended family no such exploitation would be moral.

Thus the position of Jewish law is found elsewhere centuries later. And should not the memory of such a good law be kept alive? And even if it is presently subverted, in fact is this not a fringe benefit of the legal fiction?

This rationale is actually suggested in connection with another very beautiful law, the law of the sabbatical year. Unfortunately, economic conditions did not allow Jewish farmers the luxury of a seventh-year vacation. Certainly the Romans were not going to relieve the tax burden on Jews for the year in which there was no agricultural enterprise. And that was also the year for the cancellation of all debts. What a boon for the poor – a national bankruptcy relief act!

Alas, the rabbis mercifully had to resort to legal fictions to suspend the law of the sabbatical year. But is it not better to keep the memory of that law alive even if it involves a legal fiction than to let the law be forgotten, and with it perish the thought that in a better day the magnificent law will bless not only academicians but all people?

I must make it clear that the term "legal fiction" suggests nothing pejorative to a student of the law. I was surprised that a rabbi, translating a great work by one Rabbi S. Y. Zevin, deplored the characterization of the document of sale which many Jews use to get rid of *chometz* before Passover as a legal fiction, which it is. He held that the sale was real, not fictitious.

So are all legal fictions real? They create very real legal relationships. Yet they are called legal fictions because they are designed to alter legal relationships or consequences that otherwise might have been. The Jew wants to retain his chometz until after

Passover and usually does, though this is forbidden by Jewish law. So he sells it. True, it is a real, valid sale, but who is unaware of what the purpose is and what the net result will be?

There was a time when Jews were careful to rid themselves of all chometz in their possession. It was as if they programmed their eating of bread for weeks in advance of the holiday so that all was consumed before Passover.

But then came the time when Jews owned granaries or had liquor concessions. Could they destroy their stocks before the holiday without sustaining very heavy losses? So the rabbis created the instrument of sale. It is a very real sale, by law, but in fact it was known what would be the fate of those stocks after the holiday.

I do hope that those who feel negatively about legal fictions in Jewish law will alter their attitude. If anyone thinks legal fictions do not exist in Jewish law, they are simply mistaken. Instead of denying it, they ought to help Jews appreciate how Jewish law uses legal fictions to keep the past as part of our collective memory, even as the law copes with the needs of the present and future.

Making waves:
U.S. Jewish groups must lead
the fight against "territories" lie

F ervently I pray that Jewish organizations soon will find the courage to summon American Jews to march on Washington. Not for financial help for Israel, but to put an end to the lie that Israel is violating any international law and to affirm that the so-called "occupied territories" are rightfully Israel's and the settlements are legal beyond question or doubt.

The repeated lies of Bush and Baker impel me to write as often as I do about this lest Jews begin to believe the lies because of their repetition.

One of the finest features of the Zionist movement is that it always respected and abided by international law.

Everything it achieved was by lawful purchase, not by conquest. And there is a historic, traditional Jewish law basis for it.

Jews twice have lost their independence – in 536 B.C.E., when the Babylonians captured Jerusalem, and in 71 C.E. when it was taken by the Romans. Our sages regarded the conquest of the Babylonians as legal, while that of the Romans was not. The Jews recognized the title of the Babylonians to the land but not that of Rome.

The difference was clear to them. The Babylonians took by conquest what the Jews had acquired by conquest from the Canaanites. Thus, one conquest justified a succeeding one. However, the Romans conquered what was acquired by the Jews by law – by the edict of the Persian emperor and because of their settlement on the land pursuant to an imperial grant recognized by international law. Conquest never vitiates a title lawfully acquired.

Every step the Zionists ever took was lawful. Every inch of land was paid for. What the Jordanians conquered in 1948 – illegally, brazenly, cruelly – was retaken in 1967, and what Israel now holds it is entitled to not by virtue of what happened in 1967 alone but also because of the status of the area in 1948 and even earlier. If ever any country acted with chutzpah, it is Jordan and its Arab allies.

I am no expert in international law, but the late Professor Julius Stone of Australia was one of the greatest. He was one of the most respected jurists in the world; his books are masterpieces cited as authority whenever law generally, international law in particular, is studied and practiced. Moreover, in his conclusions he draws from the writings of a colleague, Professor Stephen Schwebel, a judge of the International Court of Justice.

In 1980 Stone wrote a short work titled "Israel and Palestine" dealing with the principles of international law involved in the conflict between Israel and the world, not only the Arabs who have mesmerized humanity that justice is on their side.

It is difficult to summarize Stone's arguments in a brief essay. Suffice it to say that he holds Israel's position in the conflict to be the only just one, and that what the Arabs are arguing is "subversion both of basic international law principles, and of rights and obligations in states under them" and "grotesque reversals of the United Nations' own positions of the preceding quarter century, as part of a wide and illicit rewriting of history." Theirs is "an assault with covert as well as overt elements on the international legal order."

I was impressed especially with Stone's argument that the Palestinians have no right whatever to a state and who more than Jews have joined the wagon of their enemies to shed tears for those who would destroy them.

There is a doctrine of self-determination in international law, but the people who claim it must constitute a nation "with a common endowment of distinctive language or ethnic origin or history and tradition, and the like, distinctive from others among whom it lives, associated with a particular territory, and *lacking* (italics mine) an independent territorial home in which it may live."

The PLO itself never claimed that the Palestinians are anything but the same as Jordanians, Syrians and Lebanese. "We are one people," it says. And it is only to fight Zionism that those of them

who live in Israel claim a separate identity, and it is apparent that
the claim is for a limited period – until Israel will be reunited with
Jordan, Lebanon and Syria. Thus, can I shed tears for those who
have created a figment of imagination as the instrument to destroy my people and my homeland?

When Zionists affirm that the Palestinians have a state they
are right. They have more than one. If they do not want to move
there, they have no more right to defy Israel than African Americans in Harlem can claim a state in central Manhattan or the
Bronx. And Washington is "taken in" by the PLO as it is taken in
by Saddam Hussein, and some Americans accept the fiction as fact
– the vicious fairy tale as a plea for justice.

Yet the defense agencies of American Jewry are afraid to speak
up – not just for Jews or Israel, but for tried and established principles of law upon which the future of world peace depends.

A Legacy of Survival:
Perseverance has consistently
saved Jews from persecution

Jews often wonder why they are almost universally hated. Indeed, in a number of universities this question has become the theme for academic study and expensive research projects. And just as the investigations multiply, so do the organizations seeking to put an end to the cancer.

I prefer research on another question: Why did so many Jews remain Jews despite persecution, crusades, pogroms and, finally, the Holocaust? And why are so many Israelis calm despite the virtual lynching that Washington has orchestrated for them as all the Arab countries join with the PLO in the hope that they can precipitate another holocaust?

It is important that we rejoice in the fact that our loyalty to peoplehood and tradition is as deep as it is. Of course, there have been losses along the way: Apostasy, assimilation and even suicides. As there will continue to be falloff, what must we do to increase and assist those who wish to remain committed to Judaism?

Most Jewish universities are secularist in their commitment, and since they know the answer to be one that favors religion, they would rather ignore it. But that answer is the answer no matter how hard we try to close our eyes to it.

For millennia, Jews were loyal to Judaism because it was their faith. Sometimes the simpler the Jew's faith, the less intellectual he was, the more likely he was not to yield to the oppressor. If his vision of the hereafter was clear, if he firmly believed in its existence, he might even martyr himself when the challenge arose.

Other Jews did not want to assimilate and thus be a constituent of the Jew-hating world. They saw the hereafter in their offspring and did not want their descendants to be in the ranks of those trying to put an end to Jewish existence.

There were those who simply loved being Jewish, wanting to bequeath that love to future generations in the hope that those generations might also experience that which was loved, that they might benefit for having been blessed by the Jewish life.

Some stayed Jewish in the spirit of resistance, choosing to be heroic by saying to the anti-Semite that he will not be permitted to win. Many of us enjoy defying the villain.

Of considerable importance to our survival is an article of faith, rooted in Judaism but not exclusively religious: The belief that there will always be Jews and Judaism. No matter how hard the anti-Semite might try he will not win. The prophet Isaiah said it thousands of years ago: "No instrument used to destroy you will avail." (*Isaiah* 54:17) Many have tried but we remain an eternal people.

Why is this doctrine so powerful? Simply because it makes for a form of this-worldly immortality. It allows Jews to feel that they belong to a people that can't be knocked out, allowing us a vicarious immortality. The bearing of children is the most natural fulfillment of this; so many Jewish traditions have blossomed with regard to memorial prayers and services by children. These traditions provide continuity without terminus.

In Germany with the U.S. military after World War II, I heard some unforgettable testimony to our belief that we are indeed an eternal people.

One victim of the Holocaust was certain that he would perish, as would Jewish civilization, but that a Jew somewhere might survive. Fearing that the Nazis would destroy the Hebrew prayerbook, he hand-copied the prayerbook from beginning to end. It was passed on from victim to survivor until the war ended, when it was placed in one of the Holocaust museums for all to see.

At least one great talmudist and philosopher – who also did not survive – continued to write books throughout his ordeal. His manuscripts written in the concentration camps miraculously found their way to Rabbi M.M. Kasher, who under the auspices of Yeshiva University published a number of volumes of extraordinary value to experts in both Jewish law and Jewish philosophy.

Perhaps the most convincing testimony to our inherent spiritual optimism is the determination of so many Holocaust survivors to have large families. "Survivors have a higher birthrate than American Jews," wrote William Helmreich of CUNY's Graduate Center, "one of the clearest signs that survivors believe in the future, namely that they choose to bring children into a world that was once so cruel to them."

Jews have persistently displayed a drive not only to be identified with an eternal people but to experience the gratification that comes from making us eternal.

I am only suggesting a number of answers to my question, answers derived from personal experience. Perhaps scholarly research might help one to do better. Nevertheless, the cumulative impact of all these answers reassures me that there will always be Jews and Judaism.

God Himself has promised no less.

Needed for Jewish Survival:
Toleration, Civility

A t Bar-Ilan University's last conference on Jewish unity, I was asked whether I still believed it was possible to achieve the goal. I had to make it clear once again that if we conceived of Jewish unity as agreement by all Jews on any subject, then we were wasting our time. Indeed, there is not a single subject on which every Jew would vote the same way.

Even in their attitude toward anti-Semites they differ. Some cherish the anti-Semites who would persecute or eliminate the brethren they don't like. Many prefer to live under non-Jewish rule, Christian or Moslem, than to live under Jewish rule. And that means that even Israel does not evoke the loyalty of, or help from, more than a majority of Jews.

It must be obvious, therefore, that we are searching not for unanimity of issues or programs or beliefs but rather for civility, the traditional *derech eretz*, which ought characterize our behavior toward all people created in the image of God and especially toward our coreligionsts with whom we constitute one big family.

Perhaps to avoid giving the wrong impression, we will change the name of our conference and substitute for the term unity either civility, or derech eretz, or still another phrase that plays an important part in traditional Jewish law – *darchei shalom,* the ways of peace. These terms describe more accurately what we are seeking. And these are goals which we can hope to achieve at least from most Jews. If I believe that these were unattainable goals for Jews, then I do not know that the survival of the Jewish people would be possible or desirable.

Only to preserve the genes of genius with which many of our people seem to be endowed in order to contribute to civilization is hardly worth the price Jews have to pay in order to continue in being. And unless we can prove that we have it in us to be a model people in accordance with our historic covenant with God, then we merit the punishment He seems to be meting out to us in every generation. Our sages tell us that it was because of our hatred of each other than the second Jewish commonwealth came to an end. We should do all in our power to spare the third from a similar fate.

Fortunate we are that more and more Jews are becoming aware of the need for civility in our interpersonal relations. Pressure is being exercised on members of the Knesset to deport themselves toward each other with derech eretz. I have always admired the British members of Parliament. Their disputes are often indescribably heated. They express their views with passionate eloquence. But they never forget that the men whom they are addressing and with whom they are debating are gentlemen worthy of respectful address.

Israeli legislators have yet to master this attitude and skill. And, unfortunately, the female members are as much to be censured for their ugly performance as the males. Must a woman, even when she is angry in debate, behave like a tigress instead of as a loving mother critical of her child? It is the female members who ought, in fact, to civilize their male counterparts.

However, what hurts me more than anything else is that Jews steeped in the Torah tradition, learned rabbis and even the organizations they form do not insist on maintaining standards of derech eretz in their council and toward each other.

When I was active in New York's rabbinate, I often said it was a pleasure to attend meetings of rabbis when Orthodox, Conservative and Reform were present, and not such a pleasure when the group was all of one commitment. When the group was mixed, everyone was on his best behavior. There was mutual respect. Differences were cordially expressed. Almost never was there venom or vitriol. When the group was not mixed, outbursts of anger, intolerance, even envy and hatred, could be expected.

What can be done about it? At our last conference it was suggested that since most Jews would agree that civility is the minimum we must expect from each other, we should ignore the extremists, who are usually more guilty of uncivil behavior. We should focus only on the presumably civil majority, or at least the majority that holds civility as a value.

The suggestion may make sense. But do we not have a responsibility toward all Jews, even those who do not want what we have to offer? We are not allowed to despair about any Jew. We must try to redeem all for the good life. And it may be that if we act civilly toward those who do not cherish civility, they too may one day choose to emulate what they once rejected.

The best way to achieve civility among Jews is to practice it even with the uncivil. It is not easy to exercise such self-control. But hardly a worthy goal is ever achieved without discipline. The Talmud tells us how often people tried to overcome the great Hillel's patience and force him to lose his temper. But he was a model of both firmness and human kindness at the same time. (*Shabbat* 31a)

We must act as Hillel and never lose our temper. Yet we must also learn from him to be firm. In the overwhelming majority of controversies he and his disciples had with Shamai and his school, the school of Hillel took a lenient position for Jews rather than a demanding or exacting one. And they were not intimidated by the opposition. They did not fear that they were not adequately "religious." They did not deem their views any less in the Torah tradition that the views of their opponents. And it is likely that their opponents never taunted them as being less God-fearing, less saintly, less loyal to the covenant.

The situation is quite different today, although there is good reason to believe that this state of affairs is perennial. In the Middle Ages the opponents of Maimonides were not quite as restrained as we would have wanted them to be. And the great Rabbi Naphtali Zevi Yehudah Berlin wrote only a century ago in several places in his commentary on the Bible about those Jews who always suspected their coreligionists of not being sufficiently religious and of how God disapproves of their attitude. Toleration is a manifestation of civility. In Berlin's day in a comparatively homogenous community the malady of the present had already made its appearance. He attacked this malady vigorously and deemed those responsible for it the spiritual heirs of Korach who once led the mutiny against Moses.

Needless to say when I took the position that in Israel's present crises and its need for unity, the issue "Who is a Jew?" can easily be put aside, I knew that I would be the victim of very uncivil re-actions. This is also happening to other modern Orthodox rabbis who took the same stand.

But we must not lose our tempers. We cannot respond to venomous attacks in kind. When we know that we are in the right, we must be firm in our convictions and not be intimidated by those who question how we can hold differently from even a dozen different Orthodox organizations. Without fury and without bitterness we must make our point. We must fight for the right in the right way.

I once preached to Israel's religious Zionists that there is also a religious way to engage in politics, and if politics cannot be practiced in a religious way – consonant with spiritual and ethical requirements – then religionists had better not practice politics. This message all so-called religious political parties ought to take to heart.

The Real Meaning of a Mistranslated Biblical Verse

Very few verses of the Bible are as well known as one in the 19th chapter of Leviticus, "And thou shalt love thy neighbor as thyself." (*Leviticus* 19:18) So it pains me to tell my core-ligionists that the meaning of the original Hebrew text is quite different.

Sometimes I feel that I ought to accuse Christians of deliberately popularizing the false translation, even if the earliest Greek rendition supports what they have done. But at least we owe them thanks for making the verse universally known. They did this so well that most Jews think that the verse is derived from the New Testament.

In any event, so important a command merits more thought than we have given it. Because it sounds so good, we forget that it is impossible to perform it. And would God have commanded what mankind cannot fulfill? The Torah never commands us to do that which is beyond our capacity. Is the command to love one's neighbor as oneself therefore meaningless, or are we misreading it? Needless to say, the latter is the more correct answer.

Furthermore, the rabbis found other verses that permit men to give priority to the saving of their own lives. This would contradict the notion that we must love our neighbor as we love ourselves. If we have the right to prefer our own survival to the survival of others, then we are not loving our neighbor as we love ourselves. Is the Bible contradicting itself?

The correct interpretation is that given by Maimonides (*Hilchot De'ot* 6:3) and other medieval commentators. We are commanded to love for our neighbor that which we love for ourselves. That which we want for ourselves we should wish for our neighbors as well – wealth and health, things and status, reputation and peace of mind, all the blessings that human beings usually crave. We must not begrudge others what we enjoy. From the correct interpretation come the two general rules: Do unto others as you would have others do unto you and do not do unto others what you would not have others do unto you.

In effect, the verse is urging us to help all mankind be blessed. If we ourselves can contribute to that end, so much the better. If we cannot, then at least we should not begrudge others as we would not want to be begrudged if we had fared better.

For me the strongest argument is to be found in the 34th verse of the same chapter. Identical language is used there. First, we are told to treat the stranger in our midst as an equal, then to love for him what we would love for ourselves. It is inescapable that the verse is calling for the equality of the citizen and sojourner in our midst. It is not a plea for self-sacrifice but rather for the elimination of the difference between first and second-class citizens.

Why Christianity could not fathom this for 2,000 years I do not know. Did its teachers maliciously avoid reading the verse properly so that Jews would not be given equal status with them in their society? Or is an infidel of a lower breed than a stranger so that discrimination could be justified that way?

In any event, I feel very strongly that the time has come to stop quoting the incorrect translation of a verse which only prompts its rejection.

However, the correct translation gives us a goal which we can fulfill. We do not have to place it beyond the reach of humans. We need only promote equality and we have to our credit the performance of the mitzvah. And this is the way Jews see all the commandments. They can be performed by all men. One does not have to be superhuman to do the bidding of the Torah. The Torah was given to humans for humans – even in human language – and within our reach is total obedience.

So much for the text itself. However, its timeliness in international affairs is a good reason for giving it the look I am suggesting. What is one of the principal areas of Jewish concern today if not the almost congenital incapacity of nations to want for Jews what they want for themselves? They want their peoplehood recognized, but the peoplehood of Jews is a concept they don't grasp. They loathe accepting it.

I remember 40 years after V-E Day how difficult it was for me to make this point to American diplomats and generals. And now that there is a Jewish State, how difficult it is for them to tolerate its doing what other states do without any opposition whatever. Everyone knows that there is a double standard in the United Nations – one for all states and another for Israel. Equality of status – in rights and duties – is the rule for all but the Jewish State. They simply don't wish for us what they wish for themselves.

The same reluctance to give us equal status is especially to be found in the academic world. And Jews in academia are not even sensitive to their second-class status. Perhaps this is so because they themselves helped to create the condition. True, today they find employment – unlike the period between the world wars. But why, one asks, is Jewish civilization of less importance in the world of the intellectual than Egyptian, Greek or Roman civilization? Does Egyptian civilization play a greater role in the lives of the people of the west than Jewish civilization, the Bible and all of its values? And did the Greeks or Romans contribute more to the development of British and American political institutions than the law of Moses? Why then should Jewish civilization count only as a prelude to Christianity and not warrant in its own right the place in academia that other civilizations enjoy?

To me it seems crystal clear. The nations of the earth do not want for Jews what they want for themselves. They will quote the incorrect translation of the immortal verse in speeches and perorations. It is safe to do that. No one need take it seriously. But the correct meaning of the verse would demand a different pattern of behavior. And for that Jews must want – and wait – and wait.

As John Galsworthy once said, "From the Jew I have learned to wait." This is the existential situation of our people – to hope and wait for the Messiah.

The Importance of Voluntarism in the Welfare State

A conference was held in Israel recently on voluntarism. The subject has become especially important because the modern state, even a democratic one, has assumed most functions once performed by volunteer individuals and groups. The volunteers were not paid professionals, and what they did was in response to an inner drive to alleviate human suffering.

With the emergence of the welfare state, much of today's social work is no longer in their hands. Nonetheless, there is great need of the volunteers. Not only are they needed for the well-being of the indigent, but what they do ultimately contributes to their own well-being.

At that conference I reported on a number of insights from Jewish sources. There was a time in Jewish history when it was through donations to charitable causes that the poor were aided. It was subsequently discovered that reliance on voluntary gifts was not adequate. Jewish communities, therefore, resorted to taxing their constituents to help the needy. This was coercion of the more affluent to assist the less affluent. Yet voluntary *tzedakah*, charity, was still urged as a great mitzvah.

There was coercion with regard to specific amounts, and there was voluntarism for additional sums. By the same token, the welfare state may now do much, but it can never do enough. The professional civil servant may perform his or her duty admirably, but there is room for that extra something which the law does not provide. Thus voluntarism has its place and it is an area worthy of study. As one might have expected, Judaism has much to say about it.

Begin with the Bible. Undoubtedly, kings built castles and equipped their armies and paid soldiers from taxes. But God's tabernacle was to be built from gifts given voluntarily – "as much as a man's heart chose to give." (*Exodus* 25:2) Performance of any religious obligation must be voluntary. Otherwise, it is absurd. If it is not a willing response to God, what spiritual meaning can it have?

Indeed, even those who served God full-time – the priests and the Levites – were also compensated by gifts which were not coerced. Most people are not aware of this. They know that the institution of tithes impoverished many Christians during the Middle Ages and may have been one of the causes for the French Revolution. However, the Bible is not to be blamed.

The rabbis, millenia ago, so understood the Bible that there were no sanctions for the collection of these gifts. The state did not collect the tithes, nor were the priests and Levites permitted to solicit them. They were not even permitted to assist in the harvesting of crops lest their presence constitute an indirect hint that they should receive their share.

Jews were exhorted to pay the tithes, but that was all. As a matter of fact, a man might simply set the tithe aside and do no more. The rest of his crop might be eaten with violating any religious prohibition.

Two objectives were achieved by permitting the system of tithes to operate on a voluntary basis. First, philanthropy would remain within the province of free will. Second, the clergy would receive their due in the measure in which they were beloved by the people. Both objectives would have been defeated had the state enforced collection. And that is why, despite the great laxity that prevailed in payment of tithes by peasants, the rabbis never gave these tithes the status of a tax.

The same was generally true of gifts to the priests who took care of the sacrifices in the Temple. In most cases, priests were to receive only a share of voluntary offerings for services rendered.

All the rabbinic precautions, however, did not help prevent these servants of the Lord from aggrandizing their power and influence, and rabbis ultimately replaced them. And the rabbis' services too were to be wholly voluntary. Voluntarism was to be the hallmark of the custodians of the Law.

If the rabbi did perform a ritualistic service, he could lawfully be compensated only for the time he had given and for the loss he had sustained by being taken away from his non-rabbinic vocation, whatever it might be. The same rule applied to cantors or readers of the Law, who, because their service was rendered on the Sabbath, could only be paid for the time they spent in preparation for the Sabbath.

Centuries before the Protestant development of a non-professional clergy, Judaism was putting it into practice. This idea later found its most vivid expression among the Jews of Eastern Europe. Every Jewish community in East Europe supported at least one rabbi, but in each there were scores of others, also ordained and equally learned in the Law, who chose not to make the Torah their "trade." The yeshiva student, preparing for the rabbinate, looked forward to nothing better than to devote his life to study for its own sake (*Torah li'shmah*) rather than for the sake of a livelihood.

The Talmud mentions no fewer than 100 rabbis who were artisans by profession. In fact, the Talmudic rabbi was the true successor of the Judean prophet and the Pharisaic scribe, retaining absolute financial independence.

This limitation was based on the simple fact that God is available to people gratis. Therefore, those who act as His surrogates must do the same. They too must be available without compensation. They can be reimbursed for their pecuniary losses but no more.

The most impressive of all services that had been voluntary in Jewish life from time immemorial was service to the dead. There may be good reasons for its becoming professionalized in our day, but the traditional *chevra kadisha* – the men or women who took over when one died and rendered every necessary service until the bereaved returned to normal routines – was the most respected group in the vast array of Jewish societies attending the needy. No one would dream of taking money for this service. And it is the only communal group accorded the adjective "holy."

Indeed, the rabbis distinguished between tzedakah and *gemillat chesed*, the rendering of a kindly act. (*Sukkah* 59b) The latter ranked higher in the hierarchy of Jewish values than the former. Why? For three reasons. Charity one gives only with one's financial resources. A kindly act one renders with one's body as well. One gives charity only to the living; kindly acts are performed also for the dead. And charity one gives only to the poor. But the rich too are in need of kindly acts.

There is one more difference. The state can take the place of individuals insofar as charity is concerned. It can use its power of taxation and provide all that the needy require. But there is no way to coerce kindly acts. These can come only from volunteers, and every human being, at one time or another, want them – rich or poor, living or dead.

Voluntarism must be encouraged, especially in a society in which there is an abundance of leisure. It is the best way to make that time meaningful – and avoid ennui and depression.

Why Jews Abhor Bloodshed:
Tenets of Judaism, especially dietary laws,
instill reverence for life

How could one possibly associate God's name with such a cruel, bloodthirsty deed? A former student, now a highly respected colleague, asked me this question the day a Palestinian Arab fatally stabbed a 15-year-old Jewish girl and shouted that the heinous murder was in the name of God.

Unfortunately, this has been happening ever since God created man, and no society has as yet succeeded in eliminating acts of violence committed for a higher cause.

Most people have a conscience. When their conscience tries to inhibit them, they find justification for ignoring it. When Nero burned Rome, he did it to save Rome from the inroads of the dangerous Christians. When Nazis cremated millions, they too were protecting humanity from inferior breeds. When Arab fathers kill their daughters who shame them, they do so for the family's honor.

Unlike Gandhi – whose unqualified refusal to engage in violence is well known – Jews did not embrace that doctrine. They preferred resistance to evil and even, if necessary, a resort to violence to end violence. The best that Judaism sought to accomplish was curbing violence and, if more was possible, its humanization. If Jews had heeded Gandhi's counsel during the Holocaust, there would have been no survivors and Hitler might now be ruling the world.

But Judaism did induce in Jews a hatred for bloodshed. The dietary laws especially contributed to that aversion from the cradle to the grave.

Through our tradition we were made very aware that there is no greater threat to the human personality than homicide. Therefore, God feared that its incidence would increase because of man's carnivorous habits. It appears from a chapter of Genesis that God had hoped that man would be herbivorous. Only after the flood in Noah's day was permission granted to man to eat the flesh of animals. (*See Genesis* 9:1-4)

This, however, might cause man to esteem life lightly. Therefore, the commandment against murder and suicide was promulgated simultaneously. (*Ibid.* v. 5-6) Sharing the fears of ethical vegetarians, the Bible suggested that the shedding of the blood of an animal even for the purpose of food might make man callous to the shedding of the blood of fellow humans.

The Bible, therefore, did more than prohibit murder. It sought to induce an aversion for blood. The Law's maxim was that blood was life. (*Ibid.*) Consequently, the drinking of blood was prohibited. Moreover, the horrifying practice of barbarisms to cut steaks from live animals for food was also enjoined.

This was a minimal prohibition incumbent on all humanity. For Israel, however, there were additional proscriptions. Jews were not to eat meat unless the animal was so slaughtered that its death was immediate and the maximum amount of blood was removed from the body and tissues at the same time. Even after this manner of slaughter, the meat must be soaked and salted or broiled so that its blood content was further reduced. (*See* Shulchan Aruch Y.D. regarding the laws of Shehitah.) Perhaps some nutritive benefits were lost, but no Jew could fail to be impressed by the moral suggestion that, though the eating of meat was permitted, Jews must be ultra-careful, even squeamish, about eating blood.

Thus their almost congenital aversion to war, dueling and murder was no accident. It was definitely the consequence of the Torah's preoccupation with the prohibition regarding blood. (In one instance, the method of slaughter was varied so that the blood was not speedily removed, but that situation involved atonement for murder. This different method of slaughter was, so to speak, a reflection of the murderer's performance.)

Yet even if the manner of removing the blood had ethical significance, what of the act of slaughter itself? What could induce a greater disrespect for life than the act of killing the beast? Visitors to slaughterhouses may behold how coarse and vulgar are the men who grip the animals, swing the sledgehammers and then, in fun and frolic, cut up the cadavers. That we may have meat, alas, some human beings must be made callous.

This is something that Jewish law sought to avoid. And in order that no Jew who eats meat should do so at the cost of a brother's loss of humanity and refinement, qualifications to become a slaughterer were so numerous and so exalted that the slaughterer became a religious functionary. Upon him higher standards of ethical and ritualistic behavior were imposed than upon rabbis or cantors. To prevent degradation, requirements were exalted to the opposite extreme. He was to be learned in Torah, a man of impeachable trustworthiness and integrity, capable of great personal sacrifice and absolutely immune to any kind of pecuniary appeal.

Pious Jews were wont to boast that they ate from the *Shehitah*, or slaughter of saints. No greater compliment could be paid a man than to say that a famous rabbi ate the meat of an animal he had slain. Such was the Torah's method to save from degradation not only him who eats the meat but him who makes it available!

Jews generally abhorred human bloodshed to such an extent that though the Bible permitted capital punishment, it was almost totally abolished in Jewish society. (*Talmud Makkot* 7a) There were also laws to control cruelty and bestiality in times of war. (*See Ramban Hilchot Melachim* Chapter 6.) There were even laws to limit the circumstances in which one could be a martyr and sacrifice oneself for God's sake. (*Talmud Sanhedrin* 74a)

All of this may account for the relatively small number of Jews who commit crimes of violence. However, the daughter religions of Israel did not, as Jews did, discourage violence in general and violence for the sake of God.

Jews could engage in violence to prevent an innocent person's murder or woman's rape but not to prevent a Jew from defying God or engaging in an idolatrous practice or the desecration of the Sabbath. (*Mishah Sanhedrin* 8:7)

There was no minor brake on fanaticism or fundamentalism. In medieval Europe both Christians and Moslems massacred Jews in God's name, and even Daniel Dafoe, author of the classic "Robinson Crusoe," defended laws that outlawed religious toleration. The "heretics" were "snakes" who should be killed with impunity.

Thus, one can expect a fanatic to kill a Jewish child for God's sake more readily than a Jew would reciprocate. And it hurts when a Jewish organization – to raise funds – equates the religious extremism of Jews with the extremism of Moslems in Israel.

It is consummately to be hoped that all killing for God's sake will cease. That is His will. He is well able to take care of His enemies by Himself.

Why Not Give New Ideas a Fair Chance?

It is generally said that Judaism must cope with the fact of modern life. But one can cope in several ways. Most people resolve the problem by assuming that everything modern is good and, therefore, Judaism must be trimmed to fit.

Others are bold enough to ask whether all that is modern is truly desirable and reject much of it, preferring to concentrate on the Jewish way of life. There are some, however, who resist everything modern. If it is new they deem it bad, alleging that the Torah forbids it.

I was raised by a father who did not automatically reject every new idea of the modern world. He gave new ideas considerable thought and was willing to experiment with them. The Jewish people were even receptive to the new, especially if it might improve upon the old ways and deepen one's understanding and appreciation of the traditional faith and practice. Sometimes the new is even fulfillment of a cherished Torah objective. Thus the manner in which we relate to that which is new calls for suspended judgment, prolonged experimentation and evaluation, and, in the end, either total acceptance or rejection, or a position in between the two.

I can cite one example. Though my father received his education exclusively in Lithuanian yeshivot, he did not reject a new method in Jewish education which called for the teaching of Hebrew as the mother tongue and a living language.

Most of his colleagues preferred the study of Hebrew as we now study a second language – translating from Hebrew into Yiddish or English. My father did not feel that because a method was new it was not to be tried.

The issue is now of no significance in Israel where Hebrew is the mother tongue for all Jews except a tiny minority who reject the new only because it is new. But in the Diaspora it is still a problem and it would be folly for a rabbi or group of rabbis to pontificate whether one method is more proper halachically than another. In such matters one should retain an open mind and certainly not pronounce bans. The late president of Yeshiva University, Dr. Samuel Belkin, was often critical of the frequent resort to bans and would call it "government by *issurim* (taboos)."

Many years ago, when I served the Far Rockaway Jewish community, the board of education of its major day school debated the issue whether girls were to be taught the same curriculum as boys. It was then well-known that two opposing views were entertained – one by Rabbi Joseph Soloveitchik and the other by Rabbi Moshe Feinstein.

The board, by a vote of 9 to 6, simply decided to send the issue to Soloveitchik, whose answer was known to be in the affirmative and it was really unnecessary to submit the issue to him. But the principal of the school thought it was forbidden to teach the girls Talmud and he invalidated the board's decision.

The controversy continues today. The study of Talmud appears to be for men only. Rare is the school that makes the same opportunity available to girls as it does to boys and rare is the woman who can today become a great Talmudic scholar.

I know this will change. It happened in Israel with regard to women's suffrage. In his lifetime, Chief Rabbi Uziel did not have the courage to lift the ban against women's suffrage. His view in favor was published after his death. And the same will happen with the study of Talmud. The day will come when there will be many women who will be experts in Talmud just as there once were only isolated instances.

Now there is a new controversy – or rather an old one which has reared its head again. It is the problem of coeducation. May boys and girls be taught in the same high schools? And is the issue one which calls for the pronouncement of a ban or a taboo?

Coeducation is an issue that has concerned educators of all denominations, and even secularists. The very existence in public education of boys' and girls' high schools proves there is no consensus on what is the better way. Does the presence of girls distract the boys and give them impure thoughts? Or does the presence of girls refine the boys and give them a healthier approach to sexuality than, for example, one is apt to find in the yeshiva high schools of our day? Frankly, I do not have the answer.

There are some heads of yeshivot who are certain they know what is best and they add to the prohibitions contained in the Torah – the kind of "government by issurim" of which Belkin spoke. Would it not have been sufficient if they expressed their conviction as to what they feel is better, and not disregard the possibility that there is another view, perhaps one as legitimate, worthy of at least suspended judgment and continuing observation and study?

Do they really think yeshivot have succeeded in the context of modern society to transmit better attitudes and more wholesome approaches to sexuality than schools where boys learn early to relate with respect to girls in the same class, even as the girls avoid the seductive attire that distracts? I am not so sure, and I wish more of my colleagues would be similarly open-minded and ambivalent. A little skepticism about their own omniscience will at least yield a modicum of humility.

I repeat – I do not know which is the better way. However, to give sanction to only one way, and to prohibit the other, is to add another divisive factor to Jewish life. And will there be no end to the issues that divide us? Or do the rabbis creating the issurim really crave divisiveness so that there will be no doubt in anyone's mind as to who are the real guardians of the tradition? I prefer my father's way – to give a new idea that is clearly not prohibited a chance to prove itself before it is rejected.

ARTICLE

Thoughts on the Holocaust

Christians and Jews alike honor Elie Wiesel for many reasons, but not the least of them is the way he – like a prophet of old – has forced philosophers and theologians to ponder the impact of the Holocaust on their conceptions of God and human nature. He is not so presumptuous as to claim that he has answers to the mind-boggling questions. I certainly do not have them either, but I do want to put an end to what I consider truly sophomoric efforts by others to illuminate a darkness that is simply impenetrable.

I should say at the very outset that whenever I write about the Holocaust, I do so with fear and trepidation. For me it is like writing about the unknowable. People who experienced its horrors have a right to relate the facts, what they saw and heard, what they did, how they felt, how they reacted. They may also indulge in generalizations about the behavior of fellow victims and about what they think precipitated the indescribable tragedy. I indulge them even the right to curse or bless God.

What I cannot tolerate are attempts by historians to be judgmental about the martyrs and to decide whether their behavior was saintly or villainous. When these historians also are ignorant of the nature of Jewish life in the countries of Jewish suffering and of the content of the Jewish tradition throughout the ages, they articulate views that I often find offensive. And when anyone tries to explain why God permitted it to happen, I virtually scream. I respect the drive of those who believe in God to discover why God behaved as He did. Yet I would much rather submit that the answer is beyond man and leave it at that. Intellectual honesty sometimes demands that we admit that we cannot know what will never be known until God Himself tells us.

Why God acted or failed to act as He did is beyond us. But certainly it was not our sins that caused the Holocaust. Only non-

Jews caused it. Our sin, if any, was our blindness in not anticipating it and our inertia and silence while it was happening.

True, we may have sinned as a people and as individuals. But is the punishment commensurate with the gravity or heinousness of the sin? We would resent a human judge who acted in this way. Can we not, therefore, ask whether the Judge of all the earth should not be at least as just as a human judge?

I know many a colleague who still maintains that God punished us. I wish they would shut their mouths once and for all. Not only are they talking nonsense but they are also relieving the Christian and Moslem worlds of guilt. And they are justifying another Holocaust, for we are less righteous now than we ever were. (Even as I write this I feel myself screaming within me.)

For Jewish philosophers of all ages the problem of evil generally was one with which they could hardly cope. And there are some today who superficially or with depth still write on the subject, which is given the impressive name "the problem of the theodicy." Somehow, prior to World War II the answers may not have satisfied but we could live with the paradox that a benign God might create evil for a purpose known to Him, and we tolerated its continuance at least until the end of days. Most of the rationalization was ridden with doubt, but somehow religious faith was not shaken massively.

However, the death of six million Jews – millions of others – because of the indescribable bestiality of Hitler was too tragic a phenomenon not to upset all prior views. One simply could not believe that God would not intercede to save. The result was either a denial of God or total resignation to Him, because any hypothesis other than His existence made life meaningless. One chose God because it was the only viable alternative.

I wish that I had the infinite wisdom necessary to give a satisfactory answer. I shall delude neither myself nor anyone else by suggesting that I am even close to an explanation. If I did, I could make myself immortal – I would be as immortal as the Infinite because I fathomed His ways. But one explanation I must reject, and from that rejection perhaps one will discover a ray of light that will ennoble our lives and experiences.

The one explanation, which I first heard from the lips of Martin Buber, and thereafter from many Jewish thinkers, traditional and nontraditional, is that the period of the Holocaust was a period of *Hester Panim* for God. He simply hid His face – He turned away from man, and man and his id ran amok, with the resulting devastation. The notion is suggested in Deuteronomy. (*Deuteronomy* 31:18) At times God, so to speak, withdraws from His preoccupation with His covenanted people and havoc follows.

I do not know how I had the hutzpah thirty years ago to argue with Martin Buber. But I did, and now that I am older, I can be even more daring.

I cannot accept the idea that an omniscient, omnipotent God would ever make Himself unaware of what is happening on earth. Perforce He must know everything at all times. To take literally the biblical expression that God hides His face is to make too anthropomorphic a judgment. A God who is so petty as to yield to pique is too ignoble a God for man to worship! The verses in Deuteronomy that suggest the notion must mean something else.

I cannot imagine that Martin Buber was a literalist with regard to other anthropomorphic passages in the Bible. Would he be so literalist with regard to Moses' wish to see God's face and God's reply that only His back could be seen? Maimonides gives this passage a magnificent allegorical interpretation. Why then must we moderns become literal with regard to similar passages of the Bible and portray God as playing "hide-and-seek" with us?

If we are unequivocal in our commitment to the idea that God knows all and can do all because He is omniscient and omnipotent, then we must assume that He knew what was happening but intentionally did not act. And why He did not act is simply beyond us. Perhaps from His not acting we may learn something about His refusal to interfere with the freedom of will of even maniacs like Hitler, but then we would have to admit that He sets a bad example for me. He ordered us not to stand by idly when innocent blood is shed. Why did He? I repeat – Job's answer is still the best. It is a no answer. We do not know, but "though He slay me, I still trust in Him." (*Job* 13:15)

Yet does the phrase "hiding the face" have no meaning for us? Of course it does, but not to provide the reason for God's behavior during the Holocaust.

If we bear in mind one profound insight of Hirsch's and Heschel's, we will find meaning in the phrase. They suggested that the Bible is not a book to be used by humans primarily to arrive at an understanding of God.

It is not a textbook of man's theology. It is rather a textbook of God's anthropology. It tells us how God sees man. Thus, for example, we do not really know why God denied Adam the right to eat from one specific tree in the Garden of Eden, but we know how Adam defied God. We do not know why God favored Abel's offering and not Cain's, but we know how Cain reacted. We do not have much detail about the sins of humanity before the Flood, but we know with what arrogance new generations conspired to frustrate God. Similarly, the sins of Sodom and Gomorrah are only subtly suggested, but the response of Abraham when told about God's plan became a model for all mankind. That is what one means when one speaks of the Bible as a guidebook not to help us fathom God but rather to see ourselves – how we are and how we ought to be.

With this as our premise, it is not unreasonable that God tells us, in the Bible, what He will do under certain circumstances – not because it accords with His Being or His Justice but rather to help us see ourselves as if in a mirror.

Therefore, He told us that the day would come when we would betray Him and ignore His law. We would be punished, but even the punishment would not make us fully aware of our guilt. We would not fathom the meaning of our suffering, or sense our guilt, or take the steps necessary to achieve true penitence and a return to Him. We will hide. We will fail to see and to hear. Our hearts will be obtuse; our eyes blind and our ears deaf. And God's hiding from us will mirror our hiding from Him. Perhaps that will help us to visualize the character of our own performance and we shall be stimulated to make amends.

That is what the text tells us. God said that even when Jews reflect in their misery upon the cause of all their suffering, they will not blame themselves, but rather God, His absence, His neglect (*Deuteronomy* 31:17). How else could God teach them to reflect more profoundly, the better to discern their existential situation, than to hide Himself, which He does (*ibid.* v. 18). Perhaps as He hides, we will recognize that this is what we are doing, and we will open our ears to hear, and our eyes to see.

Now, that is precisely what happened in our lifetime and is continuing to happen. God did not hide. It was, rather, we who had lost our capacity to hear. Our self-centeredness prompted us to hear only what we wanted to hear, and God's hiding mirrored our behavior in the hope that we would see ourselves as we are and change our ways.

Were our ears not deaf during the Holocaust? We refused to listen to reports that were being transmitted to us, in ways direct and indirect, that Hitler had become the greatest human butcher in world history. We now know so much more about our deafness at that time.

First we doubted the veracity of the reports. Then we assured ourselves that we could do nothing. Lastly we even weighed – with unforgivable self-centeredness – the price of rescue against the cost of prolonging the war. We were so coldly calculating instead of hearing – simply hearing the flames of the crematoria. It was not God who hid His face but we who had hidden ours.

But it did not start with World War II. Why didn't Jews hear what was happening all about them in eastern and central Europe from almost the beginning of this century, and why were they deaf to the call of Zionism and its messianic implication? Why did they cling to the fleshpots and decline to act as the situation warranted – with emigration to Israel and the development of the land? Why did they wait so long before realizing how vicious was the voice of the anti-Semite all about them? And indeed, are we not listening to that same voice today, or are we not hiding from it?

Similarly, the United Nations, which was born as a result of World War II, has overwhelming evidence that a large bloc of its members seek the genocide of Jews again. Yet has it the capacity to listen? It does not hear or fathom anything but that which it wants to hear.

All of the resolutions of its Security Council with regard to Israel are so indescribably vile that the mere thought of them makes the heart sick.

If we had listened in the United States to the calls of distress that were coming from the ghettos for more than a generation, we might have solved our urban problems long ago.

If university administrators and faculty had listened to the complaints of students when they were first expressed, we would not have had the avalanche of campus upheavals.

If parents had listened to their own children in their teens and shared their concerns and forebodings, we would not now have hundreds of thousands in revolt against our every cherished value and institution.

The truth is that even husbands and wives do not listen to each other – each hears and knows only what he or she craves, and without the art of listening to each other, their marriages must end in divorce.

As a matter of fact, how can we ever ask God to listen to us when we do not hear Him when He speaks to us! All that is happening in and to Israel may very well be His address to us, inviting us to recognize His role in our redemption, and cautioning the rest of humanity not to permit continuing injustice to the Jew to catapult the world into another global war and the annihilation of all mankind!

All of us must learn to listen. God does not hide His face. Rather does He mirror our hiding – our burying of our heads in the sand like ostriches.

If we are to save ourselves and all mankind, we must open our ears and our eyes. If God hides His face, it is because He wants to remind us that we are hiding ours!

That also describes how I felt when I recently read a volume edited and published by Prof. Geoffrey Hartman of Yale. It is entitled Bitburg in Moral and Political Perspectives. As I reflect on what happened, I fault myself for not having been more articulate and more indignant than I was about that which the President of the United States said and did. I must have hidden my face to the horrendous implications of any attempt to "bury the hatchet" or to "come to terms with the past."

Suddenly I experienced a deja vu. In 1985 I accepted the President's explanation that forty years after the war, the time might have come for a reconciliation with the enemy, precisely as forty-odd years earlier I accepted President Roosevelt's explanation that to save the victims of Nazi tyranny would prolong the war and victimize many innocent American soldiers. I said to myself: "How many times must it happen before I detect the sham and stop hiding my face?"

It has been said that one of the deepest moral quandaries of modern times is the tension between world Judaism's need to remember the crimes of the Holocaust and post-Nazi Germany's need to forget. Bitburg represented the President's surrender to the latter need, while everything that he is now doing to meet the former need will hardly help Germans to remember.

For Elie Wiesel's role in the matter, Jewry must be everlastingly grateful. And we must also thank God that, in this instance, Wiesel did not have to stand alone. Christians and Jews proved equal to the challenge with him, and Prof. Hartman's book attests to the pluses and minuses of a historic affair called Bitburg.

In any event, we have nothing more to say other than that God's ways are unknown to man. We will never be able to explain why He permitted the Holocaust to happen. Those who think that they have an explanation only make Him look worse, and I would rather plead ignorance of His ways than blaspheme Him. All I do know is that He wishes me to live righteously. His command that I be righteous must ever be the lodestar of my existence, even if I cannot account for or justify or rationalize His inscrutable behavior during the Holocaust.

Yet what does one do with the countless references in our sacred literature and our liturgy to the fact that disobedience to Him is the cause of disaster befalling us? And were we not promised that we would be rewarded of our righteousness? Was that not God's commitment in the covenant – His side of the "bargain"?

How does one reconcile these facts with my rejection of any explanation for God's behavior during the Holocaust? I am sure that the question is still better than any answer one will receive. Yet reply I must, but with caution that in this connection too, I have no completely satisfactory rationalizations.

Many of our sages resolved the dilemma by saying that the reward for obedience and the punishment for sin are otherworldly. In another realm of existence God will fulfill His word. This view became especially central in Christian thought. Other sages did not deny the validity of this approach, but since the Bible speaks of this-worldly rewards and punishments, and not of otherworldly ones, one has reason to ask why one cannot see any connection on earth between virtue and God's bounty, on the one hand, and vice and God's wrath, on the other.

With the biblical statements which affirm the connection one can make one's peace and say that the blessings and the curses are meant for the group. If Jewish society and the Jewish state, and not only single individuals, fulfill God's will, then there will be peace and plenty. Otherwise, the consequences will be unbearable.

A basic truth is contained in this caveat – and even if the biblical language is hyperbolic, nonetheless the powerful language was intended to make Jews realize that only a just society can long endure, while a corrupt one must disintegrate. History has proven this to be generally true. Therefore, if one is not too strict a literalist, one can discern a message of lasting significance in the Torah.

This would certainly apply to the second paragraph of the Shema (*Deuteronomy* 11:13-17). In it the Jewish people were told that if they obeyed the Law, God would do everything necessary to make their sojourn in the Promised Land a blissful one. For failure to obey the Law, however, they would perish. This promise and warning were addressed to the group – the people – the state and society.

Professor Lenn Goodman of the University of Hawaii has suggested that there is no promise in this passage that God will reward the people for obedience to His Law. All that is said is that if they obey the Law, and if God rewards them, then they should be careful not to become smug because of their bliss and forget the Lord who made it possible. (*Deuteronomy* Chapter 8) Otherwise they will be punished. His suggestion makes good sense, but there are other passages which definitely make the promise to reward obedience.

One possible answer to our question is to say that to an immature people God had to speak as one does to children. For a mature people, however, the obedience itself is its own reward, as the verse in Leviticus expresses it: "I will be your God, and you will be my people" (*Leviticus* 26:12). The thought of a mutual love affair for profit is horrendous to sensitive people, and, therefore, for the truly mature, the service of God for a promised benefit is equally unthinkable. "We must not serve God in order to receive a reward," said our sages in Ethics of the Fathers. (1:3)

But what about the emphasis in our prayers on the connection between our sins and our exile, which incidentally encouraged our persecutors in the last two thousand years to do what they did? They said that they were simply fulfilling God's wish. This was widely held Christian doctrine.

To this I give what may appear to be the view of a schizoid person. I do not see that on earth the righteous are rewarded and the wicked punished, but I do believe that it is excellent exercise for a religious person to practice introspection and ponder that perhaps, when he is made to suffer, God is trying to teach him something that will make him an even better servant of man and God than he presently is. Yet, while he may think well of himself, he may never attribute other people's misfortunes to their sinfulness.

Especially troublesome is the High Holy Days prayer that tells us – on the basis of a Talmudic text (*See Talmud B. Rosh Hashanah* 8a) – that the days of judgment are the occasion for our being sentenced, "Who will live and who will die." We find it impossible to reconcile our overwhelming experience with the literal interpretation of that prayer. We discover that the most righteous are not sentenced to life and the most wicked do survive to the following year. God's ways remain inscrutable. Then why utter a prayer with whose literal meaning we cannot identify?

Needless to say, we forget that the prayer book was never intended to be a textbook in systematic philosophy or theology. Prayer is generally in the category of poetry – not logic. It is very much the product of moods, and logical coherence is not its hallmark. But so many thoughts are suggested by the prayer that who would dare to excise it!

It teaches us how flitting life is – how frail we are – how many are the threats to our existence. Then why not make the years and the days count!

It teaches us that our deeds do make a difference. One added good deed by one person can swing the balance of the survival of humanity and not only for the individual self.

It teaches us that in the imponderable "bang" of the universe, a still small voice can still be heard.

It communicates a sense of awe and trepidation, which in the modern age we need badly to reduce our arrogance and our self-assurance that we are the complete masters of our fate and captains of our destiny.

It induces a sense of solidarity with all mankind, the creatures of one Creator, who must one day account to Him for that which they did with the gift of life.

For centuries that prayer did all of this – and not only for Jews to whom its imagery was real but even for those who saw in it only the multiple meanings and reminders.

One last word. As the Bible still inspires those who take it literally as well as those who see in it much allegory, so the liturgy can inspire those who take it literally and those who see more than words in the text but also spirit, awe, adoration, commitment, and solidarity with fellow Jews in the service of God and man.

INDEX